D1314631

YALE STUDIES IN ENGLISH

Benjamin Christie Nangle, Editor

VOLUME 139

Published on the foundation established

in memory of Philip Hamilton McMillan

of the class of 1894, Yale College,

and on a grant

provided by the Horace H. Rackham

School of Graduate Studies of the

University of Michigan

Yorick and the Critics

Sterne's Reputation in England, 1760-1868

BY ALAN B. HOWES

Instructor in English, University of Michigan

New Haven: Yale University Press, 1958

The Philip Hamilton McMillan Memorial Publication Fund

The present volume is the fifty-third work published by the Yale University Press on the Philip Hamilton McMillan Memorial Publication Fund. This foundation was established December 12, 1922, by a gift to Yale University in pursuance of a pledge announced on Alumni University Day in February, 1922, of a fund of $100,000, bequeathed to James Thayer McMillan and Alexis Caswell Angell, as Trustees, by Mrs. Elizabeth Anderson McMillan, of Detroit, to be devoted by them to the establishment of a memorial in honor of her husband.

He was born in Detroit, Michigan, December 28, 1872, prepared for college at Phillips Academy, Andover, and was graduated from Yale in the Class of 1894. As an undergraduate he was a leader in many of the college activities of his day, and within a brief period of his graduation was called upon to assume heavy responsibilities in the management and direction of numerous business enterprises in Detroit, where he was also Trustee of the Young Men's Christian Association and of Grace Hospital. His untimely death, from heart disease, on October 4, 1919, deprived his city of one of its leading citizens and his University of one of its most loyal sons.

For R. E. H. and I. B. H. and in memory of I. N. H.

Preface

LAURENCE STERNE complained a few weeks before his death that he wished he "could have got an act of parliament" when his books first appeared to prevent any "but wise men" from reading them. "It is too much to write books and find heads to understand them," he concluded. The justice of his complaint has often been only too evident, although there have also been "heads to understand" and hearts to appreciate *Tristram Shandy* and the *Sentimental Journey* in every age since their first appearance. The history of Sterne criticism in England between the publication of the first two volumes of *Tristram Shandy* in 1760 and the centenary of Sterne's death in 1868 shows his gradual emergence as a classic among the masters of English fiction. But it also shows more than this: each period reveals something of its own critical sensibility in its attitude toward Sterne.

During the course of this study of Sterne's literary fortunes, which in its original form was presented as a dissertation for the doctorate at Yale University, I have incurred a number of pleasant debts. I am especially grateful to Frederick A. Pottle of the Yale University faculty, who supervised the dissertation. His constructive criticism, encouragement, and confidence have been invaluable. Benjamin Christie Nangle has given me valuable editorial counsel, and Lidie McKinney, Joan Shapiro, and Diana T. Waugh have helped in various ways in the preparation of the manuscript.

I am also grateful to members of the staffs of the various libraries which I have used. They have been most courteous in aiding my search for rare and obscure materials. In the case of materials which were particularly difficult to find, I have added statements in the notes telling where they may be found. All books which I have cited without such notation may be found in the Yale University Library.

The authorities for tabulations of editions of Sterne's various works, with abbreviations used as indicated, within square brackets, are as follows: S. A. Allibone, *Critical Dictionary of English Literature,* Philadelphia and London, 1900—[Allibone]; William T. Lowndes, *Bibliographer's Manual of English Literature,* ed. Henry G. Bohn, London, 1864—[Lowndes]; and the holdings of the following libraries: Boston Public—[Boston], New York Public—[New York], University of Chicago—[Chicago], and Yale University—[Yale]. I have also checked the holdings of the libraries at Harvard University and the University of Michigan. Where no authority for an edition is given in square brackets, the *CBEL* is the authority. In the case of editions not listed in the *CBEL,* the authority of a holding in one of the various libraries is given in preference to Allibone or Lowndes.

I wish to express my appreciation to the following publishers for permission to quote at length from works in copyright: Clarendon Press, Constable & Co. Ltd., J. M. Dent & Sons Ltd., Longmans Green and Co. Ltd., Macmillan & Co. Ltd., Odyssey Press Inc., and G. P. Putnam's Sons. I am also indebted to the Bodleian Library, Yale University Library, and the Yale Walpole Collection to quote from manuscript materials.

Finally, I am most grateful indeed for grants from the Philip Hamilton McMillan Memorial Publication Fund and from income on the endowment of the Horace H. Rackham School of Graduate Studies of the University of Michigan. Their joint subsidy has made publication possible.

A. B. H.

Ann Arbor, Michigan
December 12, 1957

Contents

Short Titles

BLANCHARD—Frederic T. Blanchard, *Fielding the Novelist,* New Haven, Yale University Press, 1927.

BOEGE—Fred W. Boege, *Smollett's Reputation as a Novelist,* Princeton, Princeton University Press, 1947.

Letters—Lewis P. Curtis, ed., *Letters of Laurence Sterne,* Oxford, Clarendon Press, 1935.

Life—Wilbur L. Cross, *The Life and Times of Laurence Sterne,* 3d ed., New Haven, Yale University Press, 1929.

NANGLE—Benjamin Christie Nangle, *Monthly Review, First Series 1749–1789, Indexes of Contributors and Articles,* Oxford, Clarendon Press, 1934; and *Monthly Review, Second Series 1790–1815, Indexes of Contributors and Articles,* Oxford, Clarendon Press, 1955. All attributions of articles in the *Monthly* are based on these two books. The difference in dates should make clear which volume is appropriate. (In the book on the second series, however, there are a few corrections and additions to the material in the earlier volume.)

WORK—James A. Work, ed., *The Life and Opinions of Tristram Shandy, Gentleman,* New York, Odyssey Press, 1940.

Works—Wilbur L. Cross, ed., *The Works and Life of Laurence Sterne,* York Ed., 12 vols., New York, J. F. Taylor, 1904. The volumes are numbered separately for individual works. (The *Life* is that of Percy Fitzgerald, 1896 ed.)

I

The "Many Handles" of Tristram Shandy *(1760–67)*

O F all the names of literary figures that appear in the columns of newspapers and magazines during the 1760's, none appears so often, over such an extended period of time, or with such a variety of praise and censure as that of Laurence Sterne. Churchill's brief fame was cut short by death; Wilkes was mentioned more as a politician than a literary figure; the Ossianic poems created a stir, but a minor one compared to that occasioned by Sterne and his work; and the various literary controversies of Garrick were of briefer duration. Sterne, on the other hand, kept pretty consistently in the public eye, both as a man and as a writer, from the publication of the first two volumes of *Tristram Shandy* early in 1760 to the time of his death in 1768.

To be sure, Sterne did not have a great deal of competition from other novelists. Smollett's *Sir Launcelot Greaves* was not considered his best work in his own time any more than it is in ours.[1] Walpole's *Castle of Otranto* did not immediately have the vogue which the Gothic novel was later to attain. Goldsmith's *Vicar of Wakefield* has had a steady popularity ever since its publication, but it never became the fad that *Pamela* and *Tom Jones* had been a few years earlier and that *Tristram Shandy* was in the sixties.

Actually, there had been no novel of note for some time before 1760. Fielding's death in 1754 and Richardson's retirement from the literary world in the same year, with the publication of *Sir Charles Grandison,* had left Smollett in sole possession of the field, although he did not publish any novel between *Ferdinand Count Fathom* in 1753 and *Sir Launcelot Greaves* in 1760. *The Expedition of Humphry Clinker* was yet to come, in 1771, after Sterne's death. Furthermore, Smollett's work had never been quite so fashionable or so popular as that of Richardson and Fielding.[2]

The periodicals of the period are constantly deploring the low level of the usual contemporary novel and its fall from past greatness. The success of Richardson and Fielding, wrote one of the *Critical's* unknown reviewers, had spread the taste for novels throughout the kingdom and

---

1. The *Monthly Review* dismissed it with a one-sentence comment: "Better than the common Novels, but unworthy the pen of Dr. Smollet"; *27* (May 1762), 391.
2. See below, p. 2. See also Boege, *passim.*

I

spawned a swarm of "imitating fools." [3] Another critic in the *Monthly Review* deplored the lack of originality in "the present race of novels" and asserted that "the common machinery by which they are all conducted, as hard-hearted, avaricious fathers, proud mothers, base, abandoned, libertine lovers, stolen or pretended marriages, sham arrests, the usual workings of the tender passions, rivals, exalted double-refined love, heroic fortitude, poverty and distress, unexampled generosity, unexpected good fortune, and improbable coincidences of events; all these constitute such a general sameness as will . . . render them at length tiresome." [4]

To a public accustomed to productions of this kind, *Tristram Shandy* must have seemed either hopelessly odd or refreshingly original, depending upon the taste of the individual; but enough people found it refreshing so that it became the talk of the fashionable world. At the same time, the imitations, attacks, and mock attacks which it inspired provided a living for numerous literary drudges. The poems alone which took Sterne and his work as their subjects during the sixties would make up a small anthology. The unknown work and its obscure author were catapulted to fame almost overnight.

It is not quite true, as Sterne's first biographer stated in the spring of 1760, that the book made its own way entirely unaided from the beginning. [5] The letter, praising the book, which Sterne had composed for Kitty Fourmantel to copy and send to an influential friend in town— probably David Garrick—had doubtless helped to introduce *Tristram Shandy* to London society. [6] Once started, however, the fame of *Tristram* continued to spread, [7] and the book lent its name to many of the fads of the day, including a soup, a game of cards, and a country dance. [8] Not since the days of *Pamela* and *Tom Jones* had any book become a success so quickly or brought so much fame to its author. [9] As one wit later

---

3. *Critical Review, 16* (Dec. 1763), 449.

4. John Noorthouck, *Monthly Review, 39* (July 1768), 84.

5. See *Works: Letters and Miscellanies, 1*, 33–46, in which Cross reprints John Hill's article from the *Royal Female Magazine* for April 1760.

6. The letter was dated January 1, 1760. Curtis sides with Cross in thinking Garrick, rather than Richard Berenger, the addressee, as Walter Sichel contended. See *Letters*, p. 86; *Life*, p. 198.

7. The book was read enthusiastically at Sterne's own university, Cambridge. During February a group at the university signed a mock deposition, stating that it contained the "best & truest & most genuine original & new Humour, ridicule, satire, good sense, good nonsense" ever published (quoted in *Letters*, p. 87) ; and William Paley, later to become famous as the author of *Evidences of Christianity*, told a group of fellow students that "the *summum bonum* of human life . . . consists in reading Tristram Shandy." [Henry Best], *Personal and Literary Memorials* (London, 1829), p. 209.

8. See *Gentleman's Magazine, 30* (June 1760), 289; *Grand Magazine, 3* (June 1760), 290–3; *London Magazine, 30* (May 1761), 269.

9. The kind of fashionable fame received by all three authors was quite similar. The *Gentleman's Magazine, 11* (Jan. 1741), 56, asserts that it was "judged in Town as great a Sign of Want of Curiosity not to have read *Pamela*, as not to have seen the *French*

remarked in one of the numerous pamphlets which were written about Sterne and his work, *Tristram Shandy* "was dedicated to a minister, read by the clergy, approved by the wits, studied by the merchants, gazed at by the ladies, and [became] the pocket-companion of the nation." [1]

The words "Shandy" and "Shandean" (sometimes spelled "Shandyan") were added to the language, and *Tristram* was often quoted and referred to in reviews of other books during the next few years. A review of Churchill's *Ghost* refers to "this Shandy in Hudibrastics," [2] and Warburton's *Doctrine of Grace* is characterized as "these little Shandean Volumes." [3] The format of *Tristram Shandy* became a topic of comment as well as a model, and critics spoke of "our modern Shandy-like pages." [4]

The initial success of *Tristram Shandy* raised Sterne and his work to a position in the public eye which he maintained practically unbroken until his death.[5] He received exceptionally large sums for his books and they ran through many editions.[6] Since the reception of the different volumes varied, however, it will be more convenient to consider this chronologically before going on to consider some general problems which are raised by the criticism of the period as a whole.[7]

The twin arbiters of taste during the 1760's were the fashionable

---

and *Italian* Dancers," evidence that Richardson appealed to the fashionable world as well as to the new reading public among the middle class. *Tom Jones* created a like furor. See Blanchard, pp. 26–78, esp. pp. 40, 50.

1. Anonymous, *Alas! Poor Yorick! or, a Funeral Discourse* (London, 1761), pp. 19–21. The minister, of course, was William Pitt, to whom the second edition of the first two volumes was dedicated, and William Warburton was among the prominent clergymen who read the book. (See below, p. 4.) Sterne also stated in a letter that "even all the Bishops have sent their Complim't[s]" to me." *Letters*, p. 101.

2. Anonymous, *Monthly Review, 29* (Nov. 1763), 397.

3. William Rose, Ibid., *27* (Nov. 1762), 370. The eminent prelate must have been none too pleased at the comparison, for by this time his patronage of Sterne was at an end. (See below, p. 28.) From the context it seems clear that the reviewer is referring not only to the format of the book but to the style as well, since he mentions that it "abounds in digressions, according to the new-fashioned mode of writing," and "lively sallies of wit and fancy."

4. See Ralph Griffiths, ibid., *32* (Jan. 1765), 20. It is ironic that Samuel Johnson, who did not approve of Sterne or his work, appears to have provided him with the idea for the format of *Tristram Shandy:* "I propose . . . to print a lean edition, in two small volumes, of the size of Rasselas." *Letters*, p. 80.

5. See below, pp. 15–17.

6. Vols. 1 and 2 of *Tristram Shandy* went through four editions and several piracies during 1760, and reached a sixth edition in 1767 (*Life*, p. 600). Vols. 3 and 4 were reprinted in 1761, and Vols. 5 and 6 were reprinted in 1767. Vols. 7 and 8 appear to have had two editions in 1765 (see *TLS*, Feb. 22, 1934), and there was a Dublin edition of Vol. 9 in 1767. Sterne received £1,500 from Dodsley for *Tristram Shandy* and the *Sermons*, and "quite as much more" from Becket (*Life*, p. 499). For information on the publication of the *Sermons*, see below, p. 12.

7. Except for remarks on the *Sermons*, critical observations by the major literary figures of Sterne's day will be reserved for the last part of the present chapter.

world and the reviewers. *Tristram Shandy* received the favorable notice of both. The *Monthly Review* in its Appendix to 1759, issued the following January, recommended the book, stating that the author was "infinitely more ingenious and entertaining than any other of the present race of novelists," and praised especially the "striking and singular" characters, the "shrewd and pertinent" observations, and the humor, which "making a few exceptions . . . is easy and genuine." In a spirit of banter the reviewer, William Kenrick, chided Tristram for making his mother continue in childbirth for so long and expressed the fear that since "Mr. Shandy seems so extremely fond of digressions" he might leave the story unfinished. Kenrick added that he would be sorry to have this happen, since he was "very willing to accompany him to the end of his tale" and had "no objection to his telling his story his own way." [8] The *Critical Review* for January, in a much briefer notice, especially commended the characters; [9] while the *Royal Female Magazine* for February gave an excerpt describing the character of Yorick to illustrate the "consequences of indiscretion and the licentious indulgence of satirical wit," which are "so humorously and affectingly displayed." This magazine also stated that since the book showed a contempt for the rules observed in other writings, it could not be judged fairly by them, although it was unfortunate that the "wantonness of the author's wit" had not been "tempered with a little more regard to delicacy." [1] Most unqualified of all in its praise was the *London Magazine,* which gave an enthusiastic bit of impressionistic criticism in February: "Oh rare Tristram Shandy!—Thou very sensible—humourous—pathetick—humane—unaccountable!—what shall we call thee?—Rabelais, Cervantes, What? . . . Thy uncle Toby—Thy Yorick—thy father—Dr. Slop —corporal Trim; all thy characters are excellent, and thy opinions amiable! If thou publishest fifty volumes, all abounding with the profitable and pleasant, like these, we will venture to say thou wilt be read and admir'd,—Admir'd! by whom? Why, Sir, by the best, if not the most numerous class of mankind." [2]

The book was already being admired by "the best class of mankind"; for Sterne had written from York on January 27 to thank Garrick for the "great Service & Honour, your good Word has done me," [3] and in a letter to Garrick dated March 7 Warburton says, "I pride myself in having warmly recommended 'Tristram Shandy' to all the best company in town." [4] The patronage of the great was still important in making a literary reputation, just as it had been when Lord Lyttelton had helped

8. *Monthly Review, 21* (Appendix 1759), 561–71.
9. *Critical Review, 9* (Jan. 1760), 73–4.
1. *Royal Female Magazine, 1* (Feb. 1760), 56.
2. *London Magazine, 29* (Feb. 1760), 111–12.
3. *Letters,* p. 86.
4. *Private Correspondence of David Garrick* (2 vols. London, 1831–32), *1,* 116.

to make the reputation of *Tom Jones*.[5] Among the enthusiastic com-
mendations of the book, besides those of Garrick and Warburton, none
was more of a feather in Sterne's cap than that of Lord Bathurst. Sterne
described his tribute in a letter written several years later:

> [Lord Bathurst] came up to me, one day, as I was at the Princess
> of Wales's court. "I want to know you, Mr. Sterne; but it is fit you
> should know, also, who it is that wishes this pleasure. You have
> heard, continued he, of an old Lord Bathurst, of whom your Popes,
> and Swifts, have sung and spoken so much: I have lived my life
> with geniuses of that cast; but have survived them; and, despairing
> ever to find their equals, it is some years since I have closed my
> accounts, and shut my books, with thoughts of never opening them
> again: but you have kindled a desire in me of opening them once
> more before I die; which I now do; so go home and dine with me." [6]

The initial interest in *Tristram Shandy* had aroused a great curiosity
in many other readers of the book to know more about its author; and it
had been while the public was indulging this curiosity that Stephen
Croft, on a day in early March, offered to pay Sterne's expenses to
London for the sake of having his company, and thus gave Sterne the
opportunity of becoming the literary lion of the London social season.
The visit was well timed, coming as it did when the name of Tristram
Shandy was on everyone's lips.

More important, the course of criticism of Sterne's works would have
been quite different had the author remained relatively unknown. None
of the reviewers knew that Sterne was a clergyman when they penned
their favorable reviews during the first two months of 1760. Had they
known this fact, as subsequent reviews prove, they would doubtless have
been much more harsh toward the production of the man whom Warburton later described as "our heteroclite parson." Furthermore, after
Sterne became known personally through his triumphal London visit, no
reviewer—and probably few readers, for that matter—was able ever
again to keep the personality and character of the man quite distinct
from the character of his work. Actually, the public learned not about
one man but about three; and Yorick, Tristram Shandy, and Laurence
Sterne became hopelessly entangled in the public mind.[7]

5. See Blanchard, pp. 27–31.
6. *Letters*, p. 305.
7. For an amusing account of this triple personality see *Grand Magazine, 3* (June
1760), 309. Sterne only increased the confusion; for he had already signed himself
"Yorick" in a letter in 1759 (*Letters*, p. 82), and in subsequent letters he refers to himself as "Tristram," "Shandy," or "Yorick." Mrs. Sterne's relatives referred to him as
"Tristram" (Emily J. Climenson, *Elizabeth Montagu*, 2 vols. London, E. P. Dutton,
1906, *1, 75*). In *Tristram Shandy*, the distinction between Tristram and Laurence Sterne
breaks down as early as Vol. 3 (ch. 11; Work, p. 179), unless we assume that Tristram
is a clergyman too. Sterne could protest, "The world has imagined, because I wrote

The best description of Sterne's transformation from an obscure
country parson to a London literary lion is to be found in a poem by the
young Boswell, who met and admired the older man. Sterne's social
life was indeed hectic during his London sojourn:

> By Fashion's hands compleatly drest,
> He's everywhere a wellcome Guest:
> He runs about from place to place,
> Now with my Lord, then with his Grace,
> And, mixing with the brilliant throng,
> He straight commences *Beau Garcon*.
> In Ranelagh's delightfull round
> Squire Tristram oft is flaunting found;
> A buzzing whisper flys about;
> Where'er he comes they point him out;
> Each Waiter with an eager eye
> Observes him as he passes by;
> 'That there is he, do, Thomas! look,
> Who's wrote such a damn'd clever book.' [8]

Sterne's own account is to be found in his letters to Kitty Fourmantel,
back in York, in which he mentions dining with Lord Chesterfield,
going to meet the Prince,[9] and being "hurried off my Legs—by going to
great People." He sums it up by saying, "I assure you my Kitty, that
Tristram is the Fashion." [1]

Notoriety, however, followed fast upon the heels of fame, and on
June 16 Warburton was writing to Garrick that he had heard enough
of Sterne's conduct in town to disable him from "appearing as his
friend or well-wisher." Ten days later, in another letter to Garrick,
Warburton continued the topic: "I have done my best to prevent his
playing the fool in a worse sense than, I have the charity to think, he

---

Tristram Shandy, that I was myself more Shandean than I really ever was" (*Letters*,
pp. 402–3); but the confusion was partly of his own making, and it has colored critical
appraisals both of his own day and of posterity.

8. This poem, which is unfinished and in draft form, has never been published in its
entirety, although this passage is quoted in Frederick A. Pottle's "Bozzy and Yorick,"
Blackwood's Magazine, 217 (March 1925), 297–313. There is a photostat in the Yale
Library of the entire manuscript, which is catalogued Douce 193 in the Bodleian. The
passage quoted may also be found in *Letters*, p. 106, and in Lodwick Hartley's *This
Is Lorence* (Chapel Hill, Univ. of North Carolina Press, 1943), p. 95.

9. Edward Augustus (1739–67), Duke of York and Albany. It was probably in his
company that Boswell met Sterne.

1. See *Letters*, pp. 96–106, passim. Cf. Gray's statement that "one is invited to dinner,
where [Sterne] dines, a fortnight beforehand" in *Correspondence of Thomas Gray*, ed.
Paget Toynbee and Leonard Whibley (3 vols. Oxford, Clarendon Press, 1935), *2*, 670.
Sterne's social triumphs in London were repeated on his visits in subsequent years,
but after 1760 they have a more purely biographical interest and hence will not be commented upon.

intends. I have discharged my part to him. I esteemed him as a man of genius, and am desirous he would enable me to esteem him as a clergyman." [2]

Just how far Sterne really "played the fool" in London is hard to determine, since many of the anecdotes that have grown up around him have an apocryphal air, and some of his detractors were clearly motivated by jealousy. A significantly large number of the reviewers refer to him, however, as being "intoxicated" with his social successes; [3] and John Croft said that "his Vanity mounted on his slowest Hobby Horse ran away with him beyond all bounds, and he boasted of Favours that he never received, and . . . flattered himself that his Person was very much admired by the Ladies, so that he turned his mind intirely to Galantry." [4] Traditions have also grown up that Dr. Johnson expressed his disapproval of Sterne in very strong terms and did his best to avoid the company of "such a contemptible priest." [5] Sterne's conduct, at best,

2. *Correspondence of Garrick, I,* 117. See below, p. 28.

3. See also Walpole's statement: "[Sterne's] head indeed was a little turned before, now topsyturvy with his success and fame." *Correspondence with Sir David Dalrymple,* ed. W. S. Lewis (New Haven, Yale Univ. Press, 1951), p. 66.

4. *Whitefoord Papers,* ed. W. A. S. Hewins (Oxford, Clarendon Press, 1898), p. 226. The passage quoted is part of a series of anecdotes and biographical notes which John Croft collected and sent to Caleb Whitefoord at the latter's request in 1795. Croft, the younger brother of Stephen Croft, spent much of his life abroad and hence did not know Sterne as well as his brother did. He also is writing nearly thirty years after Sterne's death and some of the anecdotes that he records seem to be apocryphal, although they may well have become established in Yorkshire tradition. Even after one allows for a certain amount of distortion in his account, however, Sterne still would appear to have been extremely indiscreet on his London visits. Mrs. Montagu, the cousin of Sterne's wife, later said: "The extravagant applause that was at first given to [Sterne's] works turn'd his head with vanity. He was received abroad with great distinction which made him still more vain, so that he really believes his book to be the finest thing the age has produced." She added, however, "I like Tristram better than his book. He had a world of good nature, he never hurt any one with his witt." *Mrs. Montagu,* ed. Reginald Blunt (2 vols. London, Houghton [1923]), *I,* 188.

5. Johnson is said to have told Sir Joshua Reynolds' sister that "he would rather give up the pleasure of her brother's society than meet such a contemptible priest as Sterne" (*Life,* p. 284). Writers in the *European Magazine* during the nineties mention that "the sanction of Dr. Johnson's name" has been given to the assertion that Sterne was *"licentious* and *dissolute* in conversation" (*18,* Nov. 1790, 349) and that "Dr. Johnson used to say, that the liveliness of [Sterne's] conversation had made such an impression on Garrick and Reynolds that he removed with some difficulty" (*33,* May 1798, 313). The story that Johnson was "but once in Sterne's company, and then his only attempt at merriment consisted in his display of a drawing too indecently gross to have delighted even in a brothel" (*Johnsonian Miscellanies,* ed. George B. Hill, 2 vols. Oxford, Clarendon Press, 1897, *2,* 320) rests solely on the very doubtful veracity of George Steevens, but was given wide currency by its inclusion in the *European Magazine, 7,* (Jan. 1785), 53, and Johnson's *Works,* ed. Sir John Hawkins (London, 1787), *11,* 214. The record of a meeting between Johnson and Sterne in a company where Sterne read his dedication to Lord Spencer (*Tristram Shandy, 5*) and Johnson reportedly told him it "was not English, sir" (*New Monthly Magazine, 10,* Dec. 1818, 389) has more of a ring of authenticity about it, although it is rendered somewhat suspect by a discrepancy in dates. The writer, the Rev. Baptist Noel Turner, is describing Johnson's visit to Cambridge in 1765, while Turner was at the university.

must be considered imprudent; and any imprudence found double censure from the fact that he was a clergyman.[6]

To add further to Sterne's notoriety, starting in April a flood of pamphlets and books criticizing, imitating, or purporting to explain *Tristram Shandy* began to appear. Sterne's first reaction was that they would be good publicity. "There is a shilling pamphlet wrote against Tristram," he wrote to Stephen Croft. "I wish they would write a hundred such." [7] But most of these books were either inferior imitations or merely devices to capitalize on the value of some tenuous connection with Sterne's name, often only on the title-page; and many of them were vulgar, scurrilous, and obscene.[8] Among the imitations were the *Two Lyric Epistles* of Sterne's friend, Hall-Stevenson. These poems, which bordered on the scatological and the pornographic, were thought by many, including some of the reviewers, to be Sterne's; [9] and some of the pamphlets were also attributed to him.[1] A biography of Sterne had also appeared in the *Royal Female Magazine* for April and was reprinted in the *London Chronicle* and other periodicals early in May. The article was written by John Hill, the literary hack and quack doctor who had conducted a newspaper war against Fielding a few years before.

Although he says that Johnson referred to having been "lately" in a company where Sterne had read the dedication in manuscript, it had been published more than three years previously. Since Turner also says that he had met Johnson before, perhaps he is recalling an earlier conversation. Boswell records a conversation between Johnson and Goldsmith, in which Johnson referred somewhat contemptuously to "the man, Sterne" but contradicted Goldsmith's assertion that he was "a very dull fellow." *Boswell's Life of Johnson,* ed. G. B. Hill and L. F. Powell (6 vols. Oxford, Clarendon Press, 1934–50), *2, 222.*

6. Thomas Mozeen's poem, "The Divine and Coxcomb," quoted in *Critical Review, 20* (Sept. 1765), 174, censures another clergyman for being more concerned with "ladies, card tables, and tea" than with prayers, and for appearing at the play—lapses far less serious than those attributed to Sterne.

7. *Letters,* p. 107. See also *Life,* pp. 228–30.

8. See below, pp. 28–30.

9. Warburton wrote to Sterne on June 15, referring to the poems: "Whoever was the author, he appears to be a monster of impiety and lewdness—yet such is the malignity of the scribblers, some have given them to your friend Hall; and others, which is still more impossible, to yourself. . . . But this might arise from a tale equally groundless and malignant, that you had shewn them to your acquaintances in M.S. before they were given to the public" (*Letters,* p. 113). Sterne replied on June 19, admitting that he had seen one of the poems in manuscript and "after striking out some parts," had shown it "as a whimsical performance . . . to some acquaintance." He then went on to plead Hall-Stevenson's case and promise his amendment (*Letters,* p. 115). The incident is significant because it shows the kind of indiscretion which Sterne was likely to commit and which gave fuel to the fires of his serious critics, as well as to the scribblers who were only too ready to capitalize on his name.

1. In discussing *Explanatory Remarks upon the Life and Opinions of Tristram Shandy,* the *Critical Review, 9* (April 1760), 319, voiced the suspicion that Sterne was the author. This pamphlet, although it has a certain amount of genuine humor, spends a good deal of time in capitalizing in a vulgar way on the bawdy sections of Sterne's book.

Though notably inaccurate—Hill himself admits that he is repeating anecdotes which may be untrustworthy—the article is generally friendly in tone, and Hill appears to have had no particular animus against Sterne. He presents the author of *Tristram Shandy* in a far better light than many of the scribblers were soon to do; but some of the anecdotes proved extremely embarrassing to Sterne and appear to have nettled him considerably.[2] Little more than a month after he had welcomed the appearance of the first shilling pamphlet against *Tristram* he was writing to Warburton, "the scribblers use me ill." [3] In a letter to another correspondent at this time he tries to absolve himself of blame for the flood of ribald imitations which *Tristram Shandy* had occasioned: " 'God forgive me, for the Volumes of Ribaldry I've been the cause of'— now I say, god forgive them—and tis the pray'r I constantly put up for those who use me most unhandsomely." [4]

When Sterne complained that the scribblers used him ill, he was probably thinking not only of Hill's article and the pamphleteers who had written against him but also of the treatment accorded in the *Monthly Review* to *The Sermons of Mr. Yorick,* which had appeared in May. Sterne had published the sermons with two title-pages—the second one giving his own name—and a preface which apologized for prefixing Yorick's name to the work and explained that this had been done because the name was better known than Sterne's own. The *Monthly* reviewer, Owen Ruffhead, was incensed at this manner of publishing the sermons, asserting that it was "the greatest outrage against Sense and Decency" since the beginning of Christianity and "could scarce have been tolerated even in the days of paganism." The "solemn dictates of religion" should not be conveyed "from the mouths of Buffoons and ludicrous Romancers," who "mount the pulpit in a *Harlequin's coat*"; and Sterne's second title-page in which he "does not scruple to avow his real name" shows a complete lack of "decency and discretion." [5] Though Sterne, "inflated with vanity, and intoxicated with applause" may think that the reviewer censures him out of envy, Ruffhead says that this is not the case. "The wanton Harlot," he continues, "affects to laugh at the

2. See *Letters,* passim; *Life,* pp. 220, 221, 226.
3. *Letters,* p. 112.
4. Ibid., p. 118. The addressee is Mary Macartney, later Lady Lyttelton. The fact that the words "God forgive me, for the Volumes of Ribaldry I've been the cause of" are in quotation marks (the photostat of this letter in the Yale Library is clear on this point), as well as their use in the context, would seem to indicate that Sterne is quoting someone who has upbraided him, perhaps the addressee, and not, as Cross and Work imply (*Life,* p. 228; Work, p. xxx), expressing his own contrition. A denial of responsibility would be more in character for Sterne in this situation than a statement of contrition.
5. A satirical print from the early sixties "shows *Sterne at Ranelagh* soliciting subscriptions for the sermons which he published under his pseudonym of Yorick, much to the scandal of the orthodox." See Emily Morse Symonds (pseud. George Paston), *Social Caricature in the Eighteenth Century* (London, Methuen, 1905), p. 64, pl. 92.

indignant scorn of Chastity" and tries to "persuade herself and the world, that the contempt and reproach to which she is hourly subject, arise from *envy* of her superior charms and endowments. In short, this is the common affectation of every Libertine and Prostitute, from K——— F———[6] down to TRISTRAM SHANDY." Ruffhead goes on to express the wish that "the *manner* of publication" had been "as unexceptionable as the *matter*" of Sterne's sermons, which might well "serve as models for many of his brethren to copy from." The conclusion of the review, written by William Rose, praises the "ease, purity, and elegance" of the style and asserts that "tho' there is not much of the pathetic or devotional to be found in them, yet there are many fine and delicate touches of the human heart and passions" which "shew marks of great benevolence and sensibility of mind." Considered "as moral Essays" the *Sermons* are "highly commendable, and equally calculated for the entertainment and instruction of the attentive Reader." [7]

The other periodicals were kinder to the *Sermons*. The *British Magazine* said merely that they were "plain, easy, elegant, and sensible"; [8] and the *Royal Female Magazine* paid Sterne the oblique compliment of asserting that the *Sermons* had so much merit "as will bear witness against the abuse of such abilities, to improper ends, in that day, *when every idle word shall be accounted for,* how much soever present applause may intoxicate a man to pursue the bent of a licentious turn to wit and pleasantry." [9] The *Critical Review* "took up Mr. Sterne's sermons, without being offended at Yorick's name prefixed" and expressed a willingness to "lay siege to Namur with uncle *Toby* and *Trim,* in the morning, and moralize at night with Sterne and Yorick." This reviewer says he "will ever esteem religion when smoothed with good humour, and believe that piety alone to be genuine, which flows from a heart, warm, gay, and social." [1]

Except for Dr. Johnson's dissenting opinion that in Sterne's *Sermons* was to be found only "the froth from the surface" of the cup of salvation,[2] the discourses were almost universally recommended for their style and for the strain of benevolence which the *Critical* reviewer had admired, although there were some reservations in connection with the levity of certain parts. In a letter to Anne Granville Dewes, Georgina

6. Kitty Fisher, the noted courtesan.
7. *Monthly Review*, 22 (May 1760), 422–31.
8. *British Magazine*, 1 (June 1760), 378.
9. *Royal Female Magazine*, 1 (May 1760), 238.
1. *Critical Review*, 9 (May 1760), 405.
2. *Johnsonian Miscellanies*, 2, 429. (The source is a Mr. Wickins, a linen draper from Lichfield, who knew Johnson and reported the remark from a conversation.) At another time, it is reported that Johnson grudgingly admitted having read Sterne's *Sermons,* but stated that he had read them in a stagecoach and would "not have even deigned to have looked at them, had I been at large." Joseph Cradock, *Literary and Miscellaneous Memoirs* (4 vols. in 5, London, 1826–28), *1,* 208.

Countess Cowper praised the *Sermons,* which she thought "more like Essays," and concluded, "I think [Sterne] must be a good man." [3] Richard Griffith wrote in his preface to *The Triumvirate* of the "striking and affecting" qualities of Sterne's discourses.[4] Gray thought that Yorick's *Sermons* were in the style "most proper for the Pulpit" and showed "a very strong imagination & a sensible heart," though he felt that Sterne was "often tottering on the verge of laughter, & ready to throw his perriwig in the face of his audience." [5] Even William Cowper gave qualified praise to Sterne, though he felt that the *Sermons* were lacking in the spirit of the New Testament. Sterne "is a great master of the pathetic," he wrote, "and if that or any other species of rhetoric could renew the human heart and turn it from the power of Satan unto God, I know no writer better qualified to make proselytes to the cause of virtue." He cannot admire Sterne as a preacher, however, since he "fights not with the sword of the Spirit . . . but with that wisdom which shone with as effectual a light before our Saviour came" and "therefore cannot be the wisdom which He came to reveal to us." [6]

Finally, if we may believe Boswell, the *Sermons* became fashionable and were read and talked about by many of the members of the *beau monde* who were on Sterne's distinguished list of subscribers. Boswell's half playful account occurs in another part of the manuscript poem already quoted from:

> Next from the press there issues forth
> A sage divine fresh from the north;
> On Sterne's discourses we grew mad,
> Sermons! where are they to be had?
> Then with the fashionable Guards
> The Psalms supply the place of Cards.
> A strange enthusiastic rage
> For sacred text now seis'd the age;
> Arround St Jamess every table
> Was partly gay & partly sable,
> The manners by old Noll defended
> Were with our modern chitte chat blended.

3. *Autobiography and Correspondence of Mary Granville, Mrs. Delany,* ed. [Augusta Waddington Hall] Lady Llanover, (1st Ser., 3 vols. London, 1861), *3,* 602.

4. *The Triumvirate: or, the Memoirs of A. B. and C.* (2 vols. London, 1764), *1,* xvi–xvii. A note by the author states that the preface was written in 1761.

5. *Correspondence of Gray, 2,* 681.

6. *Correspondence of William Cowper,* ed. Thomas Wright (4 vols. London, Hodder and Stoughton, 1904), *1,* 64–5. This letter, addressed to Joseph Hill, is dated April 3, 1766, but refers to Cowper's opinion at an earlier time when he read the first two volumes of the *Sermons.* Others of an evangelistic turn of mind agreed with Cowper. The Rev. Henry Venn complained that "excepting a phrase or two, they might be preached in a synagogue or mosque without offence." *Life and Letters of Henry Venn,* Evangelical Knowledge Society Ed. from 6th London ed. (New York, 1855), p. 71.

'Give me some maccaroni pray,'
'Be wise while it is call'd today';
'Heavns! how Mingotti sung last Monday'
'—Alas how we profane the Sunday.'
'My Lady Betty! hob or nob!—'
'Great was the patience of old Job,'
Sir Smart breaks out & one & all
Adore St Peter & St Paul.[7]

Thus the *Sermons* were widely read and were a financial success, in spite of the *Monthly*'s attack on them; [8] and in the next installment of *Tristram Shandy,* published in January 1761, Sterne devoted a chapter to the critics, in which he affected to be unconcerned with their attacks:

> A Man's body and his mind, with the utmost reverence to both I speak it, are exactly like a jerkin, and a jerkin's lining;—rumple the one—you rumple the other. There is one certain exception however in this case, and that is, when you are so fortunate a fellow, as to have had your jerkin made of a gum-taffeta, and the body-lining to it, of a sarcenet or thin persian. . . .
>
> I believe in my conscience that mine is made up somewhat after this sort;—for never poor jerkin has been tickled off, at such a rate as it has been these last nine months together,—and yet I declare the lining to it,—as far as I am a judge of the matter, it is not a three-penny piece the worse. . . .
>
> —You Messrs. the monthly Reviewers!—how could you cut and slash my jerkin as you did?—how did you know, but you would cut my lining too?

Sterne then promises to receive all attacks "with good temper," since the "world is surely wide enough" to hold both him and his critics.[9]

The *Monthly Review* apparently regarded this as a challenge and set out to rumple the lining of Tristram's jerkin in good earnest. Ruffhead, who had written most of the review of the *Sermons,* again wrote the review of Volumes 3 and 4 in February. He wishes to rumple the lining

7. Bodleian Library, Douce 193; see above, p. 6. The lines quoted belong to a more unfinished section of the poem as it stands in the manuscript, and have never been published. Ll. 5 and 6 are crossed out, though clearly legible. The reference in l. 11 is to Oliver Cromwell. The expression 'hob or nob' in l. 17 is a drinking salutation. In transcribing the lines, I have made a few silent corrections and additions, mainly in the punctuation, where the sense demanded them.

8. They had reached a fourth edition within a year and a ninth edition by 1768. There were also Dublin editions in 1760 and 1761. Dodsley gave Sterne £450 for the copyright of *Tristram Shandy* and the *Sermons,* having previously offered him £250 for the copyright of the two volumes of the novel alone (*Letters,* pp. 98, 111–12). Since Sterne writes in December 1762 that his publisher had gotten "400 Guineas" from "the last sermons" (*Letters,* p. 190), and the *Sermons* sold for six shillings, it is possible to arrive at an estimate of 1400 or 1500 copies as the average number for the reprintings.

9. *Tristram Shandy, 3,* ch. 4; Work, pp. 160–2.

of Tristram's jerkin, he says, "to make the owner ashamed of exposing it," for "all the world may see that it is in a filthy pickle." Although "this gumtaffeta jerkin has been a kind of heir-loom in the Shandean family," Ruffhead continues, "what an antic figure it must cut upon a prunella gown and cassock!" Sterne is urged "for shame" to hide his jerkin, or at least "send the lining to the Scowerer's," since when once thoroughly cleaned it will be "as apt to fray and fret as other people's, but at present it is covered with such a thick scale of nastiness, that there is no coming at a single thread of it." The body of Ruffhead's critical remarks is organized around a lengthy quotation from Hobbes to the effect that often "where Wit is wanting, it is not Fancy that is wanting, but Discretion" and therefore judgment "without Fancy, is Wit: but Fancy without Judgment, is not." [1] In addition to lacking discretion, Ruffhead continues, Sterne is to be taxed with "dullness," for the characters are "no longer striking and singular," and the section on noses shows a prostitution of wit which might be compared "to the spices which embalm a putrid carcase." Throughout the piece much is made of the hints of unfavorable criticism in the *Monthly*'s previous review of Volumes 1 and 2, almost as if the reviewer were apologizing for their generally favorable tone.[2]

Despite the harshness of the review, it runs to fifteen pages and contains generous excerpts from the new installment. Furthermore, the tone of the remarks is sometimes a bantering one, and the reviewer closed his discussion with an attempt to prove that he had written in good humor and good faith by giving some "friendly admonitions" to Sterne against the misapplication of undoubted talents.[3]

Critical opinion was divided in the other periodicals. The *London Magazine* told its readers that whoever had "with true relish read his former volumes, may be assured that their perusal of the 3rd and 4th will not be attended with less delight." [4] The *British Magazine,* on the other hand, lamented in a brief review : "Alas, poor Yorick! was it the nose or the cerebellum that those unlucky forceps compressed?—My service to your mother's – – – – – I'll tell you what I mean in the next chapter : but it had been well for the father, and perhaps for the public, that she had remained all her life un– – – – – You'll find the sequel in Slawkenbergius. —O, my dear *Rabelais!* and my yet dearer *Cervantes!* . . . Mr. Shandy, here's a cup of fresh caudle at your Honour's service." [5]

Perhaps the best balanced of the various criticisms is to be found in

---

1. The quotation comes from Ch. 8 of *Leviathan*. Cf. *Tristram Shandy, 3,* ch. 20; Work, pp. 192–203: Sterne says that the "wit" and "judgment" of his work are complementary, and opposes Locke's assertion that wit and judgment "never go together."
2. The *Grand Magazine,* also published by Griffiths, had printed a defense of the *Monthly*'s change of heart. *3* (June 1760), 308–11.
3. *Monthly Review, 24* (Feb. 1761), 101–16.
4. *London Magazine, 30* (Jan. 1761), 56.
5. *British Magazine, 2* (Feb. 1761), 98.

the *Critical Review* for April in an article written after some of the initial furor caused by the third and fourth volumes had died down and a more objective approach to the book and its critics was possible. The unknown reviewer believes that, like Rabelais, Sterne has written "merely *pour la refection corporelle,*" and that Rabelais rather than Cervantes has furnished the "pattern and prototype" for *Tristram Shandy* "in the address, the manner, and colouring." He continues with praise for the characters of Sterne's novel and for its "pertinent observations on life and . . . humorous incidents, poignant ridicule, and marks of taste and erudition." This is balanced by censure of the forced quality of some of the humor, the alleged childishness of most of the digressions, and the "general want of decorum." The most interesting of this reviewer's remarks, however, have to do with an analysis of the contemporary reception of the first and second installments of the book. The new installment is "no more than a continuation of the first two volumes," he says, but they had been "received with such avidity by the public, as boded no good to the sequel; for that avidity was not a natural appetite, but a sort of *fames canina,* that must have ended in *nausea* and *indigestion.* Accordingly all novel readers, from the stale maiden of quality to the snuff-taking chambermaid, devoured the first part with a most voracious swallow, and rejected the last with marks of loathing and aversion. We must not look for the reason of this difference in the medicine," he concludes, "but in the patient to which it was administered." The first installment "had merit, but was extolled above its value; the other has defects, but is too severely decried." [6]

If the third and fourth volumes of *Tristram Shandy* were "too severely decried," the fifth and sixth, which appeared in December 1761, were more kindly treated. The episode of Le Fever was universally admired and reprinted widely in newspapers and periodicals. Comparisons were frequently made between the second and third installments, to the advantage of the latter. A writer in the *Library* was typical in finding fewer offenses against decorum and delicacy in the new volumes and also thought them "much superior" in other respects. "The digressions are not so long and tedious," he says, "while there is the same spirit, the same fine ridicule of false learning, the same inimitable talent at description, the same characteristic strokes, and the same vein of humour." [7] Even the *Monthly Review,* this time in an article by John Langhorne, found that although the fifth and sixth volumes "are not without their stars and dashes, their hints and whiskers," they nevertheless "are not so much interlarded with obscenity as the former." After quoting the story of Le Fever, Langhorne concluded that Sterne's excellence lay "not so much in the humorous as in the pathetic," an asser-

6. *Critical Review, 11* (April 1761), 314–17.
7. *Library, 1* (Dec. 1761), 487.

tion that the *Monthly* was to insist upon in subsequent reviews as earnestly as ever Uncle Toby or Walter Shandy insisted upon their hobbyhorses.[8]

Meanwhile the *Critical Review* rode its own particular hobbyhorse, the resemblance of Sterne to Rabelais. The events of the new installment, the reviewer says, "are comprehended in a very few pages," while the rest of the book is filled with "the same kind of haberdashery" that Rabelais dealt in. He continues with a certain amount of banter about the oddities of style, but gives genuine praise to "some touches of character relating to Toby and to Trim . . . by which it appears, that if our author has sometimes lost sight of Rabelais, he has directed his eye to a still greater original, even nature herself." The reviewer concludes that he knows not "whether most to censure the impertinence, or commend the excellencies of this strange, incongruous, whimsical performance." [9]

Some of the magazines seemed to be running out of things to say about *Tristram.* Thus the *British Magazine* merely characterized the performance as "agreeably whimsical and characteristic, interspersed with many pathetick touches of nature," [1] while the *Court Magazine*'s reviewer thought that "those who are fond of the other volumes, may probably have pleasure in reading these," although he could not find "any thing to recommend" in the new installment.[2] The controversies over *Tristram Shandy* were dying down, and there was nothing to renew them for the next three years while Sterne was traveling in France for his health; for he published nothing until January of 1765, when Volumes 7 and 8 appeared.

This interim period, however, is by no means barren of references to Sterne and his work in the periodicals of the day, although the fifth and sixth volumes of *Shandy* apparently did not sell well after the initial sale was once over.[3] The first news to come from France after Sterne's departure was both shocking and premature. The *London Chronicle* carried a notice of Sterne's death early in February, a mistake apparently arising from the extremely discouraging prognostications of his Paris physicians; but the report was denied within a week,[4] indeed a few days before another paper printed the following graceful and appreciative poem "On the Report of the Death of the Reverend Mr. STERNE":

8. *Monthly Review, 27* (Jan. 1762), 31–41.
9. *Critical Review, 13* (Jan. 1762), 66–9.
1. *British Magazine, 3* (Jan. 1762), 44.
2. *Court Magazine,* Dec. 1761, p. 184.
3. In April 1763, Becket reported to Sterne that nearly 1,000 copies out of 4,000 remained unsold (*Letters,* p. 192). The sale of these volumes may have been more harmed than helped by the wide reprinting of the story of Le Fever; for some potential readers may have been satisfied merely to read this story, which the critics asserted to be the best part.
4. *London Chronicle, 11* (Feb. 2–4 and 11–13, 1762), 117, 145.

STERNE! rest for ever, and no longer fear
The Critic's malice, and the Wittling's sneer;
The gate of Envy now is clos'd on thee,
And Fame her hundred doors shall open free;
Ages unborn shall celebrate the Page,
Where hap'ly blend the Satirist and Sage;
While gen'rous hearts shall feel for worth distrest,
Le Fevre's woes with tears shall be confest;
O'er Yorick's tomb the brightest eyes shall weep,
And British genius constant vigils keep;
Then, sighing, say, to vindicate thy Fame,
"Great were his faults, but glorious was his flame." [5]

Meanwhile, other Sterne enthusiasts had been upset by the report, and Sterne's parishioners had gone into mourning;[6] but the quick denial must have kept the report from being widely believed for more than a short time.[7] A few months later Sterne was included in a series of biographies of the "living authors" of Great Britain,[8] and he remained very much alive to the reviewers and the literary hacks.

The flood of imitations, though definitely past its height by now, continued sporadically and included Boswell's "Cub at Newmarket," which was reviewed in March 1762.[9] Nor did the scribblers of pamphlets, humorous epistles, and verses rest entirely from their labors of capitalizing on Sterne's name and the fame of his works. In "A Paper

5. *Lloyd's Evening Post, 10* (Feb. 12–15, 1762), 158. This poem, identified only as being "by a Lady," was written by Mrs. [?J. Henrietta] Pye, and is reprinted, with minor changes, in her *Poems by a Lady,* London, 1767.

6. See *Life,* pp. 289–90; *Letters,* p. 148.

7. The impression that Cross gives (*Life,* pp. 350–1) that "the old rumor that Sterne was dead had never been quite laid" is misleading. The "Elegy on the decease of TRISTRAM SHANDY," which appeared in *St. James's Magazine, 2* (July 1763), 312, and which he cites as evidence, does not seem to bear out his contention. The poem is prefaced by a reference to "the memory of TRISTRAM SHANDY having been treated somewhat cavalierly, *under the name of Sterne*" (italics mine), and details in the poem itself make it clear that the author is referring to the decease of Tristram Shandy, not of Sterne. The whole seems to be a playful lament that no more volumes of *Shandy* have appeared for some time. Thus, the assertion of Cross that Sterne "came upon London [in 1764] almost as one returned from the dead" is, I believe, exaggerated, since the evidence, to be presented hereafter, indicates that he was far from forgotten in the periodicals during his trip to France.

8. *An Historical and Critical Account of the Lives and Writings of the Living Authors of Great-Britain* (London, 1762), pp. 19–20. This book, which was censured by the *Critical, 13* (May 1762), 441, as a "contemptible catchpenny" is very inaccurate, but is nevertheless significant as one of the first attempts of its kind. The brief account of Sterne is extremely sketchy, but on the whole appreciative, with special praise for the *Sermons.*

9. See *Monthly Review, 26* (March 1762), 233. For other reviews of works during this period which were imitations of Sterne, see ibid., *26* (June 1762), 474; *Critical Review, 15* (Jan. 1763), 13–21; *15* (May 1763), 378; *15* (May 1763), 373–7; *16* (Dec. 1763), 478.

dropt from Tristram Shandy's Pocket-book," published in 1762, one wit satirized Walter Shandy's theory of the auxiliary verbs in Volume 5 of *Tristram Shandy* by ringing the changes on the sentence "Can I write nonsense?," which was applied to Sterne and his work.[1] In September 1763 an unknown versifier wrote "The Clock-Maker's Address to Mr. Churchill, on reading his Poem on Night," in which he thanks the poet for restoring the good name of clockmakers, which had supposedly been lost by the references to winding up the clock in the first volume of *Tristram Shandy*.[2] In December of the same year another wit published a letter, supposedly written by Tristram to the Reverend John Kidgell, who had been responsible for the infamous summary of John Wilkes's infamous "Essay on Woman." In the letter Tristram is made to ask Kidgell for advice on how to handle the amours of his Uncle Toby and Widow Wadman.[3]

The reviewers also referred to Sterne and *Tristram* not infrequently in their comments on other works. Churchill's *Ghost* and Warburton's *Doctrine of Grace* brought the words "Shandy" and "Shandean" to their minds;[4] and in a review in June 1762 the *Monthly* calls the author of one of the ephemeral productions of the day "a Genius, in the current sense of the word; a star of the first magnitude in the Shandean Constellation."[5] The *Monthly* reviewer of *Letters between the Honourable Andrew Erskine and James Boswell, Esq.* compares them with the productions of "the facetious Author of Tristram Shandy."[6] In reviewing Hall-Stevenson's *Pastoral Puke* a year later, the *Monthly* compliments the work and says that "when Tristram Shandy went to France, he certainly left his mantle with this his natural brother in jocularity."[7]

Sterne returned from France in June of 1764 to reclaim his mantle from any of his "brothers in jocularity" who might have been borrowing it, although he did not complete Volumes 7 and 8 until late in the fall and

1. Anonymous, *Jack and his Whistle . . . to which is added, A Paper dropt from Tristram Shandy's Pocket-book,* Edinburgh, 1762. There is a copy of this little pamphlet, which satirizes both Sterne and John Home, in the Harvard University Library.

2. *Court Magazine,* Sept. 1763, p. 450. Much of this short poem is a poetic adaptation of the earlier pamphlet, *The Clockmakers Outcry;* see *Life,* p. 229.

3. *Court Magazine,* Dec. 1763, pp. 581–3. Although the author's main purpose is to attack Kidgell, the fact that he uses the character of Tristram to do this shows that there was public interest in Sterne at this time. Kidgell, a man of some talent although an extremely dissolute and dishonest clergyman, had procured the sheets of the "Essay on Woman" by treachery, later capitalizing on public interest in the production by printing his "summary." Though Wilkes appears not to have been the author of the piece, it was printed at his private press under his direction and was connected with his name in the public mind. (See *DNB,* arts. "Wilkes" and "Kidgell.")

4. See above, p. 3. See also *Monthly Review, 27* (Oct. 1762), 316, where Bk. III of Churchill's *Ghost* is referred to by an unidentified reviewer as "a kind of *Tristram Shandy* in *verse.*"

5. John Langhorne, *Monthly Review, 26* (June 1762), 454.

6. Ralph Griffiths, ibid., *28* (June 1763), 477.

7. Anonymous, ibid., *30* (May 1764), 415.

they were not published until January 1765. The critics had mixed feelings about the new installment, although the general tone of criticism
was not favorable. The *Candid Review* praised the novelty of the volumes, their "frequent elegance of expression," and their "fund of humour"; but censured Sterne for obscenity and irreverence and concluded
that "however witty and ingenious," the book would not give general
satisfaction "because the digressions are too abrupt, not always intelligible, and often very lewd," as well as "unexpectedly tedious" in some
parts.[8] The *Critical* observed that "an author may print a joke but he
cannot print a face, which is often the best part of a joke," and asserted
that "the principal part of the work before us is its manner, which is
either above or below criticism." Volume 7 was characterized as "an
unconnected, unmeaning, account of our author's journey to France,"
and the unknown reviewer concluded that this was all one could expect
from a man who "has pretended from his commencement of authorship,
neither to wit, taste, sense, nor argument." [9] In much the same vein was
an article which was quoted in the *London Chronicle* from Jean Baptiste
Suard's Paris review of the volumes. The author praised Sterne's
"philanthropy and humanity" but asserted that his work was "a riddle,
without an object," and by way of analogy told "the famous story
of the *man* who, some years ago, informed the public, that he
would put himself in a bottle before their eyes. The credulous multitude
. . . flocked to the theatre . . . but the droll carried away their money
and left the bottle empty; not however more empty than the two last
volumes of the life of *Tristram Shandy*." [1] Another critic, in even harsher
vein, begged to be excused for not regarding "ribbaldry and incoherent
stupidity as the genuine characteristics of humour." The public, he continued, "seems now to be awakened from its delirium, and Tristram tells
his tale, as the play-house phrase is, *to empty benches*." [2]

Tristram was hardly telling his tale "to empty benches," for Sterne
wrote to Garrick in March that "Shandy sells well," [3] and the *Monthly,*
at least, found much to praise, if it also found much to censure. In a
twenty-page review, this time written by Ralph Griffiths himself, the
reviewer accompanies Tristram on his trip through Europe and comments on the book, chapter by chapter. The main charges against the
volumes are those of obscenity and dullness. Griffiths admits that the
incident of the Abbess of Andoüillets has humor in the way it is
presented, although it is *"such* humour as *ought* to please none but

8. *Candid Review,* Feb. 1765, pp. 91–2.
9. *Critical Review, 19* (Jan. 1765), 65–6.
1. "An Account of the Two Last Volumes of the Life of Tristram Shandy, by the
Ingenious Authors of the *Gazette littéraire de l'Europe," London Chronicle, 17* (April
16–18, 1765), 373.
2. *Universal Museum, 1* (Jan. 1765), 36.
3. *Letters,* p. 235.

coachmen and grooms" and would "prohibit every modest woman in the three kingdoms" from reading the book. The description of Calais is characterized as "a dull expedient for filling up half a score pages," and the list of the streets in Paris is similarly condemned. But Griffiths' praise of the parts of the volumes which he approves is no less restrained than his censure. He rhapsodizes over the scene of the country dance at Languedoc, with the wish, "Would we had it upon two yards of REYNOLDS's canvass!" He praises the characters, saying, "I've a sincere regard for the whole family—a dog, from Shandy-hall, should always be welcome to me." Griffiths finds that the story of Uncle Toby's court-ship proves Sterne "a master of the science of human feelings, and the art of describing them"; and of the passage describing the Widow Wadman's eye he says enthusiastically: "Never was any thing more beautifully simple, more natural, more *touching!* O Tristram! that ever any grosser colours should daub and defile that pencil of thine. . . . *Richardson*—the delicate, the circumstantial RICHARDSON himself, never produced any thing equal to the amours of Uncle Toby and the Widow Wadman!" The review closes with some advice to Sterne, whose forte, Griffiths insists, lies in the pathetic. He is urged to "strike out a new plan" with "none but amiable or worthy, or exemplary characters," and deal only in "the *innocently humorous.*" "Excite our passions to *laudable* purposes," Griffiths says, and let "morality" and "the cultiva-tion of virtue be your aim—let wit, humour, elegance and pathos be the means; and the grateful applause of mankind will be your reward." [4]

Sterne was not yet ready to follow this advice, as he appears to do at least to some extent in the *Sentimental Journey;* but before giving the next installment of *Tristram Shandy* to the world, he did decide on "doing penance" for "my 7 & 8 graceless Children . . . in be-getting a couple of more Ecclesiastick ones" and thus "taxing the publick with two more volumes of sermons, which will more than double the gains of Shandy— It goes into the world," he continues in a letter to Garrick, "with a prancing list of *de toute la noblesse—*" [5] Thus accompanied with a list of subscribers which was truly im-pressive and did contain, if not all, at least a good part of the most famous names of the day,[6] Volumes 3 and 4 of *The Sermons of Mr. Yorick* appeared in January 1766, while Sterne himself was making his

4. *Monthly Review, 32* (Feb. 1765), 120–39.
5. *Letters,* pp. 235, 252. The two letters quoted from were written to Garrick in March 1765, and to Thomas Hesilrige in July 1765.
6. Vols. 3 and 4 of the *Sermons* had 693 subscribers, "thus outnumbering the [661] subscribers to the sermons of 1760 by a comfortable margin" (*Life,* pp. 238, 370). Sterne's list of subscribers included many distinguished names and the length of the list is impressive, though not unparalleled in the eighteenth century. Lansing Hammond in *Laurence Sterne's Sermons of Mr. Yorick* (New Haven, Yale Univ. Press, 1948), p. 87, mentions one collection of sermons at mid-century, which had more than 2,000 subscribers.

second continental tour. Generous extracts from these volumes soon
appeared in newspapers and periodicals, although critical comment
was somewhat sparse. There was no storm of protest at the manner of
publication, as there had been with Volumes 1 and 2. The *Monthly
Review* as usual commended the "pathetic touches," and the reviewer,
William Rose, praised Sterne's "good humour," "native pleasantry,"
and "philanthropy." Though he found serious subjects "but little suited
to Mr. Sterne's genius," Rose lauded the "many pertinent and striking
observations on human life and manners," asserting that every subject
was "treated in such a manner as shews the originality of his genius,
and as will, in some measure soften the severity of censure, in regard
to his ill-timed pleasantry and want of discretion." [7] The *Critical* was
of much the same opinion, adding at the same time a compliment to
Sterne's other work. Those who have read *Tristram Shandy,* the
reviewer says, will find "the same acute remarks on the manners of
mankind, the same striking characters, the same accurate investigation
of the passions, the same delicate strokes of satire, and the same art
in moving the tender affections of nature." [8]

Meanwhile a spurious Volume 9 of *Tristram Shandy* appeared at
about the same time as Volumes 3 and 4 of the *Sermons.* The reviewers
recognized this production as a counterfeit, but considered it a fairly
clever one, and some periodicals gave quite generous extracts from it.[9]
When the genuine ninth volume appeared a year later, most of the
critics had little left to say about it. The reviewer in the *Court Miscellany* left all criticism to his readers, saying, "Whether it has merit
or no, let the public, which formerly raised it into reputation, determine
for the present." [1] In similar vein, the *Critical* asserted that "a critic
would prove himself as extravagant as the author affects to be, should
he pretend to give a character of this work, whose wit may be termed
generical." The reviewer went on to express the wish "that it had been
a little better accommodated to the ear of innocence, *virginibus pueris-
que"*; but thought that "of all the authors who have existed since the
days of Rabelais, none can with more justice than Tristram put his
arms a-kimbo, strut through his room, and say, 'None but myself can
be my parallel.' " [2] The days when *Tristram Shandy* could cause much
of a critical furor were seemingly over,[3] and the *Monthly* was alone in

7. *Monthly Review, 34* (March 1766), 207–15.
8. *Critical Review, 21* (Jan. and Feb. 1766), 49–54, 99–106.
9. See, e.g., *Royal Magazine, 14* (March 1766), 116–18; *Critical Review, 21* (Feb.
1766), 141.
1. *Court Miscellany, 3* (Jan. 1767), 41.
2. *Critical Review, 23* (Feb. 1767), 138.
3. In some cases, however, individuals still waxed eloquent on the issue of immorality. A correspondent wrote to *Lloyd's Evening Post, 20* (March 12, 1767), 241,
that nothing "disgraces the present age more" than for Sterne, a clergyman, to write
"the most feeling compositions, to rouse our sensitive appetites; to inflame with lust,

giving extended comment on the ninth volume and a complete analysis of its contents. This review, again written by Griffiths himself, contains a good deal of banter about the misplaced chapters and the blank pages—Griffiths thinks it would have been well for Sterne's reputation if "some scores" of other pages had "been left in the like state of primaeval innocence!"—and the dedication is also the subject of pleasantry: "The volume opens with a *dedication,* to a great man :— and a *great man* he must be, indeed, who finds out the wit or the humour of this preliminary scrap. But, with this Merry-Andrew of a writer," Griffiths continues, "the jest oftentimes consists only in his setting dull readers to work, in order to *find the jest out:* while he stands by, grinning like a satyr, and enjoying the fun of seeing them busily employed, like the wise men of Gotham, in dragging the fish-pond to get out the moon." There is praise, however, for the apostrophe to Jenny, for several strokes in connection with Uncle Toby's character, and for the "art in composition" and "delicacy" in chapter 31, when Trim finally tells Uncle Toby the real reason for the Widow Wadman's solicitude. Finally, Griffiths finds a new way to characterize Sterne and his work. Though some critics have compared him to Cervantes, and others "with more propriety, to Rabelais," they are all mistaken. Sterne's "real prototype" is Harlequin and "so motley a performance" as *Tristram Shandy* "can only be denominated the PANTOMIME OF LITERATURE." [4] On this note stressing the varied character of Sterne's novel, the contemporary reviews of *Tristram Shandy* reach a fitting end.

Several things should have become apparent in this outline of the reception of Sterne's work up through the ninth volume of *Tristram Shandy.* The unprecedented popularity of the initial *Shandy;* the denunciations of Sterne's supposed obscenity and immorality; the charges of oddity, incoherence, and dullness ; and the gradual acceptance of Sterne's work and genius are all to be seen in the reviews and documents of the time. Behind this story, however, there is another story to be traced, and it is with this that we shall now be concerned.

Out of the mass of statements about Sterne, there arises the impression that despite his popularity and the fame (as well as the notoriety) which he achieved, few people in his own time could agree on the precise way his work should be regarded. The same reviewer who had praised Volumes 1 and 2 of *Tristram Shandy* later censured them for inspiring the obscenity of Hall-Stevenson's *Crazy Tales.*[5] The *Monthly*

and debauch and corrupt our youth of both sexes," and concluded that "surely our Spiritual Rulers must *frown* at these things!" Another letter was sent by a group of outraged moralists to the Archbishop of York, suggesting that strong censure of some sort be dealt Sterne, although apparently nothing came of it. (See *Life,* pp. 423–4.)

4. *Monthly Review, 36* (Feb. 1767), 93–102.
5. William Kenrick, ibid., *21* (Appendix 1759), 561–71; *26* (June 1762), 450–4.

Review was offended at the manner of publication of the *Sermons,* while the *Critical* was not. The *Critical* thought that *Tristram Shandy* was written "merely *pour la refection corporelle*" and stressed the resemblance of Sterne to Rabelais; while the *Monthly* found the Rabelaisian "nasonic Rhodomontade" of the second installment dull, not knowing whether it was "religious, political, or lascivious," and insisted that Sterne's forte lay in the pathetic.[6] One critic could find "latent lessons of virtue and morality" in Sterne's work,[7] while another writer could insist with equal vigor that Sterne "turns pander to the public, and tickles their sensuality with the feather of buffoonry and obscenity." [8]

Sterne himself was keenly aware of this diversity of opinion as to the proper interpretation of *Tristram Shandy.* Half-jokingly, perhaps, he referred to the book as "a moral work, more read than understood"; [9] but only a few weeks before his death, in writing to thank an admirer who had sent him an unusual walking stick (which he called "a shandean piece of sculpture"), he spoke in more serious vein:

> Your walking stick is in no sense more shandaic than in that of its
> having *more handles than one*—The parallel breaks only in this,
> that in using the stick, every one will take the handle which suits his
> convenience. In *Tristram Shandy,* the handle is taken which suits
> their passions, their ignorance or sensibility. There is so little
> true feeling in the *herd* of the *world,* that I wish I could have got
> an act of parliament, when the books first appear'd, "that none but
> wise men should look into them." It is too much to write books
> and find heads to understand them . . . but it is not in the power
> of any one to taste humor, however he may wish it—'tis the gift
> of God—and besides, a true feeler always brings half the enter-
> tainment along with him. His own ideas are only call'd forth by
> what he reads, and the vibrations within, so entirely correspond
> with those excited, 'tis like reading *himself* and not the book.[1]

As Sterne so clearly realized, readers and critics of *Tristram Shandy* had taken many different "handles" in approaching the book; and in their choice of these different approaches, they reveal something about the tastes and the attitudes of Sterne's time.

6. Owen Ruffhead, *Monthly Review, 24* (Feb. 1761), 104.

7. *London Magazine, 29* (Sept. 1760), 496.

8. "Animadversions on TRISTRAM SHANDY," *Grand Magazine, 3* (April 1760), 197. This essay, by a correspondent who signs himself "O," is witty in tone; but if he had found "lessons of virtue and morality" in Sterne, he would not have been disposed to write this kind of witty attack.

9. *Works: Sermons, 2, 97.* The reference occurs in the "Advertisement" to the sermon "The Abuses of Conscience Considered," as it was reprinted in 1766.

1. *Letters,* p. 411. The letter is to Dr. John Eustace in America, in answer to a letter of his accompanying the gift.

Part of the seeming disagreement at different times by the critics of the book may be explained, of course, by the differences in the character of the different installments. Many elements remain pretty much constant throughout all nine volumes, but Sterne's emphasis does change in one important respect. In the biography of Sterne already referred to, Hill had informed his readers of the quarrel in the York diocese "to which, perhaps, we owe the origin of the history of Tristram." [2] Though Sterne asserted, after his revision of the first two volumes, that "all locality is taken out of the book—the satire general," [3] Hill's article helped to spread a somewhat contrary impression; [4] and more than a trace of "locality" does remain in the satire of the first four volumes. The attacks on individuals in the characters of Dr. Slop, Didius, Phutatorius, and Kunastrokius are unmistakable, although these personal attacks are replaced in the later installments by the more generalized raillery against such targets as false learning, novel writers, guidebooks, and travelers. Nor is the satire itself as strongly emphasized in the later installments. Thus, it is not surprising that critics of the later volumes do not comment at any great length on the satirical elements,[5] while some of the critics of the early volumes saw them almost wholly in terms of satire. A writer in the *Imperial Magazine* said in 1760: "Mr. Sterne doubtless possesses in the highest degree the art of ridiculing the ruling passions, or hobby horses, as well as the vices and follies of mankind. No man is equal to him in the 'ridentem dicere verum.' " [6] The *Annual Register* for 1760, in an article almost certainly by Edmund Burke, also stressed the satirical purpose of Volumes 1 and 2: "The story is in reality made nothing more than a vehicle for satire on a great variety of subjects. Most of these satirical strokes are introduced with little regard to any connexion, either with the principal story or with each other." The satire may not always be "happily introduced," the article continues, but it is "spirited,

2. *Works: Letters and Miscellanies, 1, 36*. Hill summarizes the quarrel which resulted in Sterne's writing *A Political Romance*.

3. *Letters*, p. 81.

4. Hill refers to Dr. B[urton] as the probable original of Dr. Slop and Dr. Mead as the original for Kunastrokius. He also says that "it is scarce to be credited whose liberal purse has bought off the dread of a tutor's character" in future installments (*Works: Letters and Miscellanies, 1,* 40). Though not named, Warburton is of course the tutor referred to. (See below, p. 28.) Although he did give Sterne a purse of guineas, the inference of bribery is unsupported and was specifically denied by Sterne. See *Letters*, pp. 92–5, 102, 110.

5. In the review of Vols. 5 and 6, the *Critical, 13* (Jan. 1762), 66, merely refers to "much good satire on the follies of life"; while the *Library, 1* (Dec. 1761), 487, mentions "the same fine ridicule of false learning" which had been found in the earlier volumes. The tone of these comments is in itself indicative of the change in the character of the satire.

6. "On the Present State of Literature in England," *Imperial Magazine, 1* (Sup. 1760), 687. The article is signed "D." There is a copy of this magazine in the Harvard University Library.

poignant, and often extremely just" and Sterne "possesses in an high degree, the talent of catching the ridiculous in every thing that comes before him." [7]

As the satirical element diminishes in importance in the later volumes, Sterne focuses the spotlight on Uncle Toby, Trim, and the Widow Wadman and develops the more sentimental vein which critics referred to as "the pathetic." Barely hinted at in the passage on Uncle Toby and the fly in Volume 2 and certain parts of the story of Yorick,[8] this element is often in the ascendancy after the story of Le Fever in Volume 6. It is found, among other places, in the incident of the ass and the artichoke in Volume 7; the description of the country dance at the Languedoc vineyard, also in Volume 7; the description of the Widow Wadman's eye in Volume 8; and the story of the Negro girl in the sausage shop in Volume 9. One can see the way in which Sterne developed this side of his art and the change in his emphasis by comparing the story of Diego and Julia at the end of Slawkenbergius's tale in Volume 4 with the story of Maria in Volume 9. Both stories could have been treated in the same way, yet one is largely burlesque, while the other is thoroughly sentimental—at least until the last sentence, which the *Monthly* thought tended to *"spoil all,* by an ill-tim'd stroke of levity." [9] The tremendous popularity of the episode of Le Fever must have led Sterne to cater to the public taste in working this sentimental vein, and the critics obliged with the highest praise for it wherever it occurred. As the character of *Tristram Shandy* changed in this way with the later installments, the earlier praise for Sterne as a satirist tended to be replaced by praise for Sterne as a master of the pathetic.

Although the spotlight is focused on different groups of characters in the different parts of *Tristram Shandy,* the main characters appear and reappear throughout the book; and most of the critics agreed, from the beginning, that these characters were "striking," "singular," and "well supported." Even Horace Walpole, who found *Tristram Shandy* so dull that he never was able to get beyond the third volume, admitted that the characters "are tolerably kept up" in the first two volumes.[1] Richardson, likewise, found much more to blame than to

7. *Annual Register, 3* (1760), 247. This passage was frequently reprinted. For a discussion of the authorship of the article, see Thomas W. Copeland, "Edmund Burke and the Book Reviews in Dodsley's *Annual Register," PMLA, 57* (June 1942), 446–68, esp. 448, 468.

8. Anonymous, *The Clockmakers Outcry* (2d ed. London, 1760), p. 27, had referred to the account of Yorick as being "well imagined and pathetically written"; and the *London Magazine*'s reviewer had used the adjective "pathetik" among others in his review of Vols. 1 and 2 (see above, p. 4).

9. *Monthly Review, 36* (Feb. 1767), 99.

1. *Correspondence with George Montagu,* ed. W. S. Lewis (2 vols. New Haven, Yale Univ. Press, 1941), *2,* 255; *Correspondence with Dalrymple,* p. 66.

praise in the novel, but asserted that "Yorick, Uncle Toby, and Trim are admirably characterised, and very interesting." [2]

Particular praise, of course, was reserved for the character of Uncle Toby. Scarcely more than two years after the initial installment of *Tristram Shandy* had appeared, an unknown writer in the *Critical* asserted that Uncle Toby was a great comic character, worthy to be enshrined beside the best creations of Fielding and Smollett. "Instances of the *vis comica*" are rarely exhibited in contemporary novels, he says, for "the historian thrusts himself too frequently upon the reader" and the characters "are distinguished merely by their opposition to some other characters. . . . How different from this," he continues, "is the ridiculous simplicity of Adams, the absurd vehemence of Western, the boisterous generosity of Bowling, the native humour of Trunnion, and the laughable solemnity of uncle Toby! Each of these characters singly is complete; without relation to any other object they excite mirth." Thus, "the novels in which those characters are to be found, will furnish perpetual amusement, while others, which entertain merely from the nature of the incidents, and the conduct of the fable, are for ever laid aside after a single perusal: an engaging story will bear relating but once; a humorous character will bear viewing repeatedly." [3]

Although Uncle Toby was certainly the most universally admired and loved of Sterne's creations,[4] all of the major characters were widely praised. A writer in the *Library* was probably speaking for the majority of *Tristram Shandy*'s readers when he said: "Though we have Tristram's father and mother, and uncle Toby, and Trim, and Susannah, and Obadiah, and Dr. Slop, over and over again, yet Mr. Sterne has contrived to render them highly entertaining." [5]

At the same time that Sterne's characters were being continually praised, he was being attacked as continually for his supposed immorality. These attacks were variously motivated. First, there was a relatively small group of people who sincerely believed that both Sterne and his work were immoral. Johnson appears to have been of this number,[6] as were other moralists and divines.[7] Mary Granville

2. *Correspondence of Samuel Richardson,* ed. Anna L. Barbauld (6 vols. London, 1804), 5, 148. See below, p. 32.

3. *Critical Review, 13* (May 1762), 427–8. The remarks occur during the review of *Sir Launcelot Greaves.*

4. The wit who tried to make sport of Uncle Toby and insinuate that he got his wound not at Namur, but "in storming a castle of Venus," was practically alone in his exhibition of poor taste; see *Life and Opinions of Bertram Montfichet* (2 vols. London, [1761]), *1*, 14. Also in a decided minority was the critic who thought that Sterne's characters, modeled after those of Rabelais, "approach almost to Caricaturas." *Account of Living Authors,* p. 20.

5. *Library, 1* (Dec. 1761), 487.

6. See above, pp. 7–8. Lewis P. Curtis thinks that Sterne's being a Whig may have increased Johnson's lack of respect for him (*Politicks of Laurence Sterne,* London,

Delany, wife of the Dean of Down, wrote to her sister that *Tristram Shandy* "*has not* and *will not* enter this house.*" In another letter she admitted that the book was "read here as in London, and seems to divert more than it offends," but reported that she had had a "furious argument" with one of her friends about "reading books of a bad tendency," like *Tristram Shandy*. "I stood up for preserving a purity of mind," she says, "and discouraging works of *that kind—she* for trusting to her *own strength* and *reason,* and bidding defiance to any injury such books could do her; but as I *cannot presume* to depend on my own strength of mind, I think it safest and best to *avoid* whatever may prejudice it." [8] Unquestionably some people attacked the alleged immorality of *Tristram Shandy* from secondhand reports, not wishing to take the chance of sullying their minds by reading it.

Many of the reports which contributed to Sterne's ill fame came from the inevitable tendency to couple his name with those of his imitators and to blame him for setting a bad example, both as a clergyman and as an author. Numerous wits wrote bantering letters to magazines and newspapers, and the pamphleteers were constantly writing mock attacks to capitalize on the value of Sterne's name. "If Tristram Shandy has done any mischief," said the *London Magazine,* " 'tis in raising such a swarm of filthy pamphleteers, to din the ears and poison the eyes of the publick." [9] The *Monthly,* in censuring another priest, Charles Churchill, for a choice of subjects "somewhat free for a Clergyman," likewise noted that "*Tristram* has led the way [and] many of the cloth will probably follow him." [1] Richardson and Fielding also had their imitators who were of inferior talent, but the imitations were not able to harm the originals as much as they did in the case of Sterne: for the scurrility of Sterne's imitators was unparalleled. Even though some critics recognized the differences between Sterne and his imitators,[2] it is not surprising that he was attacked almost as much for the example he had set as for the alleged indecencies of his own works.

The figure that Sterne cut in the fashionable world also invited

---

Oxford Univ. Press, 1929, p. 136). Apparently Johnson thought *Tristram Shandy* itself beneath criticism, for no extended critical comments are recorded. See below, however, pp. 60, 72–3.

7. See, among others, William Dodd's poem, "To the Author of Tristram Shandy," in his *Poems,* London, 1767, pp. 61–2. Though not above reproach himself as a clergyman, Dodd castigates Sterne severely. See also the poem by "Telemachus" in *Lloyd's Evening Post, 6* (June 16–18, 1760), 578.

8. *Mary Granville, 3,* 588, 593. The letters, addressed to Anne Granville Dewes, are dated April 24 and May 14, 1760.

9. *London Magazine, 29* (June 1760), 328.

1. Ralph Griffiths, *Monthly Review, 25* (Dec. 1761), 451. Griffiths is reviewing Churchill's *Night.* Cf. Anonymous, ibid., *23* (July 1760), 83.

2. See, e.g., *Library, 2* (March 1762), 120; *Critical Review, 13* (June 1762), 475–80; *Candid Review,* June 1765, pp. 441–2.

attack, as one can see from a passage in Charles Johnstone's *The Reverie,* which was published in 1762. Though Sterne is not named, no reader could have been in doubt that it was he who was intended in this characterization of a "professed man of wit": "Observe that man who stands in yonder coffee-house, pumping his brain for pleasantry, and labouring for wit to entertain the sneering croud around him, whose fulsome compliments and ironical applause pass upon his vanity for a tribute justly due to his merit." The individual in question had been "raised to this eminent station," Johnstone continues, "by the success of a ballad . . . of which it may be difficult to determine whether its merit lay in its oddity, its obscenity, or its profaneness." The fame which this procured for its author gave him access to "the tables of all those who liked such buffoonery," and he took advantage of their hospitality "to sollicit subscriptions for a collection of *old saws* which he had picked up and tagg'd some how together." Thinking to make his fortune, he soon published *"a second part of the same tune,"* but since "the novelty that recommended the former [had] now worn off, there was little or no notice taken of it," even though he had included a "most plentiful measure" of obscenity and profaneness in the work to make up for its lack of quality. Angered at the public's apathy toward his second installment, he "takes the liberty, by way of reprisal, to turn every thing that it approves into ridicule, with a petulance little short of scurrility; and to support the character of a privileged wit, never misses an opportunity to being impertinent to every person he converses with." Johnstone continues with some general remarks on wit, deploring the fact that it has degenerated into "ridicule and insult" and concerns itself with "personal misfortunes and defects." Thus, "the moment a man professes himself a *wit,*" Johnstone says, he "declares war with all the rest of the world; as in return every one lies on the watch to pull down and punish so invidious a presumption. Of this he continually meets the most mortifying instances, to which the means he is obliged to make use of to support such a character, lay him constantly and defencelessly open." To support this contention, Johnstone relates a lengthy, scurrilous anecdote which is completely to Sterne's discredit.[3] Jealousy of Sterne's success may very well be one factor behind attacks of this kind, but Sterne's own conduct also gives a clue

3. *The Reverie; or, A Flight to the Paradise of Fools* (2 vols. Dublin, 1762), *1,* 189–99 (Bk. II, chs. 15, 16). Though Sterne's name is nowhere mentioned, the passage must refer to him, for the parallel is very close in all particulars except that no reference is made to his being a clergyman. John Taylor assumed that Sterne was referred to and quotes loosely from the passage in his *Records of My Life* (2 vols. London, 1832), *1,* 62. Johnstone may have invented the anecdote he relates, but more probably stories of this kind were current in the coffeehouses and the jest books of the day. Johnstone was author of the very popular *Chrysal, or the Adventures of a Guinea,* which has been called "the best scandalous chronicle of the day." *The Reverie* was reprinted at London in 1763 and 1767; copies are in University of Michigan Library.

as to their motivation. From his letters as well as from the accounts of other people, it is clear that he did sometimes play the part of a "professed man of wit"; [4] and Johnstone's account is a pretty accurate picture of the consequences. It is this side of Sterne's character which probably occasioned Johnson's disapproval of him, and it is also behind the change in his relationship with Warburton.[5]

Once Sterne had played this role of the wit in London, he found that it helped to call forth the attacks of the critics in the magazines which have been noted earlier; but he soon found that it also brought onslaughts which were of an even less dignified sort even though many

4. See above, pp. 6–8.
5. For a discussion of Johnson's attitude, see above, pp. 7–8. It is interesting to trace Warburton's relationship with Sterne. Garrick brought the two men together soon after Sterne's arrival in London in 1760. Warburton had been worried by the rumor that Sterne planned to satirize him as Tristram's tutor in the next *Shandy,* but Sterne disclaimed the intention. (See above, p. 23; *Life,* pp. 210–11; *Letters,* pp. 92–5.) The Bishop gave Sterne a purse of guineas and some books to improve his style, and sent rather pompous letters of advice to him during June after he had returned to York (*Letters,* pp. 112–16, 118–19). Meanwhile, Warburton must have been none too pleased to have one of the pamphlet imitations of Sterne dedicated to him (*The Clockmakers Outcry* was dedicated to "the most humble of Christian prelates") and he apparently felt that Sterne's conduct during his London visit had made him an undesirable object of his further patronage. (See above, pp. 6–7.) The second installment of *Shandy,* which contained an uncomplimentary allusion to the Bishop (*4,* ch. 20; *Work,* p. 298), brought the comment from Warburton in a letter to Mason that "Tristram Shandy is falling apace from his height of glory" (A. W. Evans, *Warburton and the Warburtonians,* London, Oxford Univ. Press, 1932, p. 231). The fifth and sixth volumes he thought better, since they were "wrote pretty much like the first and second," but by this time he had come to regard Sterne himself as "an irrecoverable scoundrel" (*Letters from a Late Eminent Prelate,* ed. Richard Hurd, London, [1809], p. 247). Warburton could not entirely escape from his previous associations with Sterne, however, for the *Monthly* referred to "these little Shandean Volumes" in reviewing his *Doctrine of Grace* in 1761 (see above, p. 3), and an unknown poet in *St. James's Magazine,* 2 (July 1763), 316, cited Warburton as an authority for approving of Sterne: "Where G———————r's prelate laughs why may not I?" (this is the same poem referred to in n. 7, p. 16, above). In 1766 Warburton said to Mason that Sterne was an "egregious Puppy" who had been ungrateful for his "most friendly services" (*Warburton and Warburtonians,* p. 231). Vol. 9 of *Tristram Shandy* contains Sterne's parting thrust at the Bishop when he speculates that *Tristram* has as good a chance for immortality as the *Divine Legation of Moses* (*9,* ch. 8; *Work,* p. 610). Warburton's final reference to Sterne comes in a letter to Charles Yorke at the time of Sterne's death: "Poor Sterne . . . was the idol of the higher mob . . . [and] chose the office of common jester to the many. But what is hard, he never will obtain the frivolous end he aimed at, the reputation of a wit, though at the expence of his character, as a man, a scholar, and a clergyman. . . . He chose Swift for his model: but Swift was either luckier or wiser, who so managed his wit, that he will never pass with posterity for a buffoon; while Sterne gave such a loose to his buffoonery, that he will never pass for a wit" (*Letters from Dr. Warburton to the Hon. Charles Yorke,* London, 1812, p. 89). The history of the relationship tells a good deal about the characters of the two men. If it shows something of Warburton's overbearing and pompous manner, it also reveals Sterne's imprudence as well as his independence. The rupture between the two is a good example of what sometimes happened after Sterne had played the part of a professed wit during his London visit.

of them must have been made with tongue in cheek. Thus, in the summer of 1760, one pamphleteer penned *A Letter from the Rev. George Whitfield, B.A. to the Rev. Laurence Sterne, M.A.,* in which the attack on Sterne is used as an ironic device for attacking the Methodists as well. The author, supposedly speaking in the character of Whitefield, asserts that the "prophane history of *Tristram Shandy* is as it were anti-gospel, and seems to have been penned by the hand of Antichrist himself." Sterne is told that the time will come when he will mourn his past follies and "no longer meet with a harlot at St. James's Park, or lasciviously yield to the temptations of the flesh at Ranelagh, but become a feast" where "a certain convocation of politic worms shall feed upon thy body, and there shall remain to thy soul only a fearful looking for of judgment." [6]

A year later in a mock funeral discourse, another pamphleteer undertakes to prove that Yorick is already dead, since he was "still-born" morally and the "intellectual" part of him has died, leaving only the animal part. He laments "the death of YORICK's better part . . . which was the vehicle of judgment and wit," asserting that the third and fourth volumes of *Tristram Shandy* prove "that it is now totally dead." After much pleasantry on Sterne's indecencies, he urges the reader to "learn, from the annihilation of YORICK, that licentious wit is a bubble . . . while decency and virtue are the surest paths to true honour." [7]

The depths of scurrility are plumbed by the author of an "Admonitory Lyric EPISTLE to the Rev. Tristram Shandy," which appeared in the *Grand Magazine* for June 1760. This versifier pretends to censure Sterne for his alleged lasciviousness and suggests that he either quit the priesthood and become a mountebank's assistant or submit to "an operation fit" and make himself "an eunuch for heav'n's sake: / And cheat the devil of his stake." [8]

Attacks of this kind, though seldom so contemptible, continued throughout Sterne's lifetime, but gradually abated in violence over the years. Archibald Campbell's *Sale of Authors,* which appeared in 1767, has much more savagery in its attacks on Johnson and Garrick than in its remarks on Sterne, who is nonetheless characterized as "the most harmless inoffensive poor mad Soul in the Universe." The plan of the book revolves around an auction of all the authors of the day, con-

6. *A Letter from the Rev. George Whitfield, B.A. to the Rev. Laurence Sterne, M.A.,* London, 1760. This pamphlet had two editions, one under a different title (see *Monthly Review, 23,* 85, 327). Whitefield, the prominent evangelist, was the leader of the Calvinistic branch of the Methodists.

7. *Alas! Poor Yorick!* This pamphlet was reviewed by both the *Critical* (*12,* 317) and the *Monthly* (*25,* 320) in October 1761.

8. *Grand Magazine, 3* (June 1760), 317–19.

ducted by Apollo with Mercury as his assistant. There is some genuine humor in the device of having Sterne put up for sale together with James Hervey, author of the pious *Meditations.* "The one is perpetually grinning and laughing," Mercury says, "the other praying and ejaculating. They are, like Democritus and Heraclitus, foils to one another." Sterne is finally allowed to "go about his business," because he will not bring a good price; but Hervey is sold to a "Lady of Quality," who also buys John Cleland! Cleland is included in a group of authors who "deserve to be hanged" for their works, because they "inflame the passions of mankind, and stimulate them to vice, lewdness and debauchery." [9]

It is significant that Campbell does not include Sterne in this group of writers who "inflame the passions," but agreement on this point was not complete; and this has remained the central question in connection with the charges of immorality against Sterne. Were his writings of a nature to inflame the passions, as the writings of Fielding, and indeed of Richardson himself, had also sometimes been accused of doing, or were they merely in questionable taste? A few of the reviewers, as well as many of the scribblers who wrote mock attacks and the imitators who penned vulgar imitations, inclined to the former opinion. A writer in the *Grand Magazine* asserted that "no man or woman of warm imagination" could read Sterne's dissertation on the subject of midwifery "without feeling a violent itching and propensity, to make work for the sons and daughters of Pilumnus and Lucina." His conclusion was that "by all that's luscious, *Aristotle* and *Rochester* were mere Puritans compared to Shandy." [1] In reviewing Volumes 7 and 8 of *Tristram Shandy,* Griffiths likewise accused Sterne of "setting the reader's imagination to work, and officiating as pimp to every lewd idea excited by your own creative and abominable ambiguity." [2] But many of these attacks, like the first one quoted, occurred in works whose tone was witty and humorous rather than serious; and Griffiths went on to say that "if the public will be good-natured enough to over-look your imperfections—surely I may," obviously an indication that he thought Sterne's sins more venial than one might suppose from the rest of his statements.

Even the critics who censured Sterne most harshly on this score usually found some redeeming features in his work. In *The Anti-Times,* an anonymous poem addressed to Churchill and published in 1764, the poet describes a council in hell, which has met to choose a representative to "sow dissention" in England:

9. *The Sale of Authors* (London, 1767), pp. 109–19, 130.
1. "Animadversions on TRISTRAM SHANDY," pp. 194–8. Pilumnus and Lucina are mentioned, of course, from their connection with childbirth in classical mythology. Cf. *Grand Magazine, 3* (June 1760), 308–11.
2. *Monthly Review, 32* (Feb. 1765), 125–6.

> ASMODEUS next, (amidst lascivious leers,)
> Address'd the conclave of infernal peers:
> If I have any skill, in mischief's trade,
> St-rne is the man, shou'd be our Legate made;
> A Ch-rch buffoon, a sac-rd-tal ape,
> A Merry-Andrew, dress'd in decent crape.
> His volumes, full of innuendoes nice;
> Are great provocatives to carnal vice.
> His chesnuts, STARS, and BLANKS, and NOSES are
> So many traps, to catch th' unwary Fair.
> Much of the jargon lumber of his book,
> May well be deem'd an Asmodean hook.
> 'Twas I at first inspir'd my Tristram's soul,
> To write the SLAWKENBERGIAN STARRY scrole;
> I sent the lustful vapours to his brain,
> And made concupiscence th' ascendant gain:
> Then his opinions he produc'd to view;
> From whence great gain will to our state accrue.

Belial, however, disagrees with Asmodeus as to Sterne's fitness for the task:

> Now fraudful BELIAL cut Asmodeus short,
> And rising, thus address'd the list'ning court:
> That St-rne is one of Vice's champions bold,
> Is high in Pandemonium's list inroll'd,
> All this I grant: but beg Asmodeus' leave,
> Reasons against this CANDIDATE to give.
> Tho' SLAWKENBERGIUS makes young sinners smile,
> And STARS, and BLANKS, and NOSES, may beguile;
> Tho' what he writes, almost the greatest part,
> May tend to stain with sin the humane heart,
> Flashes of wit, and sense, break radiant forth!
> And shew the man has much internal worth.
> No spleen, nor malice rank, first-born of Hell,
> Nor sland'rous thoughts within his bosom dwell.
> He's guilty of a most religious book;
> A fault, which we can never overlook.
> Rakes, bucks, and bloods, and ev'n girls of night,
> Conn'd Yorick's pages o'er with vast delight:
> The courtiers, statesmen, beaus, and men of trade,
> All read the sermons, which poor Y-rick made:
> I fear some lines flash'd veng'ance in their face,
> And kindled up a quenchless flame of grace.
> This MERRY way may work our state a spite;

Perhaps he'll JEST them into realms of light.
Some latent sparks of grace within him dwell,
He lashes faults, and hobby-horses well;
Therefore no fit ambassador from Hell.[3]

Moreover, Sterne's more discerning critics usually agreed that his
indecency was not such as to arouse the passions. Two men of such
widely differing talents and points of view as Samuel Richardson and
John Cleland agree on this. The author of *Clarissa* wrote to his friend
Mark Hildesley, Bishop of Sodor and Man: "Who is this Yorick?
you are pleased to ask me. You cannot, I imagine have looked into his
books: execrable I cannot but call them; for I am told that the third
and fourth volumes are worse, if possible, than the two first; which,
only, I have had the patience to run through. One extenuating circum-
stance attends his works, that they are too gross to be inflaming." [4]
The author of the *Woman of Pleasure* recalled a previous meeting with
Sterne, during the course of a conversation reported by Boswell:
"CLELAND. 'Sterne's bawdy [was] too plain. I reproved him, saying,
"It gives no sensations." Said he: "You have furnished me a vindica-
tion. It can do no harm." "But," I [said], "if you had a pupil who wrote
C— on a wall, would not you flogg him?" He never forgave me.' " [5]
One could hardly ask for better confirmation of the point at issue than
the statements of these two men of such different character; but the
penetrating review of Volume 9 of *Tristram Shandy* which appeared in
the *Gentleman's Magazine* also deserves quotation. The book "has
been charged with gross indecency," the reviewer says, "and the charge
is certainly true"; but indecency of this sort "does no mischief." It will
"disgust a delicate mind, but it will not sully a chaste one," for "it tends
as little to inflame the passions as Culpepper's Family Physician."
Actually, since "nastiness is the strongest antidote to desire," many
parts "that have been most severely treated by moralists and divines,
are less likely to do ill than good, as far as Chastity is immediately
concerned." But "how far he is a friend to society, who lessens the
power" of love "by connecting disgustful images with its gratifications,
is another question," the writer continues. "Perhaps he will be found

3. *The Anti-Times: Addressed to Mr. C—————— Ch--ch-ll* (London, 1764), pp.
6–8. There is a copy of this book in the Harvard University Library.
4. *Correspondence of Richardson, 5*, 146. The date of September 24, 1761 on Richardson's letter must be a mistake, for he died in July of 1761. In the letter he mentions
Edward Young's recent preferment to Clerk of the Closet of the Princess of Wales, and
implies that Vols. 3 and 4 of *Tristram Shandy* have already been published. Vols. 3
and 4 were published on January 28, 1761 (*Life*, p. 268) and Young's preferment is
recorded in the *Gentleman's Magazine* for February 1761 (*31*, 95). Hence, the letter
must have been written in late January or early February.
5. *Private Papers of James Boswell from Malahide Castle*, ed. Geoffrey Scott and
Frederick A. Pottle (18 vols. Mount Vernon, N.Y., 1928–34), *13*, 220; privately printed.
Boswell's conversation with Cleland took place on April 13, 1779.

to deserve the thanks of virtue no better than he, who, to prevent gluttony, should prohibit the sale of any food till it had acquired a taste and smell that would substitute nausea for appetite." The man who "would keep his relish of pleasure high, should not represent its objects in a ludicrous, much less in a disgusting light." [6]

This is, in effect, the same charge Goldsmith made in his attack on Sterne in Letter 53 of the *Citizen of the World,* when he said: "The veneration we have for many things entirely proceeds from their being carefully concealed. Were the idolatrous Tartar permitted to lift the veil which keeps his idol from view, it might be a certain method to cure his future superstition: with what a noble spirit of freedom, therefore, must that writer be possessed who bravely paints things as they are, who lifts the veil of modesty, who displays the most hidden recesses of the temple, and shows the erring people that the object of their vows is either, perhaps, a mouse or a monkey." The context in which this passage occurs makes it clear that Goldsmith is speaking ironically; for it comes at the center of an essay devoted entirely to denouncing Sterne and his book for the use of the twin figures of bawdy and pertness, by which "the merest blockhead" may gain "the reputation of a wit." Goldsmith attacks these two "fashionable" qualities of style as representative of the low level of the taste of the times. Sterne has revived the prurient wit which had not been in fashion since the days of Tom D'Urfey; and "though the successor of D'Urfey does not excel him in wit, the world must confess he outdoes him in obscenity." He closes the essay with some remarks on "pertness," which he sees as the natural accompaniment to bawdy:

> As in common conversation the best way to make the audience laugh is by first laughing yourself, so in writing, the properest manner is to show an attempt at humour, which will pass upon most for humour in reality. To effect this, readers must be treated with the most perfect familiarity: in one page the author is to make them a low bow, and in the next to pull them by the nose; he must talk in riddles, and then send them to bed in order to dream for the solution. He must speak of himself, and his chapters, and his manner, and what he would be at, and his own importance, and his mother's importance, with the utmost unpitying prolixity; now and then testifying his contempt for all but himself, smiling without jest, and without wit professing vivacity.[7]

6. *Gentleman's Magazine, 37* (Feb. 1767), 75–6. Cf. Walter Shandy's statement that "there is no passion so serious, as lust." *Tristram Shandy, 8,* ch. 34; Work, p. 592.

7. Letter 53, *Citizen of the World,* in *Works of Oliver Goldsmith,* ed. Peter Cunningham, Turk's Head Ed. (10 vols. New York and London, Putnam's, 1908), *4,* 308–14. Though Goldsmith's essay originally appeared after only the first two volumes of *Shandy* had been issued, his comments on the later installments would doubtless have been similar.

Much as Goldsmith appears to be blind to the genuine humor which can be found in *Tristram Shandy,* it must be admitted that he is representative of many readers of the novel in his comments upon the particular aspects which he has singled out. Such debatable examples of wit as the typographical tricks could be passed over easily as a joke which amused or not, according to the taste of the reader; but Sterne's other mannerisms were a more basic part of his style and could not be so lightly dismissed. These mannerisms unquestionably prevented some readers from seeing beyond them to the true humor of the characters and the situations. Thus Walpole thought *Tristram Shandy* "a very insipid and tedious performance" with the humor "forever attempted and missed." [8] Other leading literary figures of the day were not all so harsh in this respect, however; for Gray wrote to Wharton that "there is much good fun in [*Tristram Shandy*] & humour sometimes hit & sometimes mist." [9] Even Richardson, after castigating Sterne and his work in the letter to Hildesley already quoted from, modified his judgment to some extent: "Yet I will do him justice; and, if forced by friends, or led by curiosity, you have read, and laughed, and almost cried at Tristram, I will agree with you that there is subject for mirth, and some affecting strokes." [1]

While many people could appreciate the "good fun" and the subjects for mirth in the book, the prurient quality of some of Sterne's humor appealed to a more limited audience, composed mainly of two parts. First, there was the *beau monde* with its men and women of wit and fashion; and second, there were the coachmen and grooms for whose sole tastes, Griffiths asserted, the tale of the Abbess of Andoüillets had been adapted. Between these two extremes lay a vast number of the reading public for whom bawdy and pertness had little appeal, either on moral or aesthetic grounds.

Furthermore, reviewers of the later volumes give the impression more and more that they feel Sterne resorts to obscurity and obscenity when true wit fails him, and that the novelty of the early volumes has worn thin. Nor were the reviewers alone in this sentiment. Hume said to Boswell in the fall of 1762: *"Tristram Shandy* may perhaps go on a little longer; but we will not follow him. With all his drollery there is a sameness of extravagance which tires us. We have just a succession of Surprise, surprise, surprise." [2] A similar attitude is ex-

8. *Correspondence with Dalrymple,* p. 66.

9. *Correspondence of Gray, 2,* 681. Wharton appears to have expressed a like opinion, since Gray says: "I agree with your opinion of it, & shall see the two future volumes with pleasure."

1. *Correspondence of Richardson, 5,* 148. Richardson also goes so far as to use the word "Shandying" in a letter to Lady Bradshaigh; William M. Sale, Jr., *Samuel Richardson: Master Printer* (Ithaca, Cornell Univ. Press, 1950), p. 120.

2. *Papers from Malahide Castle, 1,* 127. For Hume's later more favorable comment see below, p. 60.

pressed two years later by an unknown writer in *Anecdotes of Polite Literature.* Extremes in composition are dangerous, he begins, for although a piece written "in a lively manner, which sets all method at defiance" will have a momentary vogue, "upstart books" of this kind "blaze a while and then are forgot." Already "men of sense and taste" regard *Tristram Shandy* as "a trifling book," not to be compared with *Don Quixote;* and a few years, he concludes, will bury it "in oblivion." [3] Though these predictions of doom were of course unfulfilled, they were perhaps to be expected from readers who could see only the novelty of the book. Such readers probably did not follow Sterne through all nine volumes.

The readers who did, apparently came to read the book less and less for the story. This was probably due to two factors, one to be found in the book itself, the other in its readers. As Sterne faced the problem of filling up each succeeding installment, he was driven more and more to include a certain amount of really extraneous material, which had much less connection with his central story than the digressions of Volumes 1 and 2 had. The prime example of this, of course, is to be found in the trip through France in Volume 7; but this is only an extreme instance of a general tendency. It certainly cannot be said of many of the digressions of the later installments that they are truly "progressive . . . at the same time," [4] in the way that those of the earlier volumes are. Furthermore, although most critics of the early installments were willing, with a few reservations, to accede to Tristram's request to "tell my story my own way," it became apparent as time went on, that not many readers fully appreciated Sterne's fundamental plan and purpose in *Tristram Shandy.* As Samuel Foote is said to have wittily remarked, "With all his *Stars* [Sterne] was but an *obscure writer.*" [5]

Sterne had given broad hints from the very first that he was following John Locke's principle of the "idea of duration and of its simple modes, [which] is got merely from the train and succession of our ideas," [6] as a means of developing his story, and that hence the seeming formlessness and the digressions were to be considered part of a general plan.

3. *Anecdotes of Polite Literature* (4 vols. in 5, London, 1764), *2*, Pt. II, 25. This collection has sometimes been attributed, though incorrectly, to Horace Walpole; see *Correspondence with the Rev. William Cole,* ed. W. S. Lewis (2 vols. New Haven, Yale Univ. Press, 1937), *1*, 57. Cf. the statement attributed to Richard Farmer that "however much [*Tristram Shandy*] may be talked about at present, yet . . . in the course of twenty years, should any one wish to refer to the book in question, he will be obliged to go to an antiquary to inquire for it." *New Monthly Magazine, 10* (Dec. 1818) 389.
4. *Tristram Shandy, 1,* ch. 22; Work, pp. 72–3. Cf. the digressions in Vols. 1 and 2 with the tale of Slawkenbergius in Vol. 4 or the digression on whiskers at the beginning of Vol. 5.
5. [John Croft], *Scrapeana* (2d ed. York, 1792), p. 130.
6. See *Tristram Shandy, 1,* chs. 4, 22; *2,* chs. 2, 8. Work, pp. 9, 72–3, 85, 103.

Churchill recognized this element in Sterne's work and paid him a very graceful compliment in Book III of the *Ghost:*

> Could I, whilst Humour held the quill,
> Could I digress with half that skill;
> Could I with half that skill return,
> Which we so much admire in Sterne,
> Where each digression, seeming vain,
> And only fit to entertain,
> Is found, on better recollection,
> To have a just and nice connexion,
> To help the whole with wondrous art,
> Whence it seems idly to depart;
> Then should our readers ne'er accuse
> These wild excursions of the Muse.[7]

None of the critics, however, makes any extended mention of Locke; and probably most readers did not understand this part of the plan of *Tristram Shandy* any better than the lady described in the fictitious "Journal of a Modern Man of Taste": "Oct. 2. Wait upon Lady L ‒ ‒ ‒ ‒, and find *Tristram Shandy* upon her toilet—She desires me to explain the stars. I excuse myself, by telling her I have not read it, and ask her what she thinks of *Locke?* She blushes—is confused—'and is surprised I should put so indecent a question to her.' " [8] Walpole had a glimmering of Sterne's plan when he said that "the great humour of [*Tristram Shandy*] consists in the whole narration always going backwards." But he did not really appreciate what Sterne was trying to do, since he thought the device was used as a joke rather than as a serious method. "I can conceive a man saying that it would be droll to write a book in that manner," he continued, "but have no notion of his persevering in executing it. It makes one smile two or three times at the beginning, but in recompense makes one yawn for two hours." [9] Walpole's friend, Sir Horace Mann, was "diverted" by the first two volumes of *Shandy,* but frankly confessed that he didn't understand the book and concluded that "it was probably the intention of the author that nobody should," since it seemed to be *"humbugging."* Of the second installment he merely commented, "Nonsense pushed too far becomes insupportable." [1] Apparently Garrick also found at least some

7. *Ghost,* Bk. III, ll. 967–78.
8. "The Adventures of an Author," *Gentleman's Magazine, 37* (March 1767), 116. For a full discussion of Locke's influence on Sterne see Kenneth MacLean, *John Locke and English Literature of the Eighteenth Century* (New Haven, Yale Univ. Press, 1936), pp. 17, 86–90, 119–20, 132–5, and passim.
9. *Correspondence with Dalrymple,* p. 66.
1. The letters to Walpole from which the quotations are taken are dated November 1, 1760, and August 1, 1761, and are in the Yale Walpole Collection. The two passages have

nonsense in *Tristram Shandy,* for in one of his poems he says that he will not "like friend *Shandy,* rattle, / And lose my matter in my prattle." [2] Even Boswell, though he admired and imitated Sterne, failed to see any sense of order in *Tristram Shandy.* Thinking of his own sketches, he set down an entry in his French exercises in the fall of 1763: "In these themes I can never resist anything laughable that presents itself, whether there is occasion for it or not. In this I follow the example of Rabelais, Tristram Shandy, and all those people of unbridled imagination who write their books as I write my themes— at random, without trying to have any order or method; and for that reason they have acquired great reputation among people of unregulated vivacity who do not wish to give themselves the trouble of thinking even in their amusements." [3] In a letter to Thomas Percy, James Grainger noted the same resemblance to Rabelais in Sterne's method, though he could not admire the "ravings" of Rabelais' "shatter-brained successor." [4]

Many readers interpreted the structural oddities of Sterne's work as the result of the rather odd sense of humor of a scatterbrained genius, a man who could sometimes tell a bawdy joke well, or write an amusing bagatelle, or even relate a truly pathetic tale upon occasion. They failed to find any relationship among these diverse elements of Sterne's work. The *Critical's* reviewer spoke for the majority when he characterized *Tristram Shandy* as "a work, which seems to have been written without any plan, or any other design than that of shewing the author's wit, humour, and learning, in an unconnected effusion of sentiments and remarks, thrown out indiscriminately as they rose in his imagination." [5] Many readers and critics alike agreed with this reviewer in thinking *Tristram Shandy* a novel in name only, for, new as the novel form was, they still had certain fairly definite ideas about what it should be. They might agree with Johnson that "if you were to read Richardson for the story, your impatience would be so much fretted that you would hang yourself" and that therefore he should be read "for the sentiment"; but they would also add, as Johnson did, that the story gave occasion to the sentiment.[6] With Sterne, not

been printed, with minor variations, in John Doran's *'Mann' and Manners at the Court of Florence, 1740–1786* (2 vols. London, 1876), *2,* 71–2. Walpole had written to Mann on May 24, 1760, that he was sending him some new books including "a fashionable thing called *Tristram Shandy*" (Yale Walpole Collection).

2. "The Sick Monkey," *Poetical Works* (2 vols. London, 1785), *1,* 39. This poem was published anonymously when Garrick returned from abroad in 1765.

3. *Boswell in Holland 1763–1764,* ed. Frederick A. Pottle (New York, McGraw-Hill, 1952), p. 67.

4. John Nichols, *Illustrations of the Literary History of the Eighteenth Century,* (8 vols. London, 1817–58), *7,* 276. The letter is dated June 5, 1761.

5. *Critical Review, 11* (April 1761), 316.

6. *Boswell's Life of Johnson, 2,* 175.

only were the sentiments and remarks pitched in many different keys, ranging from buffoonery, grossness, and a rather artificial wit in many passages to delicacy and a refined sentimentality in others; but there appeared to be no firm narrative thread to tie these varying elements together.

The fact remains that readers bought and read the book; and its tremendous popularity can be explained only by the very diversity of the work, since different aspects of it appealed to different readers. Fielding enthusiasts would find the same goodness of heart in *Tristram* that they admired in *Tom Jones,* and would also relish the comic scenes like Dr. Slop's fall. Those who had cried at *Clarissa* as her painful fate slowly overtook her, could weep with equal relish at the tale of Le Fever or that of Maria, even though they might be shocked at the Abbess of Andoüillets. Those who admired Rabelais, on the other hand, appreciated the satire and the buffoonery of his English successor. The more prurient elements of Sterne's humor furnished a momentary diversion for the fashionable world; and the wits found it a good joke to write mock attacks, like the bantering couplet,

> *If poor weak* women *go astray,*
> *Shandy's* Stars *are to blame, and not they.*[7]

Wits, imitators, scribblers, and critics alike, all capitalized on Sterne and his book for their amusement and profit. Finally, there were many things in *Tristram Shandy* which would appeal to the "impartial and judicious reader," as they did to the unknown correspondent of *Lloyd's Evening Post* who felt that "great merit" must be allowed for the "wit and good humour, impregnated with good sense and just satire." However distasteful the "loose manner of expression" might be "to the more rigid and saturnine," it "seems greatly to extenuate such faults," this writer concluded, "when we perceive, thro' the whole, that integrity and goodness of heart which remarkably characterize the Doctor's writings." [8] Wit, good humor, good sense, and just satire were the ideals of the age; and faults, indiscretions, and breaches against decorum could be overlooked, if integrity and goodness of heart lay underneath. Shaftesbury's and Hutcheson's doctrine of benevolence was nowhere better illustrated in the literature of the time than in parts of *Tristram Shandy;* [9] and much as critics might rail against Sterne for his indecency, they nevertheless appreciated this underlying current of philanthropy. The *Sermons,* in which this element was

7. *Lloyd's Evening Post, 6* (May 28–30, 1760), 513. The couplet is a parody of lines 11 and 12 of Matthew Prior's "Hans Carvel."
8. Ibid., *6* (June 25–27, 1760), 611. Although the writer is, of course, speaking only of the first two volumes, he strikes a note which is appropriate to characterize many of the reactions to the later installments as well.
9. See Work, pp. lxvi–lxvii, lxx.

supreme, were often valued above *Tristram Shandy* during Sterne's lifetime; and *Shandy* itself was most highly valued for this didactic and sentimental side. In his preface to *The Triumvirate,* an avowed imitation of Sterne, Richard Griffith said:

> In a work like this, designed for the Public at large, there must be something, in allusion to dramatic writings, to entertain the three different classes of auditors; pit, box, and gallery. . . .
>
> This then, may seem to have been the design of that anomalous, heteroclite genius, the author of Tristram Shandy, whose principal end, I hope and believe, was to inculcate that great Magna Charta of mankind, humanity and benevolence.
>
> "A tale may catch him who a sermon flies."
>
> 'Tis true indeed, that he has given us, according to the vulgar phrase, rather *more sauce than pig,* and this not sufficiently seasoned with *Attic salt,* neither. But he seems to have wrote more for the present age than the future ones.[1]

Sterne foresaw the future much more accurately than Griffith, when he thought that his book might "swim down the gutter of Time" along with the *Divine Legation* and the *Tale of a Tub;*[2] but he certainly would not have placed Griffith in the group of readers with whom *Tristram Shandy* was "more read than understood." Here, Sterne would have thought, was a reader who had grasped the right "handle."[3] What Sterne may not have realized is the fact that the readers who took other "handles" were equally important to the popularity of his book. In an age when the rapid expansion of the reading public was making it less and less homogeneous, only a book which had something for pit, box, and gallery alike could have had such a wide appeal.

1. *The Triumvirate, 1,* xiii–xiv.
2. *Tristram Shandy, 9,* ch. 8; Work, p. 610.
3. See above, p. 22.

Becoming a Classic (1768–79)

WHEN Sterne had published the slender, lone ninth volume of *Tristram Shandy* in 1767, he had obviously reached a point where further inspiration for *Shandy* was lagging, at least temporarily. He had already experimented successfully with using materials from his travels in the seventh volume of *Tristram Shandy,* however, and he had been thinking about a more extended work along the same lines. Less than a month after the publication of Volume 9 of *Shandy,* he wrote to his daughter Lydia that he had "laid a plan" for the *Sentimental Journey,* which was to be "something new, quite out of the beaten track." [1] The actual writing of the book he would defer until he got back to Coxwold, for he was busy, as usual when in London, with social engagements. His intimacy with the William Jameses began this year, and it was also at this time that he met Mrs. Draper, the Eliza whose close friendship undoubtedly influenced the tone of the *Sentimental Journey* [2] and was also to cause so much speculation and comment on the part of later biographers and critics.

Returning to Coxwold, he worked on the new project during the summer and fall, and by November of 1767 the *Sentimental Journey* was taking final shape. In a letter at this time, Sterne described it as being designed "to teach us to love the world and our fellow creatures better than we do" by emphasizing "those gentler passions and affections, which aid so much to it." [3] Two weeks later he confessed that Yorick had "worn out both his spirits and body with the Sentimental Journey," for he had torn his "whole frame into pieces" by his "feelings." [4] A few days later he described the two volumes as *"a couple of as clean brats* as ever chaste brain conceiv'd" although they were "frolicksome too." [5] Although he was obviously half joking when he called the *Sentimental Journey* his *"Work of Redemption,"* [6] he did expect it to win a favorable reception, and believed that it would not

---

1. *Letters,* p. 301.
2. See *Life,* p. 440.
3. *Letters,* p. 401. The addressee is Mrs. William James.
4. Ibid., p. 402. The addressee is an unidentified nobleman.
5. Ibid., p. 405. The addressee is Sir George Macartney.
6. This remark is reported from a conversation with Sterne at Scarborough in the early fall of 1767 by Richard Griffith in his and Elizabeth Griffith's *Series of Genuine Letters between Henry and Frances* (6 vols. London, 1766–70), 5, 83.

provoke the censure which *Tristram* had; for he predicted that "the women will read this book in the parlour, and Tristram in the bed-chamber." [7]

The initial success of the *Sentimental Journey* must have come up to Sterne's expectations, for shortly after its publication he wrote from London to his daughter Lydia: "My Sentimental Journey, you say, is admired in York by every one—and 'tis not vanity in me to tell you that it is no less admired here." [8] In some quarters, at least, the reception of the book exceeded that accorded to even the initial volumes of *Tristram Shandy,* and it won the esteem of many who had censured the earlier work. Horace Walpole, who had been unable to stomach *Tristram Shandy,* wrote to Gray early in March, "I think you will like Sterne's sentimental travels, which though often tiresome, are exceedingly good-natured and picturesque." [9] A few days later he wrote to George Montagu that Sterne's travels were "very pleasing, though too much dilated, and infinitely preferable to his tiresome *Tristram Shandy.* . . . In these there is great good nature and strokes of delicacy." [1] Richard Griffith recommended the *Sentimental Journey* to his wife, although he had censured the "loose expressions" of *Tristram Shandy.*[2] Elizabeth Montagu, the cousin of Sterne's wife, who had often upbraided him for the immorality of his earlier work, thought that "Poor Tristrams last performance was the best." [3] A year later Fanny Burney confided to her diary, "I am now going to *charm* myself for the third time with poor Sterne's 'Sentimental Journey.' " [4]

Not all the ladies read the *Sentimental Journey* in the parlor, however; and some refused to read it at all. Elizabeth Carter wrote to Elizabeth Vesey in April 1768 that she had not read the book and probably never would, "for indeed there is something shocking in whatever I have heard either of the author, or of his writings." Sterne's "benevolence," she felt, was merely "a substitute for virtue" and tended to "confound all differences of right and wrong. Merely to be struck by a sudden impulse of compassion at the view of an object of distress," she continued, "is no more benevolence than it is a fit of the gout, and indeed has a nearer relation to the last than the first." True benevolence would never allow a husband and a father to "neglect and injure" his family, though Sterne "by his carelessness and extravagance, has

7. *Letters,* p. 412. The addressee is unidentified.
8. Ibid., p. 417.
9. *Correspondence with Thomas Gray,* ed. W. S. Lewis (2 vols. in 1, New Haven, Yale Univ. Press, 1948), *2,* 183.
1. *Correspondence with George Montagu,* ed. W. S. Lewis and Ralph S. Brown, Jr. (2 vols. New Haven and London, Yale Univ. Press, 1941), *2,* 255.
2. See his preface to *The Triumvirate, 1,* xvi; *Series of Genuine Letters, 5,* 83.
3. *Letters,* p. 441.
4. *Early Diary of Frances Burney,* ed. Annie Raine Ellis (2 vols. London, G. Bell, 1889), *1,* 45.

left a wife and child to starve, or to subsist on the precarious bounty of others." [5] Mrs. Carter's disapproval of Sterne was obviously based on gossip and secondhand report; but another lady objected to the *Sentimental Journey,* after reading it, because she found Sterne's benevolence misplaced. When Elizabeth Burney praised Sterne's sensibility to the members of her reading circle, Fanny Greville exclaimed: "A feeling heart is certainly a right heart; nobody will contest that: but when a man chooses to walk about the world with a cambrick handkerchief always in his hand, that he may always be ready to weep, either with man or beast,—he only turns me sick." [6]

Unsympathetic critics of this sort were in a definite minority, however; for over the next few years the *Sentimental Journey* became as much of a fad as *Tristram Shandy* had ever been, and inspired a new deluge of imitations which continued, though somewhat sporadically, for nearly sixty years. Anything connected with Sterne's work had a better chance for a momentary hearing at least. An ode was written to Maria,[7] and we are told that prints of Angelica Kauffmann's picture of Maria "were circulated all over Europe" and "transferred to numerous articles of all sorts and sizes, from a watch case to a tea-waiter." [8] More than one author attempted to copy the pathos of Maria's story by dwelling on the description of a white handkerchief, unlaundered so that the tears of misery and affection might be preserved in it.[9] Many of the other incidents and characters from the *Sentimental Journey* were commonly imitated,[1] and the very word "sentimental," which Sterne had been instrumental in popularizing,[2] was referred to and

5. *Series of Letters between Mrs. Elizabeth Carter and Miss Catherine Talbot,* ed. Rev. Montagu Pennington (4 vols. London, 1809), *3,* 334–5. The true story of Sterne's generosity to his wife and child was not known until Mrs. Medalle's edition of her father's letters was published in 1775, and not fully appreciated until Fitzgerald's *Life of Sterne* appeared in 1864 (see below, pp. 50, 155–9). Other examples of a very practical benevolence have remained unknown even longer, among them Sterne's assiduous care in nursing George Oswald during the spring of 1763 at Toulouse; see Archibald Bolling Shepperson, "Yorick as Ministering Angel," *Virginia Quarterly Review, 30* (Winter 1954), 54–66.

6. Frances Burney D'Arblay, *Memoirs of Doctor Burney* (3 vols. London, 1832), *1,* 201. Mrs. Greville was the wife of Fulke Greville, Dr. Burney's close friend, and was Fanny Burney's godmother; Elizabeth Burney was Fanny Burney's stepmother.

7. *Sentimental Magazine, 3* (March 1775), 134.

8. Joseph Moser, as quoted in William T. Whitley, *Artists and their Friends in England 1700–1799* (2 vols. London and Boston, The Medici Society, 1928), *1,* 373. Moser was a late eighteenth-century artist.

9. See, e.g., *York Chronicle, 1* (May 14, 1773), 172; *Monthly Review, 42* (March 1770), 181.

1. See J. M. S. Tompkins, *The Popular Novel in England 1770–1800* (London, Constable, 1932), p. 51.

2. Although the word was apparently in use in fashionable conversation as early as 1749 when Lady Dorothy Bradshaigh in a letter to Richardson asked exactly what it meant, Sterne was the first to popularize it so fully through literature. Lady Bradshaigh's use of the word is the first recorded in the *OED,* and Curtis doubts that Sterne actually used it in a letter written nine years earlier (*Letters,* pp. 14–15).

used on title-pages wherever possible. Sentimental stagecoaches took journeys to all points of the compass. There were sentimental effusions, lucubrations, sketches, essays, and tales; a sentimental diary; and the story of a sentimental spy. In Sheridan's *Rivals,* Bob Acres even indulged in "sentimental swearing," and Lydia Languish had thought of a "sentimental elopement." [3] The reviewers protested that the word was a "barbarism," and that it was used so frequently that it became meaningless,[4] and moralists and literary critics alike soon attacked the new "sentimental" literature as they thought it became ridiculous or dangerous in the hands of Sterne's imitators.[5]

At the time that the *Sentimental Journey* first appeared, however, its novelty and its charm won almost unanimous praise from the periodicals. The *Court Miscellany* declared that the book "cannot fail to please every one who is not a stranger to social feelings"; [6] while the *London Magazine* referred to Sterne's "great talents notwithstanding his disregard of order." [7] The *Political Register* called it the best of Sterne's performances, expressing satisfaction that he had "added the moral and the pathetic" to the "original vein of humour which was so natural to him, and which constitutes the chief merit of his works." [8] The *Monthly's* extended review in March and April was of the same tone, for this periodical had for a long time been urging Sterne to develop his powers in "the pathetic" and use them for "moral instruction." Written by Griffiths himself, the article contains a certain amount of banter and points out a few grammatical slips, but praises Sterne warmly for his benevolence, his "delicacy of feeling," his "tenderness of sentiment," and his "simplicity of expression." "Is it possible," Griffiths asks, "that a man of *gross ideas* could ever *write* in a strain so pure, so refined from the dross of sensuality!" The *Sentimental Journey,* he concludes, was Sterne's best production, "though not, perhaps, the most admired of his works." [9]

Of the major periodicals, the *Critical* alone was unfavorable. The unknown reviewer found only "immorality, impudence, and dulness" in the book, and regretted sarcastically that "Yorick with his health lost that spirit which rendered him a favourite with thoughtless insipidity, and the dictator of lewdness and dissipation!" Sterne "set out in a

3. *The Rivals,* ii. i and v. i. In the same play, the *Sentimental Journey* is among the books that Lydia's maid brings to her from the circulating library (i. ii).

4. See *e.g.,* John Hawkesworth, *Monthly Review, 41* (Nov. 1769), 390. *Critical Review, 33* (April 1772), 325. Cf. John Wesley's comment, p. 56 below.

5. See below, pp. 68-9. Cf. the remarks of Hester Chapone, who thought that the indiscriminate reading of "sentimental" works "corrupts more female hearts than any other cause whatsoever." *Works of Mrs. Chapone* (4 vols. London, 1807), *3,* 181-2.

6. *Court Miscellany, 4* (Feb. 1768), 87.

7. *London Magazine, 37* (March 1768), 163.

8. *Political Register, 2* (May 1768), 383.

9. *Monthly Review, 38* (March, April 1768), 174-85, 309-19.

delirium," the reviewer continued, which had "the happy temporary effect of making the sufferings of others the objects of his mirth and not only rendering him insensible to the feelings of humanity, but superior to every regard for taste, truth, observation, or reflection." The reviewer further charged that the character of La Fleur had been "pieced out with shreds which Mr. Yorick has barbarously cut out and unskilfully put together from other novels." The book, he concludes, was "calculated to instruct young travellers in what the author meant for the *bon ton* of pleasure and licentiousness," but Sterne, unfortunately, "survived his art of imposing upon his countrymen *whim* for *sentiment,* and *caprice* for *humour."* [1] The main reason for the harshness of this review is doubtless to be found in Sterne's attack on Smollett in the character of Smelfungus; for even though Smollett's connection with the *Critical* had ceased some years before, the reviewer might well have felt called upon to fight back. There is no reference in the article, however, either to Smollett or to the offending passage; and it is possible that the particular reviewer also had some such bias as that of Joseph Cockfield, who wrote to a friend in March: "I have seen the reverend Prebendary's new publication; in his former writings I saw evident marks of his genius and benevolence, but who that indulges serious reflection can read his obscenity and ill-applied passages of Holy Scripture, without horror!" [2] Critical agreement had never been complete on any of Sterne's works during his lifetime, and this last was no exception.

Since Sterne's death came less than a month after the publication of the *Sentimental Journey,* in many cases reviews of the work were combined with eulogies. The passage from *Tristram Shandy* about the recording angel came to the minds of reviewers of the *Monthly Review* and the *London Magazine;* while a separate poem in the latter periodical paid tribute to Sterne for his command of both the humorous and the pathetic:

> With wit and genuine humour to dispel,
> From the desponding bosom, glooming care,
> And bid the gushing tear, at the sad tale
> Of hapless love or filial grief, to flow,
> From the full sympathising heart, were thine
> These pow'rs, O Sterne! . . . [3]

1. *Critical Review, 25* (March 1768), 181–5.
2. Nichols, *Literary History of Eighteenth Century,* 5, 780. The addressee is the Rev. Weeden Butler.
3. "On the Death of YORICK," *London Magazine, 37* (June 1768), 323. This poem was reprinted, with minor changes, in Mrs. Medalle's edition of the *Letters* in 1775, and often, thereafter, in editions of Sterne's *Works.*

A lengthier eulogy was published separately as "an humble attempt to do justice to the memory of Mr. STERNE; and screen it from the insults of those, whom levity or hunger may lead to lay hold upon the death of YORICK as an occasion of shewing their wit, or vending their Billingsgate." [4] The poet says that if heaven is a cheerful place where people who have practiced the social virtues on earth are welcomed, Sterne will be an angel there; though he will not find admittance to a heaven which must be gained by "meagre fastings" and "frantic prayers." In any event, he will be remembered on earth as long as wit, sense, and humor are valued. The poem concludes with an epitaph:

> He felt for man—nor dropt a fruitless tear,
> But kindly strove the drooping heart to chear;
> For this, the flowers by SHILOH's brook that blow,
> He wove with those that round LYCAEUM grow;
> For this, EUPHROSYNE's heart-easing draught
> He stole, and ting'd with wit and pleasing thought;
> For this, with Humour's necromantic charm,
> Death saw him Sorrow, Spleen, and Care disarm:
> With dread he saw—th' associates of his might
> Foil'd and expell'd the regions of the light;
> "If so," he cry'd, and seiz'd his sharpest dart,
> "My reign may end,"—then wing'd it at his heart.
>
> If faults he had—for none exempt we find,
> They, like his virtues, were of gentlest kind;
> Such as arise from genius in excess,
> Passions too fine, that wound—ev'n while they bless!
> Such as a form so captivating wear,
> If faults, we doubt—and, to call crimes—we fear;
> Such as, let Envy sift, let Malice fan,
> Will only shew that YORICK was a MAN.[5]

Much briefer, though perhaps more appropriate and certainly better known, is Garrick's poetic tribute:

4. A few scribblers were led by "levity or hunger" to take advantage of Sterne's death. Among the publications of this sort were *Sentiments on the Death of Sentimental Yorick By One of Uncle Toby's Illegitimate Children* and *The Fig Leaf—Veni, Vidi, Vici, Ivi; or, He's Gone! Who? Yorick! Grim Death Appears!* A copy of the latter may be found in the Harvard University Library. See also *Gentleman's Magazine, 38* (April 1768), 191, in which an earnest though untalented versifier defends Sterne from the charge which had been made in the following epigram on his death: "Wit, humour, genius, thou hadst, all agree; / One grain of Wisdom had been worth all three."

5. Anonymous, *Occasional Verses on the Death of Mr. Sterne* (London, 1768).

Shall pride a heap of sculptur'd marble raise,
Some worthless, unmourn'd titled fool to praise;
And shall we not by one poor grave-stone learn
Where genius, wit, and humour sleep with *Sterne?* [6]

Various legends have grown up around the neglect that Sterne and his memory are said to have suffered during his last illness and in the years succeeding his death. Later moralists have seized on legend and gossip, pointing a moral with stories of his "friendless" deathbed, the desecration of his corpse, and the neglect of his grave.[7] Cross has done much to dispel this impression of neglect, which seemed a strange and unfitting end for a great literary figure. One further piece of evidence may now be added. Although Cross believed that Sterne's grave was unmarked for more than ten years until "sometime near 1780," when two Freemasons erected a headstone with an inscription,[8] this headstone is reported in 1769 by the *Literary Register* as having been "lately erected." Hence, Sterne's grave cannot have remained unmarked for more than about a year. The inscription, though not completely appropriate, is appreciative:

If a sound head, warm heart, and breast humane,
Unsullied worth, and soul without a stain;
If mental powers could ever justly claim
The well won tribute of immortal fame,
Sterne was *the Man,* who, with gigantick stride,
Mowed down luxuriant follies far and wide.
Yet what, though keenest knowledge of mankind
Unsealed to him the springs that move the mind;
What did it cost him? ridicul'd, abus'd,
By fools insulted, and by prudes accused.
In his, mild reader, view thy future state,
Like him despise, what 'twere a sin to hate.[9]

These two readers, who evidently thought of Sterne mainly as a satirist and a psychologist, also added a statement that they had

6. *Poetical Works of Garrick, 2,* 484. The poem must have been written during 1768 or 1769 before Sterne's grave was marked (see below).
7. Most of these legends lie mainly outside the scope of the present study, but evidence as to the neglect of Sterne's grave is germane, since it would indicate whether his fame was soon forgotten.
8. *Life,* p. 494.
9. *Literary Register, 1* (1769), 285. (The numbers of this periodical are undated, but the position of the passage in the volume would place it in November.) The present text differs from that given by Cross in details of spelling, punctuation, and capitalization, and in the substitution of "cost" for "boot" in l. 9 and "state" for "Fate" in l. 11. Another version, halfway between the two, was printed in *Sterne's Witticisms, or Yorick's Convivial Jester* in 1782. The mistake on the stone in the date of Sterne's death, which is noted by Cross, is even harder to explain when one realizes that the stone must have been erected little more than a year after Sterne's death.

erected the stone because although Sterne was not a Mason, they felt
that "his incomparable performances" showed that he had "acted by
rule and square."

More important evidence to refute the charges of neglect of Sterne's
memory after his death and to prove the continuing interest in him
and his works is to be found in the pages of the periodicals of the day.
Biographical articles,[1] reviews of his posthumous publications, and
notices of the many imitations and forgeries connected with his name
all testify to the fact that he was far from being forgotten.

In 1769 Hall-Stevenson published his *Yorick's Sentimental Journey
Continued,* which was issued together with a reprint of the *Sentimental
Journey.* He claimed that he was carrying out Sterne's original in-
tentions as they had been related in conversation,[2] but this claim
appears to be a fraud, since the book introduces the stories of only one
or two new groups of characters and is mainly a vulgarized retelling
of the *Sentimental Journey.* It does not carry Sterne to Italy. The
biographical memoir which was prefixed contains some inaccuracies,
and not very much significant new information. The comments on
Sterne's work are taken mainly from the previous reviews in the
magazines, sometimes without acknowledgment. The publication was
universally condemned by the reviews of the day, the *Monthly* stating
that "the copy resembles the original, as much as the shadow of a
fine woman resembles the beautiful substance." [3]

The following year Richard Griffith published his *Posthumous
Works of a Late Celebrated Genius,* also known as *The Koran.* Posing
as an anonymous editor, Griffith alleged the production to be Sterne's
own attempt at an autobiography. Although the supposed editor
defended Sterne's writings by saying that they were "as indecent, but
as innocent, at the same time, as the sprawling of an infant on the
floor," [4] he nevertheless invented several biographical anecdotes which
were to Sterne's serious discredit. It is difficult to see how this work
could ever have gained a reputation for being genuine,[5] since the
Monthly Review promptly condemned it as "manifestly spurious," and
gave convincing internal evidence to back up the assertion.[6] Griffith

1. See below, pp. 53–4.
2. Although Hall-Stevenson speaks of Sterne's having "materials already prepared"
before his death, he does not claim to have used these notes, nor is he offering the
book "as the offspring of Mr. Sterne's pen." He asserts, however, that the *Sentimental
Journey* may now be considered "complete" and that the continuation is accurate in its
"facts, events, and observations."
3. Anonymous, *Monthly Review, 40* (May 1769), 428. Cf. *Critical Review, 27* (May
1769), 390; *London Magazine, 38* (June 1769), 323.
4. *Posthumous Works of a Late Celebrated Genius* (2 vols. London, 1770), *1,* v.
This defense was widely quoted and later used by Scott in his life of Sterne.
5. J. M. S. Tompkins speculates, however, that the book may contain some echoes of
Sterne's conversation. "Triglyph and Tristram," *TLS, 28* (July 11, 1929), 558.
6. John Hawkesworth, *Monthly Review, 42* (May 1770), 360–3. The *Critical,* how-

himself revealed the attempted fraud in another anonymous publication two years later.[7] Nevertheless, it has sometimes been included in complete editions of Sterne's works.

The first of Sterne's genuine posthumous publications came a little more than a year after his death, with the appearance in June 1769 of Volumes 5, 6, and 7 of the *Sermons of Mr. Yorick.* In view of the fact that Sterne had said the third and fourth volumes of the sermons were "probably the last (except the sweepings of the Author's study after his death) that will be published," [8] it is perhaps surprising that these posthumously published sermons fared critically as well as they did. Reviewers in the *Gentleman's Magazine* and the *Literary Register* pronounced them of a piece with the previous *Sermons of Mr. Yorick.*[9] The *Town and Country Magazine* and the *Critical Review* both speculated that Sterne had never intended these discourses for publication, since they were rather "superficial," but commended them for their "ease" and "sprightliness." The *Critical's* reviewer concluded that "those who admire the productions of this agreeable writer . . . would willingly subscribe for the sweepings of his study." [1] The *Monthly* carried by far the harshest review, declaring that it was "a very injudicious kindness in our surviving friends, to publish *the sweepings of our studies,*" and asserting that the sermons "might have been the work of Mr. Sterne's curate,—or of any other curate in the kingdom," if one judged them by their quality.[2] The earlier volumes of the *Sermons* continued to be popular, and several collected editions of all forty-five discourses appeared during the seventies.[3] After this they were seldom published separately, though usually included in editions of Sterne's collected works.

Shortly after the appearance of the *Sermons,* Sterne's *Political Romance,* the pamphlet concerning an ecclesiastical squabble at York which he had published but immediately suppressed in 1759, was printed both in the *Westminster Magazine* and in separate pamphlet form. The editors of the periodical had preserved the piece, though it was "of a temporary nature," so that "not a dash of this Writer's pen

ever, had accepted the piece as genuine, although with some reservations; *29* (Feb. 1770), 102–9.

7. *Something New* (2d ed. 2 vols. London, 1762 [i.e. 1772]), *2,* 67–71.

8. *Works: Sermons, 2,* 98.

9. *Gentleman's Magazine, 39* (June 1769), 310; *Literary Register, 1* (1769), 138.

1. *Town and Country Magazine, 1* (July 1769), 381; *Critical Review, 28* (July 1769), 48–53.

2. Anonymous, *Monthly Review, 41* (July 1769), 73.

3. Vols. 1 and 2 had reached a tenth edition by 1771 [Yale] and Vols. 3 and 4 were reprinted in 1768, 1770, and 1773 [Yale]. There were the following collected editions: 2 vols. 1769, 7 vols. 1773 [Boston], 6 vols. 1775, 6 vols. 1776, 6 vols. 1777, 1777, 2 vols. 1779.

may be lost." [4] Both the *Critical* and the *Monthly* found it a trifle which could have only local interest, but the latter also ventured a guarded compliment by comparing it with the work of Pope and Swift.[5]

Although the bulk of Sterne's letters were not published until the fall of 1775, two small collections, one genuine, one partly spurious and partly genuine, had been published in the preceding months. *Letters from Yorick to Eliza,* containing ten of Sterne's letters to Mrs. Draper, appeared early in 1775. The unknown editor stated in a preface that the letters had been "faithfully copied" at Bombay with Eliza's permission and characterized Sterne's friendship as "the closest union that purity could possibly admit of." Though he would not absolutely state that "the glowing heat of Mr. Sterne's affection never transported him to a flight beyond the limits of pure platonism," he hastened to add that the affair reflected no discredit upon Sterne, since "to cherish the seeds of piety and chastity in a heart which the passions are interested to corrupt, must be allowed to be the noblest effort of a soul, fraught and fortified with the justest sentiments of Religion and Virtue." [6]

The letters were generally accepted by the periodicals as genuine, but there was no general agreement as to the light in which they placed Sterne's character. Both the *Critical* and the *Monthly* stated their confidence in the innocence of Sterne's relationship with Eliza, but the *London Review* believed that the letters had thrown "a world of obloquy" on Sterne and the *Gentleman's Magazine* felt that "such cicesbeism is always unsafe, and generally suspicious; and, to virtue, prudence, and even sensibility, must give abundantly more pain than pleasure." [7] Percival Stockdale, on the other hand, felt the letters were a stain upon

4. *Westminster Magazine, 3* (July 1775), 365–70. The piece was published under the title of "The History of a Good Warm Watch-Coat" in this periodical. Both this and the pamphlet were mutilated versions (see *Life,* p. 175). For an exposition of the background for the *Political Romance,* see Curtis, *Politicks of Laurence Sterne.*

5. *Critical Review, 29* (Jan. 1770), 69–70; Anonymous, *Monthly Review, 41* (Dec. 1769), 485–6.

6. *Letters from Yorick to Eliza,* Philadelphia, 1773. Since the title-page states that this edition has been reprinted from the London one, the book must have been first issued privately in 1773, but none of the English reviews take notice of it until early in 1775.

7. *Critical Review, 39* (Feb. 1775), 129–33; *Monthly Review, 52* (April 1775), 370–1; *London Review, 1* (Feb. 1775), 155; *Gentleman's Magazine, 45* (April 1775), 188. Richard Griffith, who met Sterne at Scarborough in the fall of 1767, gives this opinion of Sterne's friendship with Eliza: "[Sterne] was making every One a Confidant in that Platonic, I suppose, as he did me, on the Second Day of our Acquaintance. But, in truth, there was nothing in the Affair worth making a Secret of—The World that knew of their Correspondence, knew the worst of it, which was merely a simple Folly. Any other Idea of the Matter would be more than the most abandoned Vice could render probable. To intrigue with a Vampire! To sink into the Arms of *Death alive!*" *Series of Genuine Letters, 5,* 199–200.

Sterne's memory only because they were "trifling" and "unpremeditated," and censured Mrs. Draper's "most injudicious vanity" in allowing them to be published.[8]

Sterne's Letters to His Friends on Various Occasions appeared a few months later, during the summer of 1775. This collection, which contained some genuine letters along with forgeries by William Combe,[9] did not draw very extended comment from the reviewers, although many periodicals printed extracts from it. The *Monthly* and the *London Review* expressed some doubts as to the genuineness of the letters,[1] but most of the reviewers accepted them as Sterne's. The *Critical* and the *London Magazine* praised the strain of benevolence which the letters showed, the latter asserting that Sterne "softens the heart, beats down every selfish barrier about it, and opens every source of pity and benevolence."[2]

Lydia Sterne Medalle's edition of her father's letters appeared in October 1775. Published in three volumes, this collection also contained a Rabelaisian fragment (apparently a discarded digression from *Tristram Shandy*) and the memoir which Sterne had written for his daughter. The dedication to David Garrick and brief preface by Sterne's daughter were followed by two poetic eulogies.[3] The memoir, the first biographical material for Sterne to bear the stamp of complete authenticity, was widely reprinted in the periodicals of the day, and all the reviewers agreed that it was a valuable source of information. They did not agree completely, however, on other aspects of the publication.

The *Critical*'s unknown reviewer found the letters "strongly marked with the feelings of conjugal or paternal affection." Though the letters "abound with the sallies of an imagination hurried away by innocent levity, and regardless of decorum," they nevertheless show Sterne to have been "an ardent lover of the social virtues, and a man of extraordinary humanity."[4] Critics in the *London Review* and the *Gentleman's Magazine* censured grammatical and stylistic slips; and the latter

8. *Miscellanies in Prose, and Verse* (Holborn, 1778), pp. 126–8.

9. For a discussion of Combe's forgeries see Lewis P. Curtis, "Forged Letters of Laurence Sterne," *PMLA, 50* (Dec. 1935), 1076–1106.

1. *Monthly Review, 53* (Sept. 1775), 266–7; *London Review, 1* (June 1775), 465.

2. *Critical Review, 40* (July 1775), 70–2; *London Magazine, 44* (Sept. 1775), 480–2.

3. One of these had originally appeared in the *London Magazine* in 1768 (see above, p. 44). The other was "A Character, and Eulogium of STERNE, and His Writings; in a Familiar Epistle from a Gentleman in Ireland to His Friend.—Written in the Year 1769." A note accompanying this latter poem praises Sterne's characters, his "power in the pathetic," and the spirit of philanthropy in his sermons, and compares him favorably with Shakespeare. The poems referred to are in *Letters of the Late Rev. Mr. Laurence Sterne, To His Most Intimate Friends*, ed. Lydia Sterne Medalle (3 vols. London, 1775), pp. xv–xx.

4. *Critical Review, 40* (Nov. 1775), 385–7. Cf. *London Magazine, 44* (Dec. 1775), 649.

condemned various "indelicacies, not to say gross indecencies, more suitable to a Martial or Petronius than a Christian divine," and was angered at some of the inconsistencies of Sterne's personal character.[5] The *Monthly,* in a review by Griffiths, thought the letters would "reflect no disgrace" upon Sterne's memory, however; and valued them for throwing more light upon Sterne's continental trips and thus serving as a supplement to Griffiths' favorite work, the *Sentimental Journey.* Though the letters are "of various and unequal importance" and few of them are written "in the rattling strain of Shandyism," nearly all of them show that Sterne wrote "from the heart." To those "who may think every thing curious from the inimitable pen" which gave us the immortal characters of *Tristram Shandy,* Griffiths concludes, there will not be "an uninteresting page" in the letters.[6] This opinion was not shared by Anna Barbauld, who thought the letters were "paltry enough"; [7] but Horace Walpole found them at least momentarily diverting, for he wrote to Mason that he had read "more unentertaining stuff." [8]

Those who found anything from Sterne's pen interesting called for some reprints of his posthumous works, and kept up a steady and more insistent demand for new editions of *Tristram Shandy* and the *Sentimental Journey.*[9] In the period under consideration there were also several collected editions of Sterne's works,[1] although it was not until 1780 that the first truly critical edition of this sort appeared. Meanwhile excerpts from all of Sterne's major works were often reprinted in periodicals, and Enfield's *Speaker,* a popular text on elocution, had ten

5. *London Review, 2* (Oct. 1775), 257-72; *Gentleman's Magazine, 46* (Jan. 1776), 27-9.

6. *Monthly Review, 53* (Nov. 1775), 403-13.

7. *Works of Anna Laetitia Barbauld* (2 vols. London, 1825), *2,* 8.

8. *Correspondence with the Rev. William Mason,* ed. Rev. J. Mitford (2 vols. London, 1851), *1,* 213.

9. There were three London editions of the *Letters from Yorick to Eliza* during 1775, as well as a Dublin edition in 1776; *Life,* pp. 606-7. *Sterne's Letters to His Friends on Various Occasions* had two editions in 1775. (Since the second edition was merely the first with a new title-page [*Life,* p. 608], it may merely have represented a device to get rid of an unsold surplus.) Mrs. Medalle's edition of the letters was reissued in 1776 and was also reprinted in Dublin in 1776, together with the other two collections mentioned above (*Life,* p. 609). The first edition of 2,635 copies of the *Sentimental Journey* was followed within a month by a second edition and later in the year by "a new edition" and an unauthorized cheaper edition. Two Dublin editions also appeared in 1768 and a third in 1769. The book was reprinted the next year in a four-volume edition together with Hall-Stevenson's continuation; and subsequent reprints appeared in 1770 [Lowndes], 1771, 1773, 1774, 1775 [Yale], 1776 [Yale], and 1778. The first two volumes of *Tristram Shandy* were reprinted in 1768 and 1769, and Vols. 3 and 4 were reprinted in 1768. Collected editions of all nine volumes appeared in 1767, 1768, 1769, 1770, 1775 [Boston, New York], 1777, and 1779, and there was a Dublin collected edition in 1779.

1. Collected editions of Sterne's works were issued as follows: 5 vols. 1773, 1774; 7 vols. Dublin, 1774; 8 vols. Dublin, 1774-78; 7 vols. 1775; 7 vols. Dublin, 1779; 8 vols. Dublin, 1779.

selections from Sterne, a number exceeded only by those from Shakespeare.[2]

Quotations from Sterne often came to the minds of reviewers as well as readers during the period, and references to him appeared in many different connections. Writers in the *Critical* and the *Monthly* often quote Sterne, and William Bewley, one of the *Monthly*'s reviewers, was probably not alone in being able to quote Sterne, though slightly inaccurately, from memory.[3] The editor of a collection of Johnson's sayings is reminded of a passage in *Tristram Shandy* as he writes his preface.[4] When traveling in Germany in 1773, Henry Man makes references to the tale of Slawkenbergius in a letter to Alexander Thomson, back in England.[5] Even John Wesley makes a reference in a letter which shows that he was familiar with *Tristram Shandy*.[6]

Another of Sterne's readers has left a more extended record of his appreciation. The actor John Henderson, who was known as "the Bath Roscius" and has been described as having "stood next to Garrick in public estimation," [7] was the leading light in a "Shandean Society" organized in the early 1770's. The club was both convivial and literary, and the members drank to the memory of the literary great, while reading from their works and composing "sentiments" about them. Henderson, who idolized Sterne, signed his letters "Shandy" and was known by that name to his intimates in the club. His biographer says that he gave readings from Sterne in a manner which "threw new light upon many passages," "called forth flashes of merriment, and drew tears from every eye." He also composed an ode for one of the meetings devoted to Sterne's memory, defending Sterne's character and deploring the unsympathetic age in which he had lived:

> When he from virtue greatest honour drew,
> And held philanthrophy to public view,
>
> . . . . .
>
> In pleasure, harmless, innocent, and mild,
> Warm as a man, forgiving as a child,
> Ev'n then they dar'd to violate his page;
> In virtue barren, fruitful in their rage,
> Vex'd, inly vex'd, that on inspection clear,

---

2. William Enfield, *The Speaker*, London, 1774. Although there are thirty-eight selections from Shakespeare, ten from Pope, and four from Milton, there are none from Richardson, Fielding, or Smollett in this text, which was often reprinted.

3. See *Monthly Review, 48* (June 1773), 450–3; *49* (July 1773), 80.

4. *Johnsoniana* (London, 1776), p. v.

5. *Miscellaneous Works of Henry Man* (2 vols. London, 1802), *1*, 170.

6. *Letters of the Rev. John Wesley,* ed. John Telford (8 vols. London, Epworth Press, 1931), *5*, 386.

7. See *DNB*, art. "Henderson."

They search'd their hearts and found no Toby there.
Stung, inly stung, they snatch'd the pen,
And told the tasteless sons of men,

. . . . .

That he, with all those powers fraught,
Was loose in language, and impure in thought;
Believing virtue, their 'monition took,
And thank'd his stars he had not read the book.

Sterne is conducted to "realms where angels hail'd him with applause," where he is received by Rabelais and Cervantes. The poem closes with a plea to the hearers to defend Sterne's memory, and a personal tribute which hints at Henderson's having met and known Sterne, although no other evidence seems to exist for such a conjecture.[8]

Henderson's defense may well be considered as going further than the facts allow, but it is nevertheless true that ignorance, misunderstanding, and prejudice often played a part in much of the adverse criticism of Sterne. One reason for this may be found in the difficulty which critics have had ever since Sterne's own time in separating the man from the author. Too often critics placed biographical criticism above literary criticism, as did the writer in the *London Review* who complained that "there was something so extremely singular and problematical in Mr. Sterne's literary character, that it is very difficult to judge of his character as a man by that of his writings." [9]

Much of the biographical material which was available consisted of inaccuracies, or at best anecdotes and legends of doubtful authenticity, supplemented by moralizing. The month following Sterne's death an article in the *Court Miscellany* stated that he had "died as he lived, the same insensible, thoughtless creature; as a day or two before he seemed not in the least affected with his approaching dissolution." [1] In 1769 the *Gentleman's Magazine* reported the rumor of the anatomization of Sterne's corpse and stated that his wife had retired to France rather than "live in England under the daily provocations of an unkind husband," since though Sterne was a great wit, he was not

8. *Letters and Poems, by the Late Mr. John Henderson, with Anecdotes of His Life by John Ireland* (London, 1786), pp. 26–39. Since Henderson was in London during part of the sixties, where he was apprenticed to a jeweler in St. James's Street, he might possibly have known Sterne. It was later that he achieved recognition on the stage, first at Bath in 1772, and that his readings from Sterne became famous. The readings brought tears from the eyes of Mrs. Siddons (James Boaden, *Memoirs of Mrs. Siddons,* Philadelphia, 1893, pp. 346–7), were referred to in a topical poem of the day in 1786 (*The Patriad,* London, 1786, p. 26), and were still remembered by a correspondent of the *European Magazine* several years later, *21* (March 1792), 167.
9. *London Review, 1* (Appendix Jan.–June 1775), 497.
1. *Court Miscellany, 4* (April 1768), 269–71.

"a desirable companion for a woman of delicacy." [2] The next year Philip Thicknesse printed the untrue story that while Sterne had been "wallowing in the luxuries of life, and expences of THE TOWN," his mother was being imprisoned for debt at York. Thicknesse professed to admire Sterne's works "as much, as any man living" and asserted that he was publishing the story, which had "crept abroad in private conversation," only "to rouze up those, who can contradict it." He did not intend, he insisted, "to stamp [Sterne's] memory with disgrace"; but at the same time he added that he had very good authority for the story.[3]

Sterne was not without his defenders. A biographical sketch, sympathetic in its general tone, appeared in the *Sentimental Magazine* early in 1774. "Yorick," the unknown author stated, "was consistent; he died as he had lived, laughing at folly, feeling for misery, and making his friends and himself happy." He likewise defends Sterne's clerical character, replying to the criticism that Sterne had "mount[ed] the pulpit in a Harlequin's coat," [4] by asserting that "it matters very little in what coat a man mounts the pulpit, if his doctrine is good." [5] Two years later John Noorthouck repeats some of the usual censures of Sterne in his *Historical and Classical Dictionary,* but he does not confuse the man with the writer. In estimating "the abilities of such a spirited flighty writer," he says, we may "so far follow his example as to overlook his profession, which perhaps was not the object of his deliberate choice; it being clearly inconsistent with his natural disposition and turn of mind." [6]

Unfortunately, however, the slurs on Sterne's character carried more weight than did the defenses of it and sometimes also played a part in the debates concerning his so-called benevolence or philanthropy. Mrs. Carter had objected to this element in Sterne's work because she believed it inconsistent with his personal character, and Mrs. Greville because she believed it overdone.[7] The objections of other critics took various forms. Richard Griffith attacked Sterne's benevolence on practical grounds, singling out the passage about Uncle Toby and the fly as "a most shining figure, among the *faux-brillants* of morals," since only a shallow philosophy could ignore the necessity

2. *Gentleman's Magazine, 39* (July 1769), 366.

3. *Sketches and Characters of the Most Eminent and Most Singular Persons Now Living* (Bristol, 1770), *1,* 117–19. No more volumes were printed of this work, which was published anonymously. For a refutation of the charge against Sterne, see *Life,* pp. 100–10. This story was later to be circulated under the authority of the names of Horace Walpole and Byron.

4. See above, p. 9.

5. *Sentimental Magazine, 2* (Jan. 1774), 4–7.

6. "Sterne," *An Historical and Classical Dictionary* (2 vols. London, 1776), *2.* This is the same Noorthouck who wrote for the *Monthly.*

7. See above, pp. 41–2.

for killing insects.[8] Religious fanatics like Thomas O'Brien MacMahon, whose *Essay on the Depravity and Corruption of Human Nature* was published in 1774, objected to Sterne's philosophy because they felt it was at variance with the bases of religion and particularly with the doctrine of original sin. MacMahon groups Sterne with Hume and Shaftesbury, all of whom are apologists "for the corrupt heart of man," and have attempted to "beatify" human nature. The "seeds of compassion" which Sterne has asserted to exist in even the hardest of human hearts are no fit substitute for more solid principles of conduct.[9] The unknown author of *Joineriana* (published two years earlier) had also attacked Yorick's clerical character, though his attack was only half serious. He advises the young clergy against following in Sterne's footsteps, for, he says, "should you chance to turn out a hare-brained wit—an irregular humourist—a rambling-scambling genius!—in the name of parochial peace and harmony! what is to become of your poor flock?"[1]

The other side of the picture may be seen in a dialogue contributed by a correspondent to the *Westminster Magazine* in 1774, who believes Sterne's religious philosophy to be based upon good humor and common sense. Yorick is made to say that the participants in religious controversies have "fought about nothing" and "sent one another pell-mell to the devil, about matters full as trifling as uncle Toby's Hobby-horses"; but that "ridicule" and "a hearty laugh" should be sufficient to "put everything to rights."[2] In much the same vein was the tribute to Sterne that Samuel Jackson Pratt (who wrote under the pseudonym of Courtney Melmoth) included in his poem, "The Tears of Genius," which had been occasioned by the death of Goldsmith. Pratt interrupts the poem for a rhapsodic prose eulogy of Sterne, praising the "milky and humane temperature" of his pulses, and the "compassion" in his turn of mind. Sterne did not have, Pratt concludes, "any parade—any ostensibility—or religious prudery" about him, but he has nevertheless "done more to the cause of Virtue" than if he had "gone scowling through life."[3]

Just as biographical prejudices often stood in the way of objective criticism of Sterne's philosophy, so preconceptions in regard to the

8. *Something New*, *1*, 141-2.

9. See *An Essay on the Depravity and Corruption of Human Nature* (London, 1774), pp. 2, 140-2, 165-80, and passim. There is a copy of this book in the University of Pennsylvania Library.

1. *Joineriana: or the Book of Scraps* (2 vols. London, 1772), *2*, 151-68. There is a copy of this book in the University of Michigan Library. This is one of the last examples of the mock attacks on Sterne, which had, in general, ceased with his death.

2. *Westminster Magazine*, *2* (Nov. 1774), 580-1. Cf. the anonymous *Voltaire in the Shades; or Dialogues on the Deistical Controversy*, London, 1770, in which Sterne is made to defend Christianity.

3. *Miscellanies* (4 vols. London, 1785), *1*, 82-3.

literary qualities of his work tended to hamper literary judgments. "Shandean" continues to be a term which can refer to a certain whimsical or risqué kind of humor; a digressive, disjointed style of writing; or even the size of a book. Reviewers repeat *ad nauseam* the critical commonplaces about Sterne's "jocularity," his "pathetic and tender strokes," and his "reprehensible passages which so justly gave offence to virtue and modesty." [4] The three brief critical tributes which were first printed in Joseph Cradock's *Village Memoirs* in 1774 were likewise widely reprinted:

> Sterne will be immortal when Rabelais and Cervantes are forgot —they drew their characters from the particular genius of the times—Sterne confined himself to nature only.

> Till my uncle Toby appeared I had used to assert, that no character was ever better drawn than that of Sir Roger de Coverly.

> A man may as well give himself the trouble to copy nature as Sterne. [5]

Though these last remarks are perceptive and appreciative, more damaging critical clichés placed Sterne in a class by himself as an "eccentric genius," who moved in a sphere of his own, and these clichés often precluded more penetrating analysis. Critics might, like Charles Jenner, find that Sterne's "natural and inexhaustible fund of humour" enabled him to please with devices which "in another man, would have been unsupportable." [6] More often, however, they shared the opinion of John Noorthouck, who thought that *Tristram Shandy* "displayed a redundancy of wild extravagant humour and wit, great knowledge of human nature, not a little indecency, absurdity, and arrant nonsense; all of which were oddly jumbled together without order, and without any discoverable end or aim, beyond that of making the reader laugh and wonder!" [7] John Wesley's comment (in his journal) on the *Sentimental Journey* is even more extreme; for he found the word "sentimental" neither "English" nor "sense." The book, he continues, "agrees full well with the title, for one is as queer as the other. For oddity, uncouthness, and unlikeness to all the world beside, I suppose, the writer is without a rival!" [8]

With such widespread misunderstandings of Sterne's talents and his method, it is not surprising that critics often disagreed when they came

---

4. For typical comments of this sort see Ralph Griffiths, *Monthly Review, 39* (Dec. 1768), 435. *Critical Review, 26* (Nov. 1768), 354.

5. *Village Memoirs* (3d ed. London, 1775), pp. 44–5.

6. *The Placid Man* (2 vols. London, 1770), *1,* 74.

7. "Sterne," *Historical and Classical Dictionary.*

8. *Journal of John Wesley,* ed. Nehemiah Curnock (8 vols. London, R. Culley, [1909–16]), *5,* 445. The entry is dated February 11, 1772.

to place him in relation to other writers. George Colman the Elder mentions him among the "bold manly wits," along with Cervantes, Rabelais, Molière, Swift, Gay, Arbuthnot, and Fielding.[9] One of the *Monthly*'s reviewers likewise places him in the first rank of the "humorous" novelists, along with Fielding, Coventry, and Smollett.[1] An essayist in the *Westminster Magazine,* on the other hand, gives first and second place among English novelists to Fielding and Smollett because they "both knew better how to *tickle*" our hearts, though he admits that Sterne deserves "infinite credit, and infinite tears for his power over our hearts when he chooses to *melt* them." Though "in the opinion of a great many" Sterne might stand first, this writer feels that he goes "too far for fun" in his humor.[2] Philip Parsons compared Fielding and Sterne at greater length, casting his discussion into the form of a dialogue between Fielding and Courtney Melmoth. Melmoth attempts to defend Sterne by emphasizing the value of "variety"; but Fielding assures him that repeated digressions and "flights under no restraint of method" are perplexing and wearying to the reader. Although Sterne's occasional "beautiful strokes of wit and tenderness" are like "vivid lightning" which "flashes surprise and pleasure upon the eye," Fielding's books please more because they have "the animating light of the sun." [3]

Meanwhile, some critics were attempting to look at Sterne's work more carefully and made more accurate judgments about it. Sir William Weller Pepys realized that *Tristram Shandy,* even though it was "a strange eccentric composition," could yet "be tried by rules adapted to the subject, & a judgment pronounc'd upon its merits, in which people of sound taste, will, upon a thorough examination of it, be found to Agree." [4] William Enfield, one of the *Monthly*'s reviewers, appreciated the fact that the true "Shandyan manner" was a "conversation-style without its defects," and that "Sterne's originality did not consist in a want of method." [5] Samuel Jackson Pratt made an equally perceptive and more extended analysis of Sterne's style in his *Observations on the Night Thoughts of Dr. Young,* clearing Sterne of the charge of "affectation." Pratt observes that there is "an *ap-*

9. *Prose on Several Occasions* (3 vols. London, 1787), *I*, 172. These remarks first appeared in the *London Packet* in 1775.

1. Anonymous, *Monthly Review, 46* (March 1772), 263–4.

2. *Westminster Magazine, 4* (Oct. 1776), 520–2. The writer has previously censured Richardson for violating probability and not following nature.

3. *Dialogues of the Dead with the Living* (London, 1779), pp. 72–6, 95. Parsons, a clergyman and miscellaneous writer, published the *Dialogues* anonymously.

4. *A Later Pepys,* ed. Alice C. Gaussen (2 vols. London and New York, J. Lane, 1904), *I*, 219. The remarks occur in a letter which, though undated, has been placed by the editor with other letters written during 1776.

5. William Enfield, *Monthly Review, 58* (Jan. 1778), 85; *53* (Sept. 1775), 269. This is the same Enfield who compiled *The Speaker* (see above, p. 52).

pearance of singularity and affectation in *Sterne*, but it is *only* an appearance"; for affectation should be distinguished only "by comparing *parts* with the *whole*." Actually, Sterne "is a very uniform writer, both in respect of thinking, and expression of thought." He may occasionally have "deviated into trifling," but Pratt believes this "the error of nature, and not of art." Since we can "trace a similar *mode* of reasoning, and a similar construction of language" through Sterne's work, its defects are to be explained by the "ardour" and "glowing fancy" with which a great genius works.[6]

Two other critics also took more careful looks at Sterne's work, though both denied him a place among the first rank of authors. Percival Stockdale felt that Swift, Pope, and Rousseau would be read by posterity "when the names of Yorick and Tristram Shandy will hardly be remembered," for Sterne's great virtues are outbalanced by his defects. He "had great knowledge of the world; he had much wit, and humour; he could move the heart: he was not deficient in imagination; but he was deficient in judgement: he had neither a vigorous, nor a comprehensive mind." He also lacked "the power of patient, and intense application"; and all these qualities are required to form "an immortal author."[7] John Ogilvie denied Sterne a place among the greatest writers for a different reason, but placed him at the top of those in his own class. In his *Philosophical and Critical Observations on Composition,* he states that the dramatic and the epic are the "two higher species of fable," which demand the greatest variety of talents. Sterne excels in an "inferior" kind of fable, along with Marivaux and Crébillon. These writers "have attempted to follow out the wanderings of the human heart, and to delineate the first impressions made upon a susceptible mind by interesting objects, as well as the manner in which it feels when insensibly familiarized to their appearance." In the *Sentimental Journey* Sterne shows the "happy talent of exciting the tenderest and most affecting sensations from the most trifling occurrences." Though he has "no uncommon depth or compass of understanding," he has "a copious imagination, and an eminent proportion of the qualities of the heart. His discernment, therefore, which as a philosopher is neither extensive nor accurate, yet as a moral painter is exquisite."[8]

Though critics might disagree on the merits of Sterne's work, the public kept buying and reading his books, and it seems appropriate to

6. *Observations on the Night Thoughts of Dr. Young* (London, 1776), pp. 71–3. I am indebted to Frederick W. Hilles of the Yale University faculty for lending me his copy of this book.

7. *Miscellanies,* pp. 129–30.

8. *Philosophical and Critical Observations, on the Nature, Characters, and Various Species of Composition* (2 vols. London, 1774) *1,* 338–42. Ogilvie was one of a group of Scottish literary clergy and fellow of the Edinburgh Royal Society.

let two unknown essayists (both presumably anonymous literary hacks long since forgotten) speak for the vast mass of Sterne's readers. The first, in a little book called *Yorick's Skull; or, College Oscitations,* published in 1777, stressed the appeal of the "benevolent" and "sentimental" side of Sterne. "I cannot help considering Tristram Shandy rather as an admirable caricature of history, than an exact portrait of private life," he says. "Let any one, after reading Le Fevre, ask his own heart, whether Uncle Toby and the Corporal are not too tender and sentimental?" The "justly-admired" amours of the Widow Wadman likewise "never did or will have existence, but in the brain. Yet it is by these means," he continues, that Sterne "has exceeded all writers in his knowledge of disposition and character. By carrying us beyond our usual feelings, he has taught us, that the human heart is capable of the greatest improvement; and that nature never feels herself more noble and exalted, than in the exercise of benevolence and humanity." [9]

The second writer recalls his first reading of *Tristram Shandy,* while he is writing a "Defense of Laughter, against Lord Chesterfield's unwarrantable Attack." The unknown essayist "was in the company of two very sensible men, who were each entertaining himself with his own reading," when he burst out laughing as he came to "the unfortunate rencounter" of Dr. Slop and Obadiah:

> I thought I saw before me the little fat Doctor, mounted on his diminutive poney, that was waddling through the narrow, dirty lane, at every step sinking to the knees in mire: I thought I saw the hasty Obadiah, mounted on a great unruly brute of a coach horse, galloping at his full speed: I thought I saw him, with this tremendous velocity, bounce upon the unsuspecting Doctor at the sudden turn of the garden-wall; I painted to myself the terror and consternation of the Doctor's face; the vain attempts he would make, in the dirt, to turn his poney out of the way of Obadiah's horse; his crossing himself, like a good Roman-Catholic, on the apprehension of inevitable death; his dropping his whip, through hurry and confusion, in crossing himself; his catching most naturally, and as if by instinct, to recover his falling whip; his losing his stirrups in consequence thereof; his falling, like a windmill, with legs and arms extended; and then sticking, when he reached the earth, like a pack of wool in the mud; then the trepidation of Obadiah at the sight of the Doctor's dirty and dangerous state; the trouble he was at to stop his great, hard-mouthed, stiff-necked brute, which he could by no other means effect, than by pulling him round and round the prostrate Doctor, and bespattering him all with mud; the rueful face of Obadiah,

9. *Yorick's Skull; or, College Oscitations* (London, 1777), pp. 34–6.

and the aukward apologies he would make: All these, I say, with
many other additional circumstances, painted themselves so
strongly on my imagination, that I laughed most immoderately
loud.

This unknown reader felt the scene so vividly that he could make
an imaginative re-creation of it for himself, since some of the details,
such as the simile of Dr. Slop's falling "like a windmill" and the
"rueful face" of Obadiah, are not to be found in Sterne.[1] More significant, however, are the reactions of his two friends, which he goes on to
describe. When he read the passage to them, one "joined very heartily
in the laugh"; but the other could not see "any thing so very witty in
the misfortune of a poor, harmless, inoffensive man-midwife" and
thought it was "cruel and insulting to laugh at his distress."[2] Most of
Sterne's readers may be placed with one or the other of these two men
when it comes to appreciating the humorous side of his works. Many of
them, of course, might appreciate the "pathetic" and "benevolent"
elements, while deprecating the humor. With Sterne, perhaps more
than with most other writers of his time, personality and individual taste
were more apt to determine the attitude of the reader than was candid
judgment.

   This may well account for Johnson's continuing antipathy to Sterne,
which led him to distort the facts when he said in 1776, "Nothing odd
will do long. 'Tristram Shandy' did not last."[3] It was likewise perhaps
prejudice, though differently motivated, which had led David Hume
to write three years earlier: "The best Book, that has been writ by any
Englishman these thirty Years (for Dr Franklyn is an American) is
Tristram Shandy, bad as it is. A Remark which may astonish you;
but which you will find true on Reflection."[4] For many more years
to come, it was to be Sterne's fate to occasion critical disagreements of
this sort, although even during the period under consideration, glim-
merings of understanding in isolated cases were enabling some critics
to make contributions toward an understanding of his books. For
many of the reading public, no such critical analysis was necessary before his works could become a cherished experience in their lives. It
was almost as if Sterne was becoming a classic without being fully
understood.

   1. Cf. *Tristram Shandy, 2,* ch. 9; Work, pp. 105–6.
   2. *Westminster Magazine, 3* (Jan. 1775), [19]–20.
   3. *Boswell's Life of Johnson, 2,* 449.
   4. *Letters of David Hume,* ed. J. Y. T. Greig (2 vols. Oxford, Clarendon Press,
1932), *2,* 269. The remarks, which occur in a letter to William Strahan, are not as
high praise in their context however, since Hume has just said that England "is so sunk
in Stupidity and Barbarism and Faction that you may as well think of Lapland for
an Author." Cf. Hume's earlier remarks, p. 34 above.

3

"Beauties" and Bowdlerization (1780–92)

STERNE's last important posthumous work, the *Letters* edited by his daughter, appeared in 1775. After this time an occasional forgery and an occasional scrap of genuine Sterne were to make their way into the magazines,[1] but in general the corpus of his works had become established. His continuing popularity, as evidenced in the demand for all his writings during the seventies, led a group of booksellers in 1780 to publish an authoritative collected edition of his works.

The advertisement prefixed to this ten-volume edition stated that "after contending with the prejudices of some, and the ignorance of others," the works of Sterne had become classics. "No writer of the present times can lay claim to so many unborrowed excellencies," the editor continued, since "in none, have wit, humour, fancy, pathos, an unbounded knowledge of mankind, and a correct and elegant style, been so happily united." The editor went on to state that he had attempted to include only genuine works, to arrive at an authoritative text, and to supply necessary annotations. Perhaps in anticipation of possible attacks on Sterne, he concluded by stressing his "sense of universal benevolence" and asserting that his works could be printed "without the least apprehension that the perusal of any part of them will be followed by consequences unfavourable to the interests of society."[2] This edition of Sterne's works became the standard one and was reprinted several times, although there were also competing editions and frequent reprints of the separate works.[3]

1. Chief among these was *Original Letters of the Late Reverend Mr. Laurence Sterne*, London, 1788, containing thirty-nine letters. Contemporary reviewers expressed doubts as to their genuineness and Curtis believes that only three are "presumably genuine," the rest forgeries by William Combe ("Forged Letters of Laurence Sterne," 1091). Various other letters have since come to light; see *Letters*, pp. v–ix.

2. *Works of Laurence Sterne* (10 vols. London, 1780), *1*, iii–vi. I have been unable to identify the editor of this edition, which was to remain the standard one for nearly 125 years.

3. A tabulation of editions of Sterne's *Works* for the period is as follows: 10 vols. 1780; 5 vols. 1780 [Boston]; 7 vols. 1780 Dublin, 1780; 5 vols. Dublin, 1780; 10 vols. 1783; 7 vols. 1783; 8 vols. 1784; 10 vols. 1788; 10 vols. 1790; 5 vols. 1790. *Tristram Shandy* was reprinted as follows: 2 vols. 1780 [Chicago]; 3 vols. Dublin, 1780 [Yale]; 1781 [Lowndes]; 6 vols. 1782; 2 vols. 1783; 3 vols. 1786. The *Sentimental Journey* was reissued in 1780; 1782; 1783; 1783, Edinburgh [Yale]; 1784 [Yale; together with Hall-Stevenson's continuation]; 1790; 1791 [Yale]; 1792; and 1792, Norwich [New York]. Mrs. Medalle's edition of the letters was reprinted

The book which was most frequently reprinted during the eighties, however, was a little volume which first appeared in 1782 and had reached a seventh edition within a year and a twelfth by 1793. It bore the title *The Beauties of Sterne; Including All His Pathetic Tales, & Most Distinguished Observations on Life,* and purported to be "Selected for the Heart of Sensibility." In his preface the editor explains that he has compiled this volume of excerpts for the benefit of "the chaste lovers of literature" and "their rising offspring," both of whom have been deprived of "the pleasure and instruction so conspicuous in this magnificent assemblage of Genius" by the admixture of obscenity in *Tristram Shandy,* and to a lesser degree in the *Sentimental Journey.* An alphabetical table of contents guides the reader in his search for Sterne's sentiments on such topics as beauty, compassion, charity, defamation, eloquence, frailty, forgiveness, generosity, and so on down through the alphabet.[4]

Sterne's work was not alone in receiving this kind of treatment, for at about this time there were "Beauties" of most of the major literary figures of the previous fifty years, as well as similar compilations for Homer and Shakespeare. Books of this kind proved so popular that Hannah More could say in 1786:

> No work in substance now is follow'd,
> The Chemic Extract only's swallow'd.[5]

The reviews were cool toward these projects from the beginning, charging the compilers with "frivolity" and "mutilation"; but the "laborious moles in the service of literature" continued to produce such volumes long after the reviewers had pronounced them "hacknied and disgustful." In 1794 the *Monthly* lamented that by that time "almost every classical writer in the English language" had been subjected to this treatment and "the man of genius" had become "like some aged oak, obscured and deformed by the ivy, the mistletoe, or other parasitical plants, which live and prey on it." [6]

---

in 1790 [Yale], and also at Dublin in 1780, together with the *Letters from Yorick to Eliza* and the "Watchcoat" [New York]. For the *Sermons,* see below, p. 69. The *Novelist's Magazine* reprinted *Tristram Shandy* in 1781 (the title-page of the copy I used bears the date 1787, perhaps a mistake or perhaps a new edition) and the *Sentimental Journey* in 1782, the latter with an illustration by William Blake (9, 52). Blake later tried at William Hayley's request to locate some of George Romney's illustrations for *Tristram Shandy,* but he does not comment on the book. *Letters of William Blake,* ed. Archibald G. B. Russell (New York, Scribner, 1906), pp. 143, 155.

4. *The Beauties of Sterne* (3d ed. London, 1782), pp. v–vi. The dedication and preface are signed "W.H." and a reference in the *Critical, 55* (Feb. 1783), 157, names "Poor Hawkesworth" as the editor for other "Beauties" of this series published by Kearsley. I have been unable to identify the Hawkesworth who may have been the editor for *Beauties of Sterne.*

5. *Florio: a Tale* (London, 1786), p. 9.

6. Nathaniel Halhed, *Monthly Review,* 2d Ser. *13* (Feb. 1794), 132–3. Comments like those quoted in this paragraph run through the reviews of the period.

Sterne fared a little better under this treatment than did some of his brother authors, since the somewhat disconnected character of his work meant that individual passages could be extracted with less real mutilation. Nor was this kind of treatment new for him, since reviewers and magazine editors had been reprinting excerpts from his work and had come to regard it as a collection of "beauties." In reviewing one of the numerous imitations of Sterne in 1783, a writer for the *English Review* was typical when he said: "In the general merit of this work we prefer it to Sterne, but when we cull out the *independent* beauties of both authors, Sterne has the majority." [7]

The Beauties of Sterne culled its selections mainly from the sentimental and "moral" parts of Sterne's work, relying heavily upon the *Sermons* and the *Sentimental Journey* and rejecting much of the more boisterous *Tristram Shandy*. Anything that might offend "the chaste lovers of literature" was carefully omitted, thus continuing the process of bowdlerization which had been begun by earlier reviewers and anthologists. When William Walbeck suggested in 1786 that some editor undertake the task of bowdlerizing *Tristram Shandy,* he perhaps did not realize that he was merely suggesting the continuation of a task that was already well under way. [8]

Many readers, however, must have been unsatisfied with the one-sided selection afforded by *Beauties;* and in the tenth edition of 1787 a new editor undertook to redress the balance somewhat. "It has been a matter of much general complaint," he explains in his preface, "that the selections hitherto made were of rather too confined a cast" and did not contain a balance between "the *utile* and the *dulce.*" Although the "dread of offending the ear of Chastity" was laudable in itself, he believed that it had "been carried to an excess, thereby depriving us of many most laughable scenes" which were harmless. Past compilers, he concludes, "keeping their eye rather upon his *morality,* than his *humour*—upon his *judgment,* than his *wit,*" have often failed to include sufficient illustrations of Sterne's most distinctive skills. In this new edition the reader, "whether of a grave or gay complexion, will find equal attention paid him," since several humorous scenes of "true Shandean colouring" have been added to the previous selections which pleased "the heart of Sensibility" and "the mind, in search of those duties we owe to GOD and MAN." [9]

Compilers of other anthologies continued to include generous selections from Sterne, just as they had during the seventies. Collections of

---

7. *English Review, 1* (May 1783), 417.

8. *Socrates and Xantippe: a Burlesque Tale.* Although I have been unable to locate a copy of this work, the passage in question is quoted in the *Critical Review, 61* (March 1786), 234. The reviewer thought it dangerous "to lay unhallowed hands on the humour of Sterne."

9. *Beauties of Sterne* (10th ed. London, 1787), pp. v–vi. The dedication is signed "A.F."

sermons usually contained one or two of Yorick's, and prose anthologies would be sure to include some of the "pathetic" pieces.[1] One of the most popular of these latter collections was *Elegant Extracts* compiled by Vicesimus Knox, which reprinted the stories of Le Fever, the Monk, Maria, and the other favorites, along with some shorter passages. Knox's *Elegant Epistles* likewise contained more than fifty of Sterne's letters.[2]

Somewhat similar to an anthology was the dramatic adaptation of *Tristram Shandy* by Leonard MacNally, which ran for several performances in 1783 and 1784 and went through two printed editions in 1783. The prologue, by another writer, states that it is the purpose of the play to "bring the beauties of poor Yorick's page" to the stage, "draw in public view the heart of man," and thus "reconcile man to his hobby-horse."[3] By changing Sterne's chronology and putting the Le Fever incident, Tristram's birth, and Uncle Toby's courtship of the Widow Wadman all at the same time, MacNally is able to include most of the famous scenes of the novel. Even such passages as that of the accusing and recording angels and the description of the Widow's eye are worked into the dialogue. The major change is that at the end of Act II Uncle Toby and the Widow go off to be married, thus producing the inevitable happy ending. Much of the dialogue, and even many of the stage directions, MacNally has transferred intact from Sterne; but unfortunately the connecting dialogue which he has written falls very flat indeed when juxtaposed with Sterne's more brilliant prose. The *Monthly* contemptuously called the performance "little else than a cento from Sterne," although the *English Review* felt that MacNally was to be commended for producing a work with "excellent stage effect," which was "suited to the general taste," since it avoided Sterne's indelicacies.[4]

The *Critical* and the *Monthly* were in agreement in their condemnation of another attempt to adapt Sterne's work to a different medium. When Jane Timbury's versification in rhymed couplets of the story of Le Fever appeared in 1787, the *Critical* expressed surprise that "the excellent story of Le Fevre, told in almost the same words as the original, should so entirely lose all its power over the mind."[5] The

1. *The Protestant Preacher*, London, 1781, and *The Narrative Companion, and Entertaining Moralist*, London, 1789, may be mentioned as typical.

2. *Elegant Extracts* in prose, 1st ed. London, 1783, had reached a tenth edition by 1816, and *Elegant Epistles*, 1st ed. London, 1790, was frequently reprinted together with the prose extracts and Knox's companion volume of poetic selections. For Knox's comments on Sterne see below, pp. 74–6.

3. *Tristram Shandy, a Sentimental, Shandean Bagatelle, in Two Acts*, 2d ed. London, 1783. The prologue was written "by Mr. Chalmers," probably Alexander Chalmers, the prolific editor of numerous standard works.

4. George Colman (the Elder), *Monthly Review*, 69 (Dec. 1783), 439. *English Review*, 2 (Nov. 1783), 378.

5. *Critical Review*, 64 (Sept. 1787), 226.

Monthly, in a comment by Griffiths himself, said that if poor
Sterne could return from his grave and see the "degradation" of his
work, it "would certainly make the *'parson swear'* worse than did
Uncle Toby, when he *resolved* that the poor sick Lieutenant should
'not die'—perhaps as bad as Dr. Slop did, when he cut his thumb." [6]

Undoubtedly some of the generation of new readers grew up after
1782 knowing Sterne only from *Beauties* and other collections of
excerpts or from adaptations; but subsequent references in diaries,
journals, and memoirs, as well as allusions in literary works and reviews,
prove that many people still read the works of Sterne in their complete form. Reviewers still expected their readers to be familiar with
the word "Shandean" and with references to the characters of *Tristram
Shandy.* The *Critical's* reviewers exhibited a particular fondness for
constructing similes which contained allusions to *Shandy,* while writers
for the *Monthly* also referred to Sterne frequently and twice summoned
the inhabitants of Shandy Hall to contribute imaginary comments on
works being reviewed.[7] The varied nature of the quotations scattered
through the periodicals during these years indicates that the reviewers
had a thorough acquaintance with Sterne's books rather than merely a
superficial one with a few of the more famous passages; and they must
have expected a majority of their readers to have the same kind of
knowledge.

Though allusions to *Tristram Shandy* were much more numerous
than those to the *Sentimental Journey,* travelers bought copies of
Yorick's travels, as Samuel Woodforde did, before setting out for
the Continent,[8] and often delighted in seeing places and meeting people
that Sterne had mentioned. Arthur Young passed the house of the
Marchesa di Fagnani near Milan on an October evening in 1789 and
remembered that she was "the lady with whom our inimitable Sterne
had the rencontre at Milan." [9] Frederick Reynolds, traveling on the
Continent in 1782, took pains to ask Dessein about Sterne while he was
at Calais. Reynolds also gave the name La Fleur to his French valet,
thus, as he says, "affording me the opportunity of fancying myself,
either a Sterne, or a Glorieux." [1]

Sterne and his works came to people's minds in many different
connections. Bishop Hurd quoted him during a conversation with a
young lieutenant in 1783.[2] When writing his *Memoirs* in 1791, James

6. *Monthly Review, 78* (Jan. 1788), 78.
7. See ibid., *62* (June 1780), 429–30; *78* (Feb. 1788), 167. Other references to Sterne
are scattered throughout the *Monthly* and the *Critical.*
8. *Woodeforde Papers and Diaries,* ed. Dorothy Heighes Woodforde (London, P.
Davies, 1932), p. 95.
9. *Travels in France & Italy During the Years 1787, 1788 and 1789,* Everyman ed.
(London, J. M. Dent, [1915?]), p. 238.
1. *Life and Times of Frederick Reynolds* (2 vols. London, 1826), *1,* 180–1, 231.
2. Rev. Francis Kilvert, *Memoirs of the Right Rev. Richard Hurd* (London, 1860),
p. 150.

Lackington, the self-educated man who became one of the most important London booksellers, made allusions to Sterne.[3] George Colman the Younger thought of a kindness rendered him during his college days in Scotland as having "an Uncle Tobyism about it." [4]

Writers of fiction likewise mentioned Sterne. Mrs. Lewston, a servant in the anonymous novel *The Amicable Quixote,* claims to be educated, since she has belonged to a circulating library and read "a volume of *Mr. Shandy's Travels*" among other books, though how much she profited from any of them may be judged by the fact that she speaks of "Mrs. Slipslop, in one of 'Squire Richardson's stories— let me see which was it—ay, God's Revenge against Adultery." [5] In *The Sentimental Mother,* a comedy attributed to Baretti, Lady Fantasma Tunskull, the character used to satirize Hester Thrale Piozzi, counts *Tristram Shandy* among her favorite books and reads the more "moral" parts of it on Sunday when she has retired to her devotions.[6]

Mention of Sterne's name still helped to sell publications, as some of the jest books of the period prove. Typical of these was *Sterne's Witticisms, or Yorick's Convivial Jester,* published in 1782, which began with "Yorick's Memorandum Book" containing various anecdotes of Sterne and fragments allegedly from his pocket book. The editor quickly ran out of Sterne material, however, and went on to give anecdotes of other people and jokes of the day. Garrick is mentioned almost as frequently as Sterne, but it is Yorick's name which the editor relies upon to sell his work.[7] Other authors refer to Sterne on title-pages and in dedications and prefaces.[8]

Material about Yorick also found a prominent place in the magazines. A writer in the *European Magazine* in 1782 found the Monk and Maria standing guard when he paid an imaginary visit to Sterne's grave, and he walked away as happy "as Addison when he visited Virgil's tomb: or even Garrick himself when he shed a tear of rapture on the shrine of Shakespeare." [9] A few years later an enterprising

3. See *Memoirs of the Forty-Five First Years of the Life of James Lackington,* in *Autobiography* (33 vols. London, 1826–33), *18,* 112, 292.

4. Richard Brinsley Peake, *Memoirs of the Colman Family* (2 vols. London, 1841), *2,* 88.

5. *The Amicable Quixote; or, the Enthusiasm of Friendship* (4 vols. London, 1788), *1,* 106–7.

6. *The Sentimental Mother* (London, 1789), pp. 14, 129.

7. Cf. Croft's *Scrapeana,* which has a motto from Sterne on the title-page and gives numerous anecdotes, probably many of them apocryphal, of Sterne.

8. Typical of these was the unknown author of *Unfortunate Sensibility,* London, 1784, who told the story "in a Series of Sentimental Letters" which were "dedicated to Mr. Yorick, in the Elysian Fields" and addressed a long passage in the preface to Yorick. (See p. 71, below.) There is a copy of this book in the Harvard University Library.

9. "Sterne's Grave," *European Magazine, 2* (Nov. 1782), 325–6.

journalist wrote a series of articles for the same periodical which purported to be based on interviews with La Fleur. Picturing Sterne through La Fleur's eyes, he finds "confirmation of such traits in the *Sentimental Journey* as indicate the refinement of his feelings and the exquisite sensibility of his soul," and defends Sterne against the assertion, "malevolently sent abroad under the sanction of Dr. Johnson's name," that he was "licentious and dissolute" in conversation. The author also includes some biographical material on La Fleur himself (which sounds suspiciously like an attempt to add a chapter to the *Sentimental Journey*), and he identifies some of Sterne's characters, giving the impression that Sterne's work was an artful blend of fact and fiction. His comparison of Sterne with Voltaire is fairly perceptive. "The levity of Sterne," he says, "is a lancet that lightly produces a smart, which we blush at while we acknowledge it. The ridicule of Voltaire is malevolent merriment, which applies a CAUSTIC to what is festering, and enjoys the pain of its corrosion." Though both are "excellent satirists," one "is the favourite of the *gloomy growler* at his species; he who joys at discovered depravity—the other, of that best of men, who can readily find an extenuation for the foibles of other characters, in the FAULTS that he feels with sensibility about his own." [1] Few other critics had tried to show the relationship between Sterne the satirist and Sterne the man of sensibility.

Almost none of Sterne's imitators achieved this happy blend of satire and sensibility, though the flood of imitations continued nearly unchecked. Reviewers were quick to point out imitations of Sterne's style and typography; playwrights drew upon *Tristram Shandy* in creating their characters; and one novelist even introduced a sermon into a scene at a masquerade, in imitation of Yorick's sermon in the first installment of Sterne's novel.[2] Charles Dibdin was exaggerating only slightly when he said in 1790, "All the would-be lady writers have sprung from RICHARDSON, just as all the would-be gentlemen writers have sprung from STERNE." [3]

Although Sterne's style and manner were copied in all sorts of productions, the majority of outright imitations were of the *Sentimental Journey* rather than of *Tristram Shandy*. More than one author at-

---

1. "Sterne's La Fleur," *European Magazine, 18* (July–Dec. 1790), 173-4, 268, 346-9. Cross calls these articles "quite untrustworthy as a whole," although they have behind them "a real La Fleur and vague traditions" (*Life,* p. 408). Sir Walter Scott later used some of this material. For a discussion of Johnson's attitude toward Sterne, see above, pp. 7–8. Cf. also the remarks of a writer in the *Westminster Magazine, 13* (Nov. 1785), 587, who declared it impossible to "give the faintest imitation of Sterne" without blending "the finest satire, and the most delicate sympathy."

2. See *Monthly Review* and *Critical Review,* passim, for the numerous notices of imitations of Sterne.

3. *The By-Stander; or, Universal Weekly Expositor* (London, 1790), p. 273. See below, pp. 79–80.

tempted a continuation of Yorick's travels,[4] while other writers enlarged upon hints thrown out by Sterne and told the complete stories of characters he had sketched more briefly. Typical of these latter productions was *Letters of Maria*. The anonymous "editor" pretends to have met one of Maria's friends at Moulines and obtained her letters, which give all the details of her unhappy love affair. St. Flos, her sweetheart, goes away after their marriage has been forbidden by the curate, ostensibly being sent overseas as a soldier. When she receives no answer to her letters, Maria's mind begins to give way and she makes a pilgrimage on foot to Rome. She returns to her home, at which time Sterne apparently meets her, and later finds that St. Flos had not entered the army after all, but has become a monk at a nearby monastery. After resolving to meet in the next world, they indulge in a tearful farewell. Maria's mind is restored, but both she and St. Flos soon die and are buried together.[5] The reviews were unanimously harsh in their comments on this production, the *English Review* calling it a "milk and water dilution of the simple pathos" of the original.[6] The *Monthly* felt it was "sacrilege for any unhallowed hand" to treat the woes of Maria, while the *Critical* echoed these sentiments, asserting that the story was "enshrined and secured from all attack" in Sterne's amber.[7]

Meanwhile, other literary hacks took sentimental journeys of their own to all points of the compass. Typical of these was *Adventures of a Hackney Coach,* published anonymously by Dorothy Kilner in 1781. In her dedication the authoress claims to have found "an old worn-out pen of Yorick's," which she has put in repair, feeling certain of success while she has "this renowned Talisman." [8] The book itself imitates the more obvious elements of Sterne's style and brings in such contemporary events as Garrick's retirement from the stage, William Dodd's execution, and the funerals of Lord Chatham and Ned Shuter. The "renowned Talisman" failed, however; for the *Critical* found it "as execrable a hack as any private gentleman would wish to be drove in," and the *Monthly* asserted that the author could not be "any relation of the Shandy family" and lamented the uses which had been made of Sterne's name: "Prithee come hither, honest grave-digger, and cover

4. *Continuation of Yorick's Sentimental Journey* (1788) was condemned by the *Monthly,* the *Critical,* and the *English Review;* while *A Sentimental Journey. Intended as a Sequel to Mr. Sterne's* (1793) was likewise condemned by Thomas Holcroft in the *Monthly.*

5. *Letters of Maria,* London, 1790.

6. *English Review, 17* (March 1791), 232.

7. William Enfield, *Monthly Review,* 2d Ser. *4* (March 1791), 355. *Critical Review, 70* (Dec. 1790), 698.

8. *Adventures of a Hackney Coach* (London, 1781), pp. 5–6. There is a copy of this book in the University of Chicago Library.

up *Yorick's* skull. The flies have blown on it.—Cover it up!—Maggots and all!" [9]

The two productions discussed above are fairly typical of the kind of thing which was being turned out in imitation of Sterne, and the comments of the reviews are also typical. Even the best of Sterne's imitators were open to the charges of lacking freshness and originality, while the worst were accused of being servile copyists or of merely imitating Sterne's "frivolity" or his "indecency and extravagance." In 1780 Boswell had said: "How many writers have made themselves ridiculous by dull imitation of the sudden sallies of fancy and unconnected breaks of sentiment in Sterne?" [1] But during the next few years a goodly number of literary hacks continued to make themselves ridiculous.

While the excesses of Sterne's imitators were calling forth adverse comments from the critics, some of the excesses in Sterne's own style were likewise being attacked. Thus Noorthouck said in the *Monthly* that "Sterne was credited with profundity, till the public were profoundly tired with the investigation of his hidden meanings." [2] William Creech echoed these sentiments and compared Sterne to those men who speak to you "for a whole evening" without saying "any thing which is worth remembering, or affects the judgment." Sterne, "under an air of pretended mystery, endeavours to conceal nothing at all"; and though the reader may be "now and then tickled," he will conclude that there is "more real wit and just satire in a very few pages in Swift or Fielding" than in Sterne's whole book. [3]

The style of the *Sermons* was often singled out for condemnation, as these discourses, which had been so popular in Sterne's lifetime, gradually declined somewhat in popularity. [4] John Stedman found the humor in them "inconsistent with the dignity of the pulpit"; [5] and after the publication of Gray's letter to Wharton which had contained some fairly restrained praise of the *Sermons*, [6] John Mainwaring felt impelled to characterize Gray's remarks as "rather hasty and unguarded." Sterne's *Sermons* lack propriety, he continues, since the "gaiety of

9. *Critical Review,* 52 (Aug. 1781), [159]. Samuel Badcock, *Monthly Review,* 64 (June 1781), 468; 65 (Nov. 1781), 390.
1. *The Hypochondriack,* ed. Margery Bailey (2 vols. Stanford, Stanford Univ. Press, 1928), 2, 12.
2. *Monthly Review,* 2d Ser. 2 (Aug. 1790), 421.
3. *Edinburgh Fugitive Pieces* (Edinburgh, 1815), pp. 151–2. The remarks first appeared in 1783.
4. They were reprinted separately only twice (1784 and 1787), although they were included in complete editions of Sterne's works and were anthologized.
5. *Laelius and Hortensia* (Edinburgh, 1782), p. 78. Stedman was a physician, probably at Edinburgh, whom I have been unable to identify further.
6. See above, p. 11.

polite conversation" is not suited to the pulpit; and further, "besides
their strange indecorum, and air of burlesque," they are "incorrect,
verbose, and affected." [7]

Opinion was still divided about the sincerity and the tendency of
Sterne's philanthropy. Sir John Hawkins, Johnson's biographer,
observed that sentimentalists like Sterne are "in general men of loose
principles, bad œconomists, living without foresight," who try to excuse themselves "by professions of greater love to mankind" and "finer
feelings than they will allow men of more regular lives, whom they
deem formalists, to possess." Men of this sort, though they have "good
hearts," feel themselves above "that rule of conduct which is founded
in a sense of duty." Fielding, Rousseau, and Sterne are "the principal
teachers" of this "new school of morality," and "great is the mischief
they have done." [8] Hawkins' daughter, Laetitia-Matilda, hints that
her father's strictures on Sterne may have been partially responsible
for the unfavorable review in the *Gentleman's Magazine* of his *Life of
Johnson.* She agrees with him that Sterne's work is not fit "to be put
into the hands of a female," although she explains that his "affectionate
injunction" never "openly or clandestinely to read what he did not
approve" has prevented her from reading Sterne.[9] Ely Bates, whose
Chinese Fragment was published in 1786, was even more violent in
his condemnation of Sterne's principles. Though Yorick has been
"extolled as a philanthropist, and even as a philosopher," Bates pro-
nounces him a "villain" and a "hypocrite," since "he that wantonly
stabs the *morals* of his country is a villain; and he is a hypocrite, if,
under such a conduct, he makes pretensions to benevolence." [1]

Hannah More, the close friend of Johnson, likewise casts aspersions
on Sterne's sincerity, though her strictures are not quite so severe:

> Oh, bless'd Compassion! Angel Charity!
> More dear one genuine deed perform'd for thee,
> Than all the periods Feeling e'er can turn,
> Than all thy soothing pages, polish'd STERNE! [2]

Gilbert Wakefield echoed these sentiments with the exclamation, "Oh!
that the sentiments of benevolence and pity, which adorn [Sterne's]

7. *Sermons on Several Occasions* (Cambridge, 1780), pp. v–vii, xxix–xxx.
8. *Life of Samuel Johnson* (London, 1787), p. 218.
9. *Memoirs, Anecdotes, Facts, and Opinions Collected and Preserved by Laetitia-
Matilda Hawkins* (2 vols. London, 1824), *I,* 238–40.
1. *A Chinese Fragment. Containing an Enquiry into the Present State of Religion in
England* (London, 1786), pp. 102–3. A copy of this book, which was published anonymously, may be found in the University of Michigan Library.
2. "Sensibility," *Sacred Dramas* (London, 1782), p. 285. This immensely popular
volume had reached a twenty-fourth edition by 1850. For Miss More's later remarks see
below, pp. 92–3.

writings, had been transferred to the embellishment of his life!" [3]

In general, however, biographical treatments of Sterne were some-what kinder; [4] and there were many who were ready to forgive his faults. Sometimes these were somewhat carried away in their enthusiasm, as was the author of *Unfortunate Sensibility*, who admits that Sterne was "a rational being, whose *gaieté de coeur* but ill became the sable vestment," but goes on to imagine him as "the father of some happy convent," where he might have heard "the soft confession of the female penitent" and consoled her with "the tear of sympathy" and an easy penance. [5] The sentimental approach to Sterne's character lent itself to cliché almost as readily as did the harsher approach of the moralists.

Clichés were also still common in the literary assessments of Sterne's work, [6] and when critics attempted to place him in relation to other writers there was no more agreement than there had been before. He might be classed by one writer with Richardson, Rousseau, and Goethe for his "sentimental" and "pathetic" side; [7] while another might place him with Butler, Rabelais, and Swift before going on to state, paradoxically enough, that it was the story of Le Fever which had made his fame secure. [8] William Hayley applauded the mixture of the humorous and the pathetic which he found in Sterne, instancing "the song of ANSTEY, and the tale of STERNE" as works of genius with "moral grace and comic power." [9] Martin Sherlock, on the other hand, credited Sterne with wit rather than genius, placing him with Voltaire and Addison rather than with Richardson, Milton, and Shakespeare. Both wit and genius are "compounded of imagination and judgment," Sherlock says, but the imagination in a man of genius has more "heat." "The object of wit is to please; the object of genius is to invent"; and hence genius "resembles a conflagration; wit an artificial firework." [1]

Sterne began to invite more frequent comparison with the other great novelists, although critics again differed in their conclusions. Lord

3. *Memoirs of the Life of Gilbert Wakefield Written by Himself* (London, 1792), p. 75. Wakefield was famous both as a classical scholar and as a controversial writer on religious and political subjects.

4. The edition of the *New and General Biographical Dictionary* published in 1784, for example, contains no strong personal censure. The extreme popularity of Sterne's sentimental side may partially account for the kinder biographical treatments.

5. *Unfortunate Sensibility*, 1, vii–viii.

6. See, e.g., *English Review*, 7 (Feb. 1786), 154. Cf. the more incisive remarks in *Critical Review*, 69 (March 1790), 358. The former are the rule, the latter the exception in the criticism of this period.

7. *English Review*, 8 (Nov. 1786), 354.

8. *The Patriad*, pp. 10, 26.

9. "The Triumphs of Temper," *Poems and Plays* (6 vols. London, 1785), 5, 131–2.

1. *Letters on Several Subjects* (2 vols. London, 1781), 1, 68–73. Elsewhere in the *Letters* Sherlock, who was chaplain to the Earl of Bristol, credits Sterne with a certain amount of genius for producing something "new" in the *Sentimental Journey* (1, 25–6), but censures him, along with Congreve and Vanbrugh, for indecency (1, 126).

Chedworth ranked Fielding as "a very great master of human nature" who was "far, far above Sterne"; [2] but many critics would have agreed with the *Critical*'s unknown reviewer who thought Sterne "without an equal, and almost without a predecessor." [3] Henry James Pye, poet laureate and classical scholar, sided with Lord Chedworth in preferring Fielding to Sterne, though for different reasons. In his commentary on Aristotle's *Poetics,* he wrote, "Perhaps there is not a stronger instance of the difference between manners introduced as secondary to the action, though arising immediately, and necessarily, from it; and their holding the first place, than the novel of Tom Jones compared with Tristram Shandy." The "masterly contrivance of the fable" in *Tom Jones* "at once astonishes and delights us"; but though we are "struck with the high coloring" of *Tristram Shandy,* "we soon perceive it is laid on promiscuously" and we are "amused," but not "interested," except when "our passions are engaged by incident," as in "the admirable story of Le Fevre." [4] James Beattie, another scholarly critic, brought a slightly different charge against Sterne, for he thought that both Sterne and Smollett sometimes attempted "to raise laughter by unnatural exaggeration." [5] Gradually, however, Sterne and the other great novelists of the eighteenth century were all coming to be accepted as classics in the new genre which they had helped to develop. John Noorthouck mirrored the attitude of the time when he wrote in the *Monthly* in 1791: "Richardson, Fielding, Smollet, and Sterne, were the Wedgwoods of their days; and the imitators that have since started up in the same line, exceed all power of calculation!" [6]

In general, the older generation of critics, who had seen the gradual emergence of the novel as a form and had read *Tristram Shandy* when it was first published, did not have much new to say about Sterne. Johnson apparently remained unrelenting in his opposition. His last recorded mention of Sterne involves an incident in May 1781, when Mary Monckton (later Countess of Cork) "insisted that some of

2. *Letters from the Late Lord Chedworth to the Rev. Thomas Crampton* (Norwich, 1840), p. 111. The letter was written in 1788. Cf. the comment of Enfield in the *Monthly,* 2d Ser. 8 (May 1792), 107, that Fielding "in the general judgment of the public, still possesses the first place among English novelists."

3. *Critical Review,* 53 (June 1782), 402.

4. *A Commentary Illustrating the Poetic of Aristotle* (London, 1792), p. 165. The passage quoted is in illustration of Aristotle's statement that "the professed end of tragedy is to imitate an action: and, chiefly by means of that action, to shew the qualities of the persons acting."

5. *Dissertations Moral and Critical* (London, 1783), p. 177. It is significant, however, that Beattie does not include Sterne in his censure of Aristophanes and Rabelais for "indecent buffoonery." Beattie, who was professor of moral philosophy and logic at the University of Aberdeen, discusses Richardson, Fielding, and Smollett in his essay *On Fable and Romance,* but makes no reference there to Sterne.

6. *Monthly Review,* 2d Ser. 5 (July 1791), 338.

Sterne's writings were very pathetick. Johnson bluntly denied it. 'I am sure (said she) they have affected *me*.'—'Why (said Johnson, smiling, and rolling himself about,) that is, because, dearest, you're a dunce.' When she sometime afterwards mentioned this to him, he said with equal truth and politeness; 'Madam, if I had thought so, I certainly should not have said it.' " [7] Mrs. Piozzi apparently agreed with Miss Monckton, for she was surprised to have Susan and Sophia Thrale come home from school and "repeat some Stuff in an odd Tone of Voice, & laugh obstreperously," when she realized that they were reciting the passages about Sterne's Maria. She concludes that the youth of the children was responsible for their unfeeling conduct, since compassion is not a "native Sentiment of the Soul" and must be taught.[8]

Boswell thought of Sterne occasionally as he was writing the series of essays which he entitled *The Hypochondriack*,[9] and a simple scene of industry and frugality which he saw in 1780 likewise brought him to mind.[1] His reference to Sterne in one of the essays as "a writer of temporary fashionable fame in this age," who displayed "much levity" and "much contaminating extravagance of effusion," may represent a cooling of his former enthusiasm toward the works of Yorick. It is more likely, however, that he is merely trying to write in the character that he has adopted for the essays.[2] Walpole, who had liked the *Sentimental Journey* but found *Tristram Shandy* unsupportably dull, referred in a letter written in 1782 to "Sterne's capricious pertness, which the original wore out: and which having been admired and cried up to the skies by foreign writers of reviews, was on the contrary too severely treated by our own." [3] Time had mellowed his opinion somewhat, although it remained basically unchanged.

Among the outstanding authors and critics in the newer generation of men of letters, comments were varied. Henry Mackenzie, who was regarded as a disciple of Sterne, nevertheless imitated only the more sentimental side of his master and could not appreciate his wit and humor. He was probably summing up a lifelong attitude when he wrote many years later: "Sterne often wants the dignity of wit. I do

7. *Boswell's Life of Johnson, 4,* 108.

8. *Thraliana,* ed. Katharine C. Balderston (2 vols. Oxford, Clarendon Press, 1942), 2, 823-4.

9. This series, which originally appeared Nov. 1777-Aug. 1783 in the *London Magazine,* contains two definite references to Sterne (*1,* 153; *2,* 11) and two probable allusions (*1,* 143; *1,* 314).

1. *Papers from Malahide Castle, 14,* 125. The scene, which is described in Boswell's "Journal in Edinburgh, 1780," is said to be "equal to any one in Sterne."

2. *Hypochondriack, 1,* 153. Boswell, writing "On Conscience," is especially anxious to stress the importance of revelation, which, he feels, goes far beyond Sterne's "decent and clear piece of induction" in his "Sermon on Conscience."

3. *Correspondence with William Cole, 2,* 301.

not speak of his licentiousness, but he often is on the very verge of buffoonery, which is the bathos of wit, and the fool's coat is half upon him." [4]

Both Sterne and Mackenzie were the "bosom favorites" of Robert Burns, who prized Mackenzie's *Man of Feeling* "next to the Bible," but also spoke enthusiastically of both *Tristram Shandy* and the *Sentimental Journey*.[5] In one of his letters he identifies himself with Sterne, thinking of his relationship with one of his women friends as similar to that of Sterne and Eliza.[6] And he also appreciated Sterne's lighter side. In speaking of the power of David's harp, which chased the evil spirit out of Saul, he says: "This Evil Spirit, I take it, was just, long-spun Sermons, & many-pag'd Epistles, & Birth-day Poetry, & patience-vexing Memorials, Remonstrances, Dedications, Resolution-Addresses, &c. &c. &c. while David's harp, I suppose was, mystically speaking, Tristram Shandy, Laugh & be fat, Cauld kail in Aberdeen, Green grows the rashes, & the rest of that inspired & inspiring family." [7]

The same instinctive and warmly appreciative attitude toward Sterne is evidenced in the remarks of Leonard MacNally in his *Sentimental Excursions to Windsor and Other Places,* one of the many imitations of the *Sentimental Journey*. "I have always read STERNE with delight," MacNally says, "and never read him but I felt him in my heart more than in my head; yet I hope his precepts have improved my understanding in the same proportion they have expanded my humanity." Sterne's precepts, MacNally continues, affect him like "a conjunction of love and wine," since they make him "generous and gay." The work of Sterne will be read and loved, he concludes, "when the laboured works of labouring philosophers, travellers, historians, politicians, and other *mouseingendering* compilers shall lie sleeping in dust upon the upper shelves of shops and libraries." [8]

One of the most extended treatments of Sterne and his works is to be found among the essays of an author of a quite different character. Vicesimus Knox, headmaster of Tunbridge School and ordained priest, first published his *Essays Moral and Literary* in 1778 and augmented the collection in subsequent editions during the eighties.[9] These dis-

4. *Anecdotes and Egotisms of Henry Mackenzie,* ed. Harold W. Thompson (London, Oxford Univ. Press, 1927), p. 182. These remarks were written sometime between about 1825 and 1831; but the character of Mackenzie's own novel, *The Man of Feeling,* Edinburgh, 1771, indicates that the more jocular side of Sterne's work would not have been attractive to him even in his younger days.

5. See *Letters of Robert Burns,* ed. J. D. Ferguson (2 vols. Oxford, Clarendon Press, 1931), *1,* 14, 100, 111, 346; *2,* 166.

6. Ibid., *2,* 265.

7. Ibid., *1,* 278–9.

8. *Sentimental Excursions to Windsor and Other Places* (London, 1781), pp. 60–2. See also above, p. 64.

9. None of the four essays which are quoted below appear in the first edition of 1778, and three of them were added in the "new" edition of 1782; see *Monthly Review, 68*

courses were widely read, going into a sixth edition by 1785 and a thirteenth by 1793.

Knox takes as his basis for criticism "the effect which a literary work is found to produce," asserting that "sentiment or feeling, after all that has been urged by theoretical critics, is the ultimate and infallible touchstone." In all works "of true taste and genius," there is something "which cannot be pointed out by verbal description, and which can only be perceived by the vibrations it produces on the nervous system." [1]

When he comes to consider the works of Sterne, he finds that their effect is both good and bad. Though "far below Shakespeare in the scale of genius," Sterne shares with him the "power of shaking the nerves" and "affecting the mind in the most lively manner in a few words, and with the most perfect simplicity of language." Sterne possesses the further merit of effectively recommending "a general philanthropy" and smoothing "the asperities of natural temper." At the same time, Knox believes, Sterne's work has also been a harmful influence, since its hold upon the mind and heart has promoted immorality. "That softness, that affected and excessive sympathy at first sight, that sentimental affection, which is but *lust in disguise,*" he says, "have been the ruin of thousands of our countrymen and countrywomen, who fancied, that while they were breaking the laws of God and man, they were actuated by the fine feelings of *sentimental affection.* How much are divorces multiplied since Sterne appeared!" Sterne himself "is said to have displayed in private life, a bad and a hard heart"; and thus it is only natural that he should be "the grand promoter of adultery, and every species of illicit commerce." [2]

Among the other "faults and follies, which render the writings of Sterne justly and greatly reprehensible," Knox lists their obscurity and lack of unity.[3] His wit is "of the lowest kind, and the easiest of invention," since it is "for the most part allusive obscenity." His characters are not "natural," nor do they exhibit "true humour in their manners and conversations."

Knox goes on to admit that he knows "this censure will be considered as blasphemy by the idolaters of Sterne" and expresses the hope that it will not "sour that milk of human kindness which they may have

---

(April 1783), 304–5. The fourth, "On Simplicity of Style in Prosaic Composition," must have been added in 1779, although I have been unable to locate a copy of this edition. The present text is taken from the 13th ed. 3 vols. London, 1793.

1. "On Modern Criticism," *Essays Moral and Literary,* 1, 250.
2. Cf. Knox's *Winter Evenings* (2d ed. 2 vols. London, 1790 [1st ed. 1788]), 2, 159, in which he states that "Mr. Sterne and Mrs. Draper have too many imitators" and that "a goat is a personage of as great sensibility and sentiment as most of them."
3. Knox admits that perhaps Sterne's works should not be judged by the rules of Aristotle but asserts that "even by the decisions of reason and common sense" his books "abound with faults."

imbibed from his writings." He likewise admits that Sterne excels in the "exquisite touches of the pathetic interspersed throughout all his works," though he believes that this is their sole excellence "which admits of unalloyed applause." [4] Knox also has high praise for the "true simplicity of style" and "faithful adherence to nature" of the *Sentimental Journey.* But though the book can make our nerves "vibrate with every tender emotion," it also contains a subtle and dangerous poison, since it arouses and inflames those passions which "after all that the novelist can advance in their favour, are the copious sources of all human misery. Many a connection, begun with the fine sentimentality which Sterne has recommended and increased," he continues, "has terminated in disease, infamy, want, madness, suicide, and a gibbet." No matter what a writer's private life may be, Knox concludes, he "should take the side of virtue in his public writings." [5]

Thus Knox revived the old charge that Sterne inflames the passions, and it is this assumption, together with a certain amount of antipathy to Sterne's personal character, that lies behind most of his censure. He seems somewhat uncertain as to just what his final conclusions about Sterne should be, since the harshest censure is mingled with the strongest praise. One hesitates as to whether he would rather have his last word on the subject be that Sterne was "the grand promoter of adultery, and every species of illicit commerce," or that "the works of an Addison and a Sterne, and the reception they have met with, will vindicate the nation from the charge of wanting taste for simple beauty." [6]

Though Knox had glimpsed both great faults and great virtues in Sterne, his brother moralist, George Gregory, could see no "simple beauty" in Sterne's style. In his *Sermons,* first published in 1787, Gregory says : "I know no author so likely as Sterne to corrupt the style and taste of his readers; all his writings are full of trick and affectation . . . and are at best only calculated to excite the momentary admiration of the unthinking part of mankind." [7] Gregory echoes these sentiments in a footnote to his translation of Bishop Robert Lowth's *Lectures on the Sacred Poetry of the Hebrews,* published the same year, and also charges that Sterne "has borrowed from others all the tolerable thoughts which are thinly scattered through his writings." [8]

When Gregory's friend Anna Seward read these remarks, she jumped to Sterne's defense in her letters to Gregory. She is astonished

4. "On the Moral Tendency of the Writings of Sterne," *Essays Moral and Literary,* *3*, 212–18. Badcock stated in the *Monthly, 68* (April 1783), 305, that this censure had been "too severe" but Knox was apparently regarded as an authority on Sterne, for he is quoted in the *British Plutarch* (3d ed. London, 1791), *8*, 90–1.
5. "On the Manner of Writing Voyages and Travels," *Essays Moral and Literary,* *1*, 223–4.
6. "On Simplicity of Style in Prosaic Composition," ibid., *1*, 145.
7. *Sermons* (2d ed. London, 1789), p. xxiv.
8. *Lectures on the Sacred Poetry of the Hebrews* (3d ed. London, 1835), p. 181.

at his statement that "no classic ear can endure" Sterne's style, since she has always admired "that happy, thrice happy, mixture of the humorous and the pathetic, in which he stands alone amongst all other writers out of the dramatic scale," and her ear has found his style "so natural, easy, animated, and eloquent." She also commends the "penetration which seems to have an hundred eyes with which to look into the human heart." Replying to Gregory's charges of plagiarism she minimizes the influence that Swift and Rabelais may have had on Sterne, since "Swift has not any of Sterne's pathos, and Sterne has none of the filthiness of Swift,—though too apt to sport licentiously with comic double-meanings." This fault, she continues, "however justly censurable, has no tendency to injure the minds of his readers by inflaming their passions." Neither Swift nor Rabelais ever "interest[s] the affections, while Sterne guides, turns, and precipitates them into any channel he pleases." She praises the "dramatic spirit" which Sterne has infused into Walter Shandy and comments on the naturalness of the other characters: "We see and hear the little domestic group at Shandy-Hall; nor can we help an involuntary conviction, not only that they all existed, but that they had been of our acquaintance." Even "the most shadowy prototype" of Uncle Toby, Trim, Mrs. Shandy, or Dr. Slop is not to be found in any other book. Finally, she dares to suggest, though very tactfully, that Gregory's failure to appreciate Sterne may be a kind of literary blindness. "I never knew a man or woman of letters," she says, "but there was some one fine writer, at least, to which their 'Lynx's beam became the mole's dim curtain.'" There have been famous writers who were "moles" to Ossian, Rousseau, or Milton; and "envy made Johnson a mole to all our best poets, except Dryden and Pope. You are a mole to Sterne," she concludes.[9]

Gregory may have concluded that he was in good company in indulging in "literary molism"; at any rate Anna Seward's plea seems to have had little effect upon him, for in the second edition of his *Essays Historical and Moral*, published the next year, he shows no change of heart. In the first edition, published in 1785, he had deplored those who prefer "the tinsel of Sterne, to the classic gold of Addison." In a footnote to this passage in the second edition, Gregory says that he is "sorry to find, that the admirers of Mr. Sterne have thought their favourite author degraded by this comparison," but that he is "one of those insensible and incorrigible beings, who can read trite sentiments and mock pathos without being overwhelmed with admiration or melted into tenderness, merely because it is the fashion to be so." [1]

9. *Letters of Anna Seward*, [? ed.] Archibald Constable (6 vols. Edinburgh, 1811), *1*, 365, 375–8. The quotation comes from La Fontaine's *Fables*, Bk. 1, fable 7.
1. *Essays Historical and Moral* (2d ed. London, 1788), p. 140. In reviewing the first edition, the *Critical's* reviewer had thought that "Sterne deserves a better character"; *60* (July 1785), 42.

Impelled by these remarks and probably also by similar ones in Gregory's letters to her, the "Swan of Lichfield" sprang back to the attack. She is especially zealous to defend Sterne from the charge of plagiarism, pointing out that Shakespeare and Milton, among others, also borrowed freely and that "taking designs from others, was never reckoned plagiarism." She asserts that "Tristram Shandy, in natural humour, in dramatic spirit, and in truth of character, [is] superior to the Scribleriad Family in Pope's Miscellanies," from which she thinks that Sterne probably derived his plan. Every person in the Shandy family, "down to the fat scullion, lives," she says, "and they are, by those happy characteristic touches, that mark the hand of genius, brought to our eye, as well as our ear." Replying apparently to a suggestion which Gregory must have made that Uncle Toby was an imitation of Smollett's Commodore Trunnion, she states that although it is a long time since she has read *Peregrine Pickle,* the Commodore "made so little impression" on her that she has "no remembrance" of him. On the other hand, "even after the slightest perusal" she could never have forgotten "the warm-hearted, honest, generous Toby Shandy, by whose absurdities, so happily mingling with his kindness, and with his virtues, we are betrayed at once into the tears of admiration, and into the convulsions of laughter." Praise of the other characters follows, together with enthusiastic comments on both comic and pathetic incidents in the book. She then continues by showing the superiority of Sterne's Maria over Cervantes' Dorothea, a comparison which Gregory has apparently hinted at. Miss Seward again hints that Gregory's failure to appreciate Sterne is a literary blind spot in him and concludes: "If your dislike is invincible, we will mention him no more—since, were I to become your proselyte on this subject, it must be at the expence of my gratitude, for many an hour that has been softened by his pathos, and gilded by his wit." [2]

During the period under consideration, some critics remained as "invincible" in their dislike of Sterne as Gregory, just as others were as confirmed in their enthusiasm as was Anna Seward. Some of course, like Knox, found themselves torn between praise and censure by the different elements in Sterne's work. Meanwhile the public continued to call for new editions of Sterne; the reviewers continued to quote him; and many who did not read his works in their entirety, nevertheless read and cherished the famous passages in *Beauties of Sterne.* The selections in this volume eliminated the problem of his alleged immorality and emphasized Sterne's sentimental side, and the numerous imitations of the *Sentimental Journey* served to reinforce this tendency of the public to think of him more and more as a master of the pathetic. Many a man and woman of "sensibility" probably read Sterne's pa-

2. *Letters of Anna Seward, 2,* 182–8.

thetic tales together in the way described by the author who addressed
these lines "to a lady called Maria, on reading to her Sterne's beautiful
story of that name":

> As Sterne's pathetic tale you hear,
>   Why rudely check the rising sigh?
> Why seek to hide the pitying tear,
>   Whose lustre aids the brilliant eye?
>
> Tears which lament another's woe,
>   Unveil the goodness of the heart:
> Uncheck'd, unhided, these should flow—
>   They please beyond the pow'r of art.[3]

People of this sort would obviously not appreciate the lighter side of
Sterne's work, and critics likewise were often not quite sure what value
posterity would place on the humorous elements in Sterne. Clara Reeve,
casting about for a comment on *Tristram Shandy* which she could
make "with safety," was perhaps typical of many when she said that
Sterne had had "the good fortune to make himself and his writings
the *ton of the day,*" although she would not "presume" to say "what
value posterity will set upon them." Of his pathetic side she could say,
with less hesitation: "Where *Sterne* attempts the Pathos, he is irresistible. . . . His *Maria* and *le Fevre* and his *Monk,* are charming
pictures, and will survive when all his other writings are forgot." [4]

Charles Dibdin, writing in the *By-Stander* in 1790, was much surer
of Sterne's place and even suggested that he might have successfully
"disputed the literary throne" with Johnson, had he wished to do so.
Dibdin believes that Sterne's powers were superior to "Oliver's" (his
name for Johnson under the analogy between his literary dictatorship
and Cromwell's political one): "STERNE, with many other merits as a
writer, possessed great good sense. He could either surprise or pene-
trate the heart at will, but he generally chose surprise," since this was
"the surest chance for popularity, unless, as I hint before, he had fairly
entered the lists with Oliver, and contended for the throne. Had he
done this," Dibdin continues, "the pretender would have sat in a most
uneasy situation.—STERNE had genius enough for any thing, and he
knew human nature so well that he had it in his power to have begot the
most awkward and clumsy anxiety in Oliver. I have not the smallest
doubt that if STERNE had invented a series of dogmas in opposition to
those which were daily uttered by Oliver, and credited as gospel by his
adherents, an universal laugh would have been raised to the honour of

---

3. Quoted in *Critical Review, 68* (Aug. 1789), 159-60, in a review of some anonymous poems.
4. *The Progress of Romance* (2 vols. Colchester, 1785), *2,* 29-31.

STERNE, and at the expence of the pretender, and perhaps the credit of his pretensions." [5] Certainly, if one measures in terms of popularity, the countless imitations of Sterne and the numerous references to his works would tend to suggest that he had fully as much literary influence during the sixties, seventies, and eighties as Johnson had, even though, at that time the final verdict of more distant posterity was felt by many to be still in doubt.

5. *By-Stander,* pp. 321–2. This series of essays was first published serially in 1789–90, the quotation coming from a "History of Literature," which is continued throughout the series. In previous numbers Fielding has been given high praise, Richardson has been severely criticized, and Smollett has been characterized as mediocre.

4

"Borrowed Plumes" (*1793–1814*)

ALTHOUGH the originality of Sterne's work had strongly impressed most of his contemporary readers as well as those of the next two decades, the charge had been made more than once that he was indebted in various ways to his predecessors. The *Critical Review* had insisted upon the resemblance of *Tristram Shandy* to Rabelais, and had also accused Sterne of creating the character of La Fleur "with shreds . . . barbarously cut out and unskilfully put together from other novels." [1] Mrs. Piozzi, strolling into a bookshop at Derby in the summer of 1774, had picked up a copy of *The Life and Memoirs of Corporal Bates* (1756) and fancied that she had found "the very Novel from which Sterne took his first Idea." [2] It seems doubtful that the book had this much, if any, influence upon Sterne; [3] but a few years later Anna Seward had suggested the Scribleriad family as a more likely source for the general plan of *Tristram Shandy*, insisting, however, upon the essential originality of Sterne's work. [4]

In 1792 a correspondent of the *European Magazine* reported that Sterne's ardent admirer, John Henderson, [5] had been perusing Burton's *Anatomy of Melancholy* just before his death and had "extracted various parallel passages, which Mr. Sterne had availed himself of in the course of his entertaining works." The correspondent would have sent these to the *European Magazine,* he continues, had he not been informed that "a very learned and ingenious Gentleman at Manchester had already been travelling over the same ground," and intended to publish the results of his research. [6]

The "ingenious Gentleman at Manchester" was the versatile John Ferriar, [7] whose "Comments on Sterne" were to create far more of a

1. See above, pp. 14, 15, 44.
2. *Thraliana, 1,* 23–4.
3. A modern critic, Helen S. Hughes, has agreed that there are "parallels in matter and method" with *Tristram Shandy,* although "one's final judgment may be less positive than Mrs. Piozzi's." See "A Precursor of *Tristram Shandy,*" *JEGP, 17* (1918), 227–51. Cf. Edward Bensley's remarks in *Notes and Queries, 159,* (Aug. 2, 1930), 84.
4. See above, pp. 76–8.
5. See above, pp. 52–3.
6. *European Magazine, 21* (March 1792), 167–8.
7. Ferriar was active in the Literary and Philosophical Society of Manchester, preparing papers on a wide variety of subjects, as well as writing for the *Monthly* between 1799 and 1806. He came to Manchester about 1785 after receiving his medical degree in Edinburgh. He may have been first drawn to Sterne's work by the obstetrical dis-

critical furor than the correspondent of the *European Magazine* might have supposed. First embodied in a paper read at a meeting of the Literary and Philosophical Society of Manchester on January 21, 1791, Ferriar's remarks were printed in the *Memoirs* of the society in 1793. Ferriar begins the essay by observing that Sterne is "almost the only satirical and ethical writer of note" who has not had a commentator. "The works of Rabelais, Butler, Pope, Swift, and many others," he says, "are over-loaded with explanations, while Sterne remains, in many places, unintelligible to the greater number of his readers." Sterne's originality is not at stake, he insists, since he is "considered as the inventor of a new style in our language." "I do not mean to treat him as a Plagiarist," he continues; "I wish to illustrate, not to degrade him. If some instances of copying be proved against him, they will detract nothing from his genius, and will only lessen that imposing appearance he sometimes assumed, of erudition which he really wanted." [8]

Partially echoing the comments of the *Critical Review* of some thirty years back, Ferriar finds that Rabelais has "furnished Sterne with the general character, and even many particular ideas," if one considers *Tristram Shandy* as "a general Satire, levelled chiefly against the abuse of speculative opinions." "From that copious fountain of learning, wit and whim," he continues, "our author drew deeply. Rabelais, stored with erudition, poured lavishly out, what Sterne directed and expanded with care, to enrich his pages. And to this appropriation, we owe many of his most pleasing sallies. For being bounded in his literary acquirements, his imagination had freer play, and more natural graces. He seized the grotesque objects of obsolete erudition, presented by his original, with a vigour untamed by previous labour, and an ardour unabated by familiarity with literary folly." Ferriar goes on to quote various passages which are "founded on" Rabelais, but hastens to add that "any degree of imitation" is "greatly to Sterne's honour," since "a higher polish was never given to rugged materials." [9] Later in the essay, Ferriar alludes to the comparison between Sterne and Rabelais which Voltaire had made, saying that he "has done neither of them justice." While Rabelais "derided absurdities then existing in full force, and intermingled much sterling sense with the grossest parts of his book," Sterne "laughs at many exploded opinions, and abandoned fooleries, and contrives to degrade some of his most solemn passages by a vicious levity." None of the three, Ferriar believes, is ideally

cussions in the early part of *Tristram Shandy;* but once aroused, his interest led him to an extensive study of all Sterne's possible literary sources.

8. "Comments on Sterne," *Memoirs of the Literary and Philosophical Society of Manchester, 4* (1793), 45–7. Ferriar seems to be using the word "illustrate" in the sense of "shed lustre upon" as well as that of "explain." The former meaning was still current in his day.

9. Ibid., pp. 47–8, 54–5.

qualified for the office of "a literary Censor," since "Rabelais wanted decency, Sterne learning, and Voltaire fidelity." [1]

Although Ferriar is somewhat reluctant to ascribe much direct influence to Rabelais, he states that "there can be no doubt" about Sterne's indebtedness to Burton's *Anatomy of Melancholy*. The "singularities" of Walter Shandy's character, "with all the stains and mouldiness of the last century about him," may be traced to Burton's *Anatomy* and "the peculiarities of Burton's life." He points out several passages which Sterne has "borrowed" from Burton "without variation"; and suggests the influence that Burton's style may have exerted in Sterne's fondness for digressions. At the same time Ferriar speaks of Sterne's "improvements" in the passages "wherever he has imitated or borrowed"; and he cautions against ascribing too much influence to the earlier writer.[2]

The "pathetic manner" of Sterne's work, Ferriar believes, may have been inspired by Marivaux and Crébillon, although he states that he has not had time to explore this possibility at length. He also mentions borrowings from Donne, Montaigne, and various other authors and suggests that "the manner, the style, and the selection of subjects" in Sterne's *Sermons* "were derived from Bishop [Joseph] Hall. There is a delicacy of thought, and tenderness of expression in the good Bishop's compositions, from the transfusion of which Sterne looked for immortality." [3]

Ferriar's treatment is sympathetic throughout the essay. He nowhere applies the term "plagiarist" to Sterne; and although he points out passages that have been taken over from other authors with little change, he also insists in many instances upon the imaginative use that Sterne made of his borrowed materials. His final conclusion is that his remarks "leave Sterne in possession of every praise but that of curious erudition, to which he had no great pretence, and of unparallelled originality, which ignorance only can ascribe to any polished writer." [4]

The review of Ferriar's essay in the *Critical* quoted this last passage, which the unknown reviewer felt "evinces equal judgment and liberality

1. Ibid., pp. 84–6. Ferriar is referring to Voltaire's review in 1777 of the French translation of the first four volumes of *Tristram Shandy*. Voltaire mentions Swift and Sterne as the two Englishmen who have written in the style of Rabelais, but the comparison between Rabelais and Sterne is not developed. (See *Oeuvres complètes de Voltaire*, ed. A. J. Q. Beuchot, 52 vols. Paris, 1877–83, *30, 379–82*.) Voltaire had also referred to Sterne as "le second Rabelais d'Angleterre" in "Conscience," *Dictionnaire philosophique* (1771). In this earlier discussion of Sterne he summarizes the sermon in the second volume of *Tristram Shandy*, but apparently has misunderstood at least some parts of the English text, since he credits Dr. Slop with defending the Anglican church against the papists. See *Oeuvres complètes, 18, 237*.
2. "Comments," pp. 55, 57–60.
3. Ibid., pp. 80–1. Lansing Hammond states that Hall "stands third among those to whom Yorick was most indebted," the first two being Tillotson and Clarke. *Sermons of Mr. Yorick*, p. 81.
4. "Comments," p. 84.

in the writer";[5] but opinion in the other periodicals was divided. The *Analytical Review* concluded that Sterne's merits "have been too highly estimated," since "some of the most striking passages in his works have been almost servilely copied" from Burton.[6] Thomas Beddoes, in his review for the *Monthly,* says that he has heard that Sterne sometimes made "such free use" of Hall-Stevenson's library "as occasionally to copy with the closeness of a plagiary." Although Ferriar has said that Sterne's reputation will be little affected by the disclosures, Beddoes thinks it would "be prudent to forbear summing-up, till the evidence be all before us"; and this must be collected from the books which Sterne had access to.[7]

Some critics, however, were ready to do their summing up without waiting for all the evidence. Among these was "Eboracensis," a correspondent of the *Gentleman's Magazine,* whose comments in 1794 foreshadowed the tone that many future moralists were to take. Sterne's borrowings, he says, "leave him in possession of as little eminence as a writer, as his conduct, while living, gained him esteem as a man and respect as a divine." His works are on "the level of the lowest of all literary larcenies; they are found to shine with reflected light, to strut in borrowed plumes."[8]

Critics who judged the question from a literary rather than a moral point of view came to quite different conclusions. Isaac D'Israeli, although he thought that Ferriar's essay "might be considerably augmented," nevertheless classed Sterne among the writers "who imitate, but are inimitable."[9] William Jackson, the famous musician and composer of Exeter, elaborated the same attitude in his essay "On Literary Thievery," published in 1798. He instances Prior and Voltaire as other writers who have borrowed freely, but concludes that in all three cases the "thievery" has been justified. "The thievery of a fool is never excused," he says, "because no one can return the compliment; but, we pardon a genius, because if he takes, he is qualified to give in return."[1]

The sympathetic attitude which had been so marked in Ferriar's "Comments" is not so apparent in his *Illustrations of Sterne,* published in 1798. In *Illustrations* he revises and expands his earlier discussion, augmenting his list of Sterne's borrowings, adding a good deal of background material,[2] and for the first time elaborating a possible

5. *Critical Review,* 2d Ser. *9* (Sept. 1793), 4.
6. *Analytical Review, 20* (Dec. 1794), 415.
7. *Monthly Review,* 2d Ser. *13* (Feb. 1794), 183–4.
8. *Gentleman's Magazine, 64,* Pt. 1 (May 1794), 406–7.
9. *Miscellanies; or, Literary Recreations* (London, 1796), p. 318.
1. *The Four Ages* (London, 1798), pp. 244–57. Jackson also minimizes the importance of extensive plagiarism in the *Sermons,* since the practice is common among clergymen.
2. Ferriar's "Comments" runs to 41 pages; the 1798 edition of the *Illustrations,* to 185. Sometimes, however, Ferriar appears to be using his discussion of Sterne merely

source for the *Sentimental Journey*. The plan for Yorick's travels, he says, "seems to have been taken from the little French pieces" of Chapelle, Bachaumont, and Fontaine, "the merit of which consists in making trifles considerable." [3]

Although Ferriar still speaks of the "improvements" which Sterne has made over his originals,[4] his emphasis has shifted decidedly on this matter. Thus one of the key passages in "Comments" is changed to read as follows in *Illustrations:*

> [Sterne's] imagination, untamed by labour, and unsated by a long acquaintance with literary folly, dwelt with enthusiasm on the grotesque pictures of manners and opinions, displayed in his favourite authors. It may even be suspected, that by this influence he was drawn aside from his natural bias to the pathetic; for in the serious parts of his works, he seems to have depended on his own force, and to have found in his own mind whatever he wished to produce; but in the ludicrous, he is generally a copyist, and sometimes follows his original so closely, that he forgets the changes of manners, which give an appearance of extravagance to what was once correct ridicule.[5]

While the earlier passage represents an incisive insight into Sterne's use of his comic materials, the later one does not rise above the clichés which dated from Sterne's own time but were still common in Ferriar's day. The same idea is expressed in a brief prefatory poem for the 1798 volume, which speaks of "borrow'd mirth" but asserts that *"Le Fevre's* woes, / Maria's wand'rings, and the *Pris'ner's* throes" fix Sterne "conspicuous on the shrine of glory." [6] Although Ferriar had treated Sterne mainly as a humorist and a satirist in "Comments," his discussion in *Illustrations* served to reinforce the picture which had been built up in the public mind of Sterne as a master of the pathetic whose humorous side was not to be so highly valued.

Finally, in *Illustrations* he does not scruple to speak of the borrowings as "plagiarisms," [7] and his previous statement that Sterne is entitled to "every praise but that of curious erudition" is greatly modified. If the reader's "opinion of Sterne's learning and originality be lessened," he says, "he must, at least, admire the dexterity and the good taste with

---

as a peg on which to hang the accumulations of his reading and research in topics which may have been suggested originally by his study of Sterne but are not germane to the main issue.

3. *Illustrations of Sterne: with Other Essays and Verses* (London: printed in Manchester, 1798), p. 178.

4. See ibid., pp. 51, 55, 91, 112, 181, and passim.

5. Ibid., pp. 6-7. Cf. above, p. 82.

6. Ibid., p. 2.

7. See ibid., pp. 68, 90.

which he has incorporated in his work so many passages, written with very different views by their respective authors. It was evidently Sterne's purpose to make a pleasant, saleable book, *coute que coute*; and after taking his general plan from some of the older French writers, and from Burton, he made prize of all the good thoughts that came in his way." [8] Elsewhere in *Illustrations* he refers to *Tristram Shandy* as "a desultory book, apparently written with great rapidity," [9] a judgment which contrasts sharply with his statement in "Comments" that Sterne had "directed and expanded with care" the materials which he had taken from Rabelais.[1]

It is difficult to explain the change in Ferriar's attitude, since the mere accumulation of a greater number of parallel passages does not seem a sufficient reason for so great a shift in his position. It also seems unlikely that before writing *Illustrations* he became newly acquainted with some of the similar clichés about Sterne as a master of the pathetic rather than the humorous, since these were certainly as widespread in 1791 as in 1798. Perhaps the best explanation lies in the fact that "Comments" was originally prepared as a paper to be read within a small group, while *Illustrations* was designed for the public at large. In the five years between the publication of the two, some reviewers and correspondents had intimated that Ferriar had been too lenient on Sterne; and hence he may have felt obliged to yield to what he thought the generally accepted attitude of the day.

The main body of the evidence was now assembled, although from time to time during the next few years other borrowings were pointed out in the magazines. Ferriar also further expanded his *Illustrations* in the second edition of 1812, adding two chapters. In one of these he attempts to suggest real-life prototypes for the characters of *Tristram Shandy*, at the same time lamenting the "waste of talents . . . occasioned by temporary satire," since we "know hardly any thing of Sterne's objects" and his "resentment against blockheads" was not worthy of recording.[2] In general, his conclusions remain unchanged from those given in the edition of 1798.[3]

Critics differed in their reactions to Ferriar's expanded discussion

8. Ibid., pp. 181–2. Cf. above, pp. 82–3.

9. Ibid., p. 43.

1. See above, p. 82. In a review for the *Monthly* two years later, Ferriar refers to Fielding, Sterne, and Goldsmith as writers whose style is adequate, though not "of first rate reputation." *Monthly Review,* 2d Ser. *32* (June 1800), 145.

2. *Illustrations of Sterne: with Other Essays and Verses* (2d ed. 2 vols. London: printed in Warrington, 1812), *1,* 144.

3. Apparently Ferriar did not revise the material of the 1798 edition very carefully, but merely fitted in the two extra chapters and a few other passages in 1812. In 1798 he had thought that Sterne had "conceived the first precise idea of his Tristram" from Bouchet's *Evenings;* and he allowed this passage to stand in the edition of 1812, although in one of the added chapters he states that he "cannot perceive that [Sterne] has made much use" of Bouchet. See *Illustrations* (1812 ed.), *1,* 60, 76,

of Sterne's borrowings. None of the reviewers appears to have noted the change of attitude between "Comments" and *Illustrations*.[4] The *Monthly* dismissed *Illustrations* with the brief remark that it was "a piece of much entertaining research," and later said that Ferriar had "certainly made out his point, whatever be the consequences in regard to the merit of the lively and pleasing writer whose works are the subject of it." [5] The *Critical* was more markedly sympathetic, asserting that the authors from whom Sterne had "fertilised his fancy" had not "suffered" from his "disingenuity." "If he had referred to them," the reviewer says, "there would have been little inducement to turn to the passage quoted; but the book from which Yorick pilfered becomes an object of research and value." A few years later the *Critical* again commented that Ferriar's had been "an ungracious task." [6]

Other critics were more violent in their views both pro and con. John Corry, a miscellaneous writer who was evidently an enthusiastic reader of Sterne, accused Ferriar of being a "forager on other's wisdom" and stated sarcastically that he might "claim the merit of having discovered a new method of embalming, for, by interspersing some of the fragrant spices of Sterne's wit with his own ideas, he has preserved the inert mass." [7] Correspondents of the *Gentleman's Magazine,* on the other hand, wrote in from time to time to disclose additional borrowings and disparage Sterne's character at the same time. In 1798 one of these, signing himself "R.F.," quoted parallel passages to "pluck another quill from Sterne's wing" and prove that he "was in the habit of making free with the apophthegms of other men, which, when varnished and disfigured with the dramatic style, he put into the mouths of his own heroes." Sterne "has been stript of many of his borrowed plumes," he concludes, and "the sorry reputation of a servile imitator is almost all that remains." [8] "M.N." wrote to the same periodical a few weeks later, agreeing that Ferriar had proved Sterne "a literary pilferer," but attempting a somewhat half-hearted defense against the strictures of "R.F." Sterne has displayed "ingenuity in so nicely blending the sentiments of other writers," he says, and even in the places where he "has most servilely copied" he has introduced "some slight, but characteristic, touches." [9] A different sort of apology was made by a large group of slightly more sympathetic critics who took their cue from

4. This is all the more remarkable since a reprint of the "Comments" in its entirety was published in 1798 in the *Annual Register* for 1793.
5. John Aikin, *Monthly Review,* 2d Ser. *28* (Feb. 1799), 131. William Tooke, ibid., 2d Ser. *39* (Oct. 1802), 220.
6. *Critical Review,* 2d Ser. *26* (June 1799), 153; 3d Ser. *6* (Oct. 1805), 163.
7. *The Detector of Quackery, or, Analyser of Medical, Philosophical, Political, Dramatic, and Literary Imposture* (2d ed. London, 1802), p. 162. There is a copy of this book in the University of Chicago Library.
8. *Gentleman's Magazine, 68,* Pt. I (June 1798), 471.
9. Ibid., *68,* Pt. II (Aug. 1798), 673–5.

Ferriar's conclusion in *Illustrations* that Sterne's originality lay in his "pathetic" side, although most of his humor had been copied.[1] These critics were relatively unaffected in their judgments by the intimation that Sterne's humorous side was not original, since they did not regard that portion of his work very highly in any case.

Although for different reasons, many of the critics who were equipped to take a broader view of Sterne's work also felt that Ferriar's disclosures made little difference. Andrew Becket, whose *Lucianus Redivivus* was published in 1811, took the same tone that Ferriar had originally taken in "Comments" and suggested that Sterne should "be rather styled an *imitator* than a *plagiary*," since the borrowed passages are "improvements" rather than "thefts."[2] Mrs. Barbauld likewise felt that though Sterne "exhibits a good deal of reading in [Burton] and many other books out of the common way . . . the wit is in the application, and that is his own."[3] T. J. Mathias, author of the extremely popular *Pursuits of Literature,* commented in much the same vein that Ferriar's disclosures have not detracted "from the absolute *originality*" of Sterne's genius, since "his *manner* and his wit are still . . . exclusively his own."[4] The more discerning critics agreed that Sterne had transformed whatever he had touched.

In the light of Ferriar's careful documentation, no future critic could afford to ignore the fact of Sterne's borrowings; but, once the initial furor had died down, the effect of the disclosures upon his standing was not as great as might have been expected. Even the moralists, who thought that the discovery of Sterne's indebtedness would eventually reduce his literary reputation to the level on which they believed his indecency ought to place him, found that their predictions were unfulfilled. Among the last of these was "J.N.," who may be tentatively identified as John Nichols, author of the *Literary Anecdotes.*[5] Writing in the *European Magazine* in 1816, he is forced to admit that Sterne has "long amused the public" and "will continue to do so in spite of every discovery of the critics," although his sole merit is that of "a very skilful compiler, and an ingenious alterer of language."[6]

At the same time that the moralists tried to capitalize on the evidences

1. See, e.g., Nathan Drake, *Literary Hours* (3d ed. 3 vols. London, 1804), *3,* 16. See also below, p. 94.

2. *Lucianus Redivivus* (London, 1811), dialogue 16, p. 141. There is a copy of this book in the University of Michigan Library.

3. "The Origin and Progress of Novel-Writing," *British Novelists* (50 vols. London, 1810), *1,* 41–2. See below, pp. 108–9.

4. *Pursuits of Literature* (12th ed. London, 1803), p. 57. Although the first part of the poem had been published anonymously in 1794, the comments quoted were added in a note in 1800.

5. The communication is dated from Islington, where Nichols lived.

6. *European Magazine, 69* (April 1816), 320.

of borrowing to lower Sterne's literary reputation, the widespread circulation of several anecdotes to his serious discredit furnished them with even better ammunition for the disparagement of his character. During the period in question, Sterne's personal reputation fared worse than at any time since his death, as gossip and doubtful tradition became accepted in the place of more solid biographical research. At best Yorick was shown to be a frivolous, imprudent, and unrespected individual; while at worst he was stigmatized as a callous scoundrel. Ferriar had alluded to Sterne's friendless deathbed,[7] and authors like William Cook, the biographer of Samuel Foote, retailed stories about Sterne's debts.[8] An anecdote was widely circulated concerning Sterne's ludicrous mistake during his Continental visit when he had given an insulting description of a fellow guest to his face without realizing his identity.[9] Henry Brougham, later Lord Brougham, seized upon this incident as "one among many proofs of that sentimental person's contemptible character." [1] When John Almon edited the correspondence of Wilkes in 1805, he repeated the story that Sterne's wife had been forced "to retire to France . . . under the daily provocations of an unkind husband," since Sterne was not a desirable companion "for a lady of delicacy." [2]

The most damaging story, however, was the untrue one connected with Sterne's alleged neglect of his mother. This calumny had been circulated as early as 1770 by Philip Thicknesse,[3] but it remained for the epigrammatic wit of a later version to fix it in the public mind, after remarks attributed to Horace Walpole were printed in *Walpoliana* in 1799: "What is called sentimental writing, though it be understood

7. "Comments," p. 80; *Illustrations* (1798 ed.), pp. 174–6.
8. See *Memoirs of Samuel Foote* (2 vols. New York, 1806), *2, 56.*
9. The incident is recounted by Louis Dutens in his *Memoirs of a Traveller* (5 vols. London, 1806), *2,* 5–8: "We were very jovial during dinner; and drank, in the English manner, the toasts of the day. . . . Mr. Sterne, addressing himself to me, asked me if I knew Mr. D***, meaning me. I replied, 'Yes, very intimately.' The whole company began to laugh; and Sterne, who did not suppose me so near him, imagined that this Mr. D*** must be a very singular character, since the mention of his name alone excited merriment. 'Is not he rather a strange fellow?' added he, immediately. 'Yes,' replied I, 'an original.'—'I thought so,' continued he; 'I have heard him spoken of:' and then began to draw a picture of me, the truth of which I pretended to acknowledge; while Sterne, seeing that the subject amused the company, invented from his fertile imagination many stories, which he related in his way, to the great diversion of us all." Sterne came to apologize the next day, but Dutens assured him that he had been "as much amused at his mistake as any of the party," and the two parted friends. I have quoted this account of the incident because several later critics, including Thackeray, used it in making unfair attacks on Sterne's character.
1. *Edinburgh Review,* 5th ed. 7 (July 1806), 351. The attribution to Brougham is based on Walter A. Copinger, *On the Authorship of the First Hundred Numbers of the "Edinburgh Review,"* Manchester, Priory Press, 1895, privately printed.
2. *Correspondence of the Late John Wilkes* (5 vols. London, 1805), *5,* 20. For the source of these remarks see above, pp. 53–4.
3. See above, p. 54.

to appeal solely to the heart, may be the product of a bad one. One would imagine that Sterne had been a man of a very tender heart—yet I know, from indubitable authority, that his mother, who kept a school, having run in debt, on account of an extravagant daughter, would have rotted in jail, if the parents of her scholars had not raised a subscription for her. Her son had too much sentiment to have any feeling. A dead ass was more important to him than a living mother." [4] The authority of Walpole's name seemed to stamp the story as authentic, and the clever turn of expression rendered it memorable. More than a decade later Byron wrote in his *Journal,* chiding himself for not doing his duty in Parliament: "Ah, I am as bad as that dog Sterne, who preferred whining over 'a dead ass to relieving a living mother'—villain— hypocrite—slave—sycophant! but *I* am no better." [5]

The authority of anecdotes of this sort was reinforced by the generalizations about Sterne in supposedly more trustworthy works of reference. In 1797 the *Encyclopaedia Britannica* said that although Sterne wrote in praise of benevolence, "we have heard anecdotes of him extremely well authenticated, which proved that it was easier for him to praise this virtue than to practise it." [6] Even John Aikin, who had given a fairly sympathetic account of Sterne's work in his *General Biography,* another standard reference work, concluded the article by observing that it was "unpleasant" to have to admit that "Sterne's private and domestic character by no means corresponded with the effusions of tenderness and generosity so frequent in his works." [7] Most writers who treated Sterne's life and works at any great length felt called upon to make at least perfunctory references to the lapses which were pointed up by the various anecdotes.

This picture of Sterne's private life which was being built up in the public mind tended to color judgments of his work and especially of

4. "Walpoliana," *Monthly Magazine,* 7, Pt. 1 (May 1799), 300. This collection of Walpole's *bons mots,* compiled by John Pinkerton, was also printed in book form the same year.

5. *Works of Lord Byron: Prose,* ed. Rowland E. Prothero (6 vols. London and New York, J. Murray and Scribner's, 1898–1904), *2,* 359. Although the *Journals* were not published until 1830, the passage is significant in showing the wide currency of this anecdote at an earlier date. Cf. the account of the same story in *Monthly Repository, 3* (Jan. 1808), 9–13, wherein John T. Rutt quotes from correspondence during 1776 between the Rev. Daniel Watson and George Whatley. See also ibid., *3* (July 1808), 376–7, in which a correspondent adds insult to injury by relating a story accusing Sterne of neglecting his daughter as well. The censures of Sterne's relationship with Mrs. Draper had practically disappeared, although an occasional critic might repeat them (see *Critical Review,* 2d Ser. *33,* Dec. 1801, 461). The charges of Sterne's neglect of his family probably seemed to most critics to rest on firmer ground, however, since they would be supposed to be a matter of fact rather than of interpretation.

6. *Encyclopaedia Britannica* (Edinburgh, 1797), *17,* 795. Sterne had not been included in earlier editions of the *Britannica.* George Gleig was the editor of this volume of the *Britannica,* but the article on Sterne is not signed.

7. *General Biography* (London, 1814), *9,* 243.

the *Sermons*. As less and less respect was paid to his clerical character, the discourses, which had apparently been even more popular than *Tristram Shandy* in many quarters during his lifetime, declined continually in the public estimation.[8] Few critics make more than passing references to them, although Robert Alves, the minor Scotch poet, found them "good practical discourses, composed in an easy, simple style, which is better than . . . that affected, quaint, though sparkling wit, that seems to pervade all his other compositions." [9] George Ensor was more typical of the general attitude of the time, however, when he asserted that Sterne "wrote sermons as his son Tristram did biography," and called them "flippant and pompous." [1]

The *Sermons* are seldom even mentioned by the group of moral philosophers who discuss Sterne entirely from an ethical rather than a literary point of view. Robert Hall, the Baptist divine who was noted for his pulpit oratory, is typical of this group in repeating the two serious charges which critics of this sort had been making ever since Sterne's own day. The whole tendency of Sterne's work, he believes, "is to degrade human nature, by resolving all our passions into a mere animal instinct . . . of the grossest sort. It was perfectly natural for such a writer to employ his powers in panegyrising an ass." To this charge of promoting licentiousness he adds the further one that by diverting the mind "from scenes of real to those of imaginary distress" Sterne weakens the character, since "those feelings which were designed to stimulate to active benevolence are employed in nourishing a sickly sensibility." [2] Other critics echoed these clichés that Sterne's writing was "a channel of licentiousness" and had done infinite "mischief to the world" by setting up "casual benevolence as an excuse for the neglect or the breach of positive duty" and "confounding the limits of right and wrong." [3] A certain D. Whyte, former surgeon to English prisoners in France, was even more virulent, combining his attack on Sterne with strictures on the French Revolution. Like Rabelais, Vol-

---

8. Though usually included in collected editions of Sterne, the *Sermons* appear to have been issued separately only three times during the period: at London in 1794 [Boston] and 1796 [Yale], and at Edinburgh in 1796.

9. *Sketches of a History of Literature* (Edinburgh, 1794), p. 236.

1. *The Independent Man* (2 vols. London, 1806), *1*, 333, 517. There is a copy of this book in the Harvard University Library. Ensor was an Irish political writer.

2. *Reflections on War* (2d ed. London, 1804), p. 56 and n. This sermon was preached in 1802.

3. For remarks of this kind see *Christian Observer, 4* (Sept. 1805), 548. William Wilberforce had been instrumental in founding this periodical, which was "Conducted by Members of the Established Church." See also the remarks of the Rev. Montagu Pennington in his edition of *Letters between Mrs. Carter and Miss Talbot, 3,* 335. Cf. the remarks of the Rev. Archibald Arthur, professor of moral philosophy at the University of Glasgow, in his *Discourses on Theological & Literary Subjects* (Glasgow, 1803), pp. 451–2, 455. There is a copy of the latter book in the Harvard University Library.

taire, Bolingbroke, and Hume, Sterne has advocated a "system of impiety and corruption of manners," he says, thus weakening the "bonds of religion and government." Sterne is even more dangerous than these other writers because he "concealed his cloven foot under a flowing tunic, and endeavoured to allure by the gaudy gilding of his nauseous pill." Whyte also repeats the old charge that Sterne arouses the passions, asserting that the immorality of his work shows a very cold-blooded plan to corrupt his readers, for he is not "a man of real gallantry, a Rochester," but rather "an apathist," [4] a "second Satan." Whyte concludes his diatribe with the warning that writers like Sterne may bring to England the depravity of the French and consequences similar to those of the French Revolution.[5]

The obvious fanaticism and illogic of a writer like Whyte must have precluded his denunciation from having much weight,[6] but more impartial and better-known writers also saw vicious implications in Sterne's sentimental philosophy. The *Annual Register* for 1800 pointed out that, starting with Shaftesbury, a school "which founded morality in some principle analogous to sensation or sense" rather than in justice and duty had grown up, culminating in "such lax moralists as Sterne, and the myriads who condescend to imitate that unprincipled though humorous buffoon." [7] Remarks of this same kind were also made by two much more famous writers in evangelical works which achieved tremendous popularity. In his *Practical View* of Christianity, first published in 1797, William Wilberforce asserted the superiority of "practical benevolence" over "delicate sensibility." Sterne, he says, has employed his talents "to the pernicious purposes of corrupting the national taste, and of lowering the standard of manners and morals," for the whole tendency of his writings is to produce "a morbid sensibility in the perception of indecency." [8] A few years later Hannah More also condemned the sentimental side of Sterne's work, basing her

4. It is interesting to note that, however unperceptive his overall evaluation of Sterne may be, Whyte has anticipated some of Sterne's modern critics in the psychological interpretation implied in this term. Cf. Work's statement, p. lx: "And with a curiously perverse and possibly self-revelatory sense of the incongruous [Sterne] grins again and again over sexual impotence, the suspicion of which hovers like a dubious halo over the head of every Shandy male, including the bull." See also Arie de Froe, *Laurence Sterne and His Novels Studied in the Light of Modern Psychology* (Groningen, P. Noordhoff, 1925), pp. 172, 190, and passim.
5. *The Fallacy of French Freedom, and Dangerous Tendency of Sterne's Writings* (London, 1799), pp. 2–10, and passim. There is a copy of this book in the New York Public Library.
6. See *Monthly Review*, 2d Ser. 29 (May 1799), 115; *Critical Review*, 2d Ser. 26 (Aug. 1799), 479.
7. *Annual Register*, 1800 (London, 1801), p. [233.
8. *A Practical View of the Prevailing Religious System of Professed Christians* (1st Amer. ed. Philadelphia, 1798), pp. 202–3. The quotation appears in a note to a lengthy section (pp. 177–202) discussing "the generally prevailing error, of substituting amiable tempers and useful lives in the place of religion."

strictures on moral as well as aesthetic grounds. In *Coelebs in Search of a Wife,* her evangelical novel which was first published in 1808, she refers to Sterne's "corrupt, but too popular lesser work" which made him "the mischievous founder of the school of sentiment. A hundred writers communicated, a hundred thousand readers caught the infection," she continues. "Sentimentality was the disease which then required to be expelled." Now, however, "the reign of Sterne is past" and the "vapid puling of the sentimental school" has been discarded.[9] The influence that these two works must have had may be judged from the fact that the *Practical View,* which has been called the "manifesto of the evangelical party of the time," sold 7,500 copies in six months and had reached a fifteenth edition by 1824; while *Coelebs,* its counterpart in fiction, went through eleven editions within a short time after its publication and had a sixteenth edition in 1826.

Sterne was not without his champions, though many of their tributes to his works and character seem hopelessly ephemeral when placed side by side with such solidly popular works as those of Wilberforce and Hannah More. Among these defenders was the Honorable Mrs. M. A. Cavendish-Bradshaw, who had read *Coelebs* with disgust and was particularly incensed at the strictures on her "favourite Sterne." Attacking *Coelebs* at length in the preface to one of her own novels published in 1810, she deplores the "mistaken zeal" of "bigotted disciplinarians." She concludes, moreover, that an acquaintance with "the methodistical proser, Mr. Coelebs," is fully as apt to lead to moral "contamination" as is an acquaintance with Sterne's "Sentimental Traveller," since *Coelebs* presents a distorted picture of society and of human nature. An apostrophe to Sterne follows, concluding with the statement that sensibility is the only defense against "the insidious poison of bigotted and metaphysical barbarism, whose baleful introduction must extinguish every sentiment of liberality and refinement, levelling in its progress the proud distinctions of intellect and education." [1] Mrs. Bradshaw was well aware that she moved in quite different circles from those of the author of *Coelebs*; and though the enthusiasts of methodism and the stricter moralists might find Sterne abhorrent, the members of

---

9. *Coelebs in Search of a Wife* (1st ed. 2 vols. London, 1808), *2,* 83–4. Although published anonymously, *Coelebs* was almost immediately attributed to Hannah More. She praises Richardson for the morality of his work (*2,* 210–11), and in the second edition (2 vols. London, 1809) adds a passage condemning the heroes of Fielding and Smollett as "worthless fellows" (*2,* 5) and another censuring Sterne's personal character (*2,* 12–13).

1. *Ferdinand and Ordella* (2 vols. London, 1810), *1,* xi, xiii, xxv–xxvii, xxxi–xxxii. Though Miss More's authorship of *Coelebs* was common knowledge by this time, Mrs. Bradshaw, who published under the pseudonym of Priscilla Parlante, takes no cognizance of the fact. There is a copy of *Ferdinand and Ordella* in the University of Minnesota Library. Mrs. Barbauld expressed surprise at some of Mrs. Bradshaw's remarks when she reviewed the book for the *Monthly,* 2d Ser. *63* (Oct. 1810), 217.

Mrs. Bradshaw's social circle still praised the "liberality and refinement" of his sensibility.

There were other tributes of this sort, both in prose and poetry, as literary pilgrims recorded visits to Sterne's grave and that of his Eliza,[2] or imagined the resting place of Yorick's shade. George M. Woodward, the caricaturist, imagined a scene with Uncle Toby, Trim, the Monk, Maria, Eliza, Le Fever, and the Recording Angel clustered around Sterne's resting place;[3] while Alexander Thomson, the minor Scotch poet, gave Yorick a slightly less crowded niche in the Elysian "Vale of Pity." [4] In his "Ode to Pity" Nathan Drake also sought the shade of Sterne in Elysium and pictured him surrounded by various other literary great who might be expected to appreciate his talents, including Petrarch, Rousseau, Otway, Collins, and Shakespeare. In his introduction to the poem, however, Drake feels obliged to make it clear that he is appealing "not to the life, but to the *pathetic* writings" of Sterne, since he believes his personal conduct to have had "a levity, very inconsistent with the profession he had chosen to exercise." [5]

In general, the authors of the encomiums referred to above eulogized the sentimental side of Sterne, either overlooking or deprecating any irregularities in his personal life and ignoring the other aspects of his work. One or two writers, however, paid tribute to Sterne in better-balanced eulogies. In his *Hobby Horses,* published in 1797, Jenkin Jones asserts that criticism of Sterne has been too harsh and unsympathetic and even suggests that he may be read by girls in their teens. At fifteen, he says, the "lively Romp" begins a course of reading which takes her through the *Arabian Nights, Gil Blas,* Richardson, and Fielding, until she comes to the *Sentimental Journey* and finally to "Shandy's bolder height." Sterne's work is characterized as follows:

> Too little understood! too seldom read!
> Where is the gen'rous taste of letters fled?
> Shall some light faults, ye captious critics say,
> A mighty load of massy worth outweigh?
> Is there no medium in the candid mind,
> Can moderation no fair balance find?
> When ye the merits of a work would learn,
> Why do ye thus all rules of justice spurn?
> Indeed ye fall on very honest means,
> To try *one heart*—a jury of *twelve spleens.*

2. See Anne Grant, *Letters from the Mountains* (2d ed. 3 vols. London, 1807), *3,* 173–4.

3. *Eccentric Excursions* (London, 1796), pp. 17–18.

4. "The Vale of Pity," Canto iv, *Paradise of Taste* (London, 1796), p. 64. There is a copy of this book in the Harvard University Library. Thomson was the friend of Robert Anderson the publisher.

5. *Literary Hours, 3,* 16–20. The "Ode to Pity" appears for the first time in the third edition.

Praise of Sterne's benevolence follows; and although Jones gives first place to "the softest beams of feeling," he is also aware of the excellence of Yorick's satire and wit.[6]

A still more judicious panegyric of Sterne was included in the poem which Sir Martin Archer Shee wrote in 1814 at the time of a celebration paying tribute to the memory of Sir Joshua Reynolds. Sterne, who is mentioned along with other famous men whose portraits had been painted by Sir Joshua, is described as

> The soul alike of sympathy and whim,
> Who struck the heart's full chord with skilful hand,
> And smiles and tears held equal at command.

Though it contains nothing strikingly original, Shee's graceful tribute reminds Sterne enthusiasts that "the fires of Wit and Humour" are as much a part of his work as the "tenderest touches" of his sentimental side.[7]

Tributes of the sort quoted above would prove little more than that there was still a Sterne cult during the period in question,[8] but more substantial evidence for his popularity is to be found in the continuing demand for his work across the counters of the booksellers. Scarcely a year went by without a reprint of some of Sterne's work, and between 1793 and 1810 more than fifteen collected editions were published.[9] The thirteenth edition of *Beauties of Sterne* appeared in 1799, and a new edition of this anthology was published in 1810. The previous year another somewhat abridged edition of *Beauties* had appeared, illustrated with two caricatures by Thomas Rowlandson.[1] Other anthologies also included the work of Sterne.

6. *Hobby Horses* (London, [1797]), pp. 15–17. There is a copy of this book in the New York Public Library.

7. *Commemoration of Reynolds* (London, 1814), pp. 38–9. Shee was president of the Royal Academy.

8. Sterne enthusiasts still sent in occasional contributions to the magazines. As late as 1814 a correspondent spoke for "Irish Shandeans" in claiming the "immortal author of Tristram" for Ireland and stating that Tristram himself was really "an O'Shandy, of the county of Tipperary." *Monthly Museum; or, Dublin Literary Repertory*, 1 (Jan. 1814), 233.

9. Sterne's *Works* were issued as follows: 5 vols. 1793; 10 vols. 1793; 7 vols. 1794 [New York]; 8 vols. 1794; 8 vols. 1795; 10 vols. 1798; 8 vols. 1799; 8 vols. Edinburgh, 1799 [Yale]; 8 vols. Berwick, 1800; 7 vols. 1802; 4 vols. 1803; 8 vols. 1803; 8 vols. Edinburgh, 1803; 4 vols. 1808; 3 vols. 1808 [New York]; 7 vols. 1810 [Yale]. Editions of *Tristram Shandy* appeared in six and three volumes in 1793 and 1794, respectively. The *Sentimental Journey* was reprinted separately in 1794, 1800 (Liverpool, in *Mirror of Amusement*), 1801, 1803, 1803 (Glasgow), 1807, 1809, 1810 (in Mudford's *British Novelists* together with *Tristram Shandy*), and 1814 (Dublin). All of these editions of the *Sentimental Journey* may be found in the New York Public Library. There was also an edition of Sterne's travels in 1804 [Yale]. Mrs. Medalle's edition of the letters was reprinted in 1794.

1. This edition omitted all but two of the selections from the *Sermons,* but retained most of the other material of the earlier editions. Other books of selections from Sterne included *Gleanings from the Works of Laurence Sterne* (London, 1798) and another

Further evidence of the fact that Sterne was widely read during this period is to be found in the numerous references to him among the younger generation of literary great. In 1796 Dorothy Wordsworth mentions in a letter that she has read *Tristram Shandy,* though she gives no comment on it.[2] It must also have been during the nineties that Jane Austen first read Sterne, and in the early *Love and Freindship* a passage has been pointed out which appears to be a parody of similar scenes in *Tristram Shandy.*[3] A few years later she refers to Uncle Toby in a letter to her sister;[4] and in *Mansfield Park,* written toward the close of her life, she has Maria Bertram think of Sterne's starling as she faces the iron gate at Sotherton and waits for Mr. Rushworth to get the key.[5]

Both Byron and Lamb refer to Sterne's foolish fat scullion: the former in a note in Canto ii of *Childe Harold's Pilgrimage,* published in 1812;[6] the latter in a letter to John Rickman written in 1801.[7] Other allusions to Sterne are to be found elsewhere in Lamb's letters, one parodying Sterne's famous proverb in a comment on one of Lamb's friends who has suffered financial reverses. Adverting to the fact that his friend may be forced to sell some of his art treasures, he exclaims, "God should temper the wind to the shorn connoisseur."[8]

The early letters of Southey contain affectionate references to Sterne. A letter in doggerel verse to Thomas Lamb, written in 1792 when Southey was nineteen, mentions various of the characters in *Tristram Shandy.*[9] The letters to Grosvenor Bedford, his friend from his school days at Westminster, also contain allusions to Sterne. Writing to Bedford in 1796 he says that he does not know "anything more delightful" than "to Shandeize," and alludes to their future reunion with the words, "Grosvenor, when we sit down in Shandy Hall, what pretty speculations shall we make! You shall be Toby, and amuse yourself by marching to Paris, I will make systems, and Horace shall be Doctor Slop."[1]

book of selections, *Extracts from Laurence Sterne,* Poughnill, George Nicholson, n.d. (the outer cover reads: *"Selections from Sterne,* Stourport, 1813").

2. *Early Letters of William and Dorothy Wordsworth,* ed. Ernest de Selincourt (Oxford, Clarendon Press, 1935), p. 152. Dorothy's more famous brother does not seem to have recorded any comments on Sterne. See below, p. 128.

3. See Archibald B. Shepperson, *The Novel in Motley* (Cambridge, Harvard Univ. Press, 1936), pp. 138-9.

4. *Jane Austen's Letters to Her Sister Cassandra and Others,* ed. R. W. Chapman (2 vols. Oxford, Clarendon Press, 1932), *1,* 140. Chapman assigns the letter to 1804.

5. Ch. 10, *Mansfield Park.*

6. *Works of Lord Byron: Poetry,* ed. Ernest H. Coleridge (7 vols. London and New York, J. Murray and Scribner's, 1898-1904), *2,* 176.

7. *Letters of Charles Lamb,* ed. E. V. Lucas (3 vols. New Haven, Yale Univ. Press, 1935), *1,* 289. For another early comment by Lamb see below, p. 102.

8. Ibid., *2,* 27. See also *1,* 200, 307.

9. *Selections from the Letters of Robert Southey,* ed. John Wood Warter (4 vols. London, 1856), *1,* 9-10.

1. *Life and Correspondence of Robert Southey,* ed. Rev. Charles Cuthbert Southey

A few years later, when *Madoc* was being published, he again referred to Dr. Slop in a letter to Coleridge: "I look on Madoc with hopeful displeasure . . . this coming into the world at seven months is a bad way; with a Doctor Slop of a printer's devil standing ready for the forced birth, and frightening one into an abortion." [2] A letter in 1799 had referred to Sterne's "quick strokes of feeling that . . . surprise you into a tear before you have finished a smile." [3]

Finally, Coleridge, Hazlitt, and Scott, the three men who were later to make the most significant contributions to the criticism of Sterne during the Romantic Period, all date their familiarity with him from this time. As early as 1803, Coleridge wrote to Southey, suggesting that the latter undertake a history of English literature and mentioning Sterne among the "great names" who have either "formed epochs in our taste" or at least are "representative." [4] Hazlitt showed a similar admiration for Sterne in a letter written to the *Morning Chronicle* in 1813. In opposing the notion that the Restoration and the eighteenth century lacked "refinement," Hazlitt includes Sterne among the writers whose chief excellence was that "they have every kind and gradation of character" because their portraits were taken from life. "They were true to nature, full of meaning, perfectly understood and executed in every part. Their coarseness was not mere vulgarity," he continues, "their refinement was not a mere negation of precision. They refined *upon* characters, instead of refining them away." Strength and refinement, he concludes, are "far from being incompatible," but rather "assist each other, as the hardest bodies admit of the finest touches and the brightest polish." [5] Hazlitt's early essays likewise contain numerous passages which attest his complete familiarity with the works of Sterne, and Sterne's characters have become so much a part of Hazlitt's background that he often thinks of them in nonliterary contexts. [6]

Allusions of the same kind are frequent in Scott. As early as 1796 he mentions Corporal Trim in a letter to Alexander Boswell, and in other letters discussing his military interests he thinks of Uncle Toby. [7] A letter written in 1811 gives an amusing account of the circumstances

---

(6 vols. London, 1849–50), *1*, 291–2. "Horace" is presumably Grosvenor's brother, Horace Walpole Bedford.

2. Ibid., *2*, 154.

3. *Letters of Southey, 1*, 68.

4. *Letters of Samuel Taylor Coleridge,* ed. Ernest Hartley Coleridge (2 vols. Boston and New York, 1895), *1*, 425.

5. *Complete Works of William Hazlitt,* ed. P. P. Howe (21 vols. London and Toronto, J. M. Dent, 1930–34), *20*, 8.

6. For references to Sterne in Hazlitt's early essays, see the exhaustive index of Howe's edition. Hazlitt also mentions reading Sterne during his youth; ibid., *12*, 223.

7. *Letters of Sir Walter Scott,* ed. H. J. C. Grierson (12 vols. London, Constable, 1932–37), *2*, 159, 264; *12*, 375.

surrounding the birth of one of his children. His wife, he explains, once nearly made a "blunder in very awkward circumstances. We were invited to dine at Mellville Castle," he continues,

> with the Chief Baron and his Lady, then its temporary inhabitants, when behold, the Obadiah whom I despatchd two hours before dinner from our cottage to summon the Dr. Slop of Edinburgh, halting at Mellville Lodge to rest his wearied horse, make apologies, and so forth, encountered the Mellville Castle Obadiah sallying on the identical errand for the identical man of skill, who like an active Knight Errant relieved the two distressd dames within three hours of each other. A blessed duet they would have made if they had put off their crying out, as it is calld, till they could do it in concert.[8]

Both Hazlitt and Scott were so steeped in the works of Sterne that allusions of many different kinds came naturally to their pens.

Sterne was often in the minds of less well-known figures of the period. An incident during his travels in Germany in 1800 recalled a passage in *Tristram Shandy* to Henry Crabb Robinson.[9] William Hutton, who has been called "the English Franklin," quoted Sterne in his autobiography and thought of "the jocund Yorick" when he visited Skelton Castle and remembered that Sterne had been Hall-Stevenson's frequent guest.[1] Mary Wollstonecraft Godwin quoted Sterne twice in her posthumously published letters to Imlay.[2] During a Parliamentary debate, William Windham mentioned Sterne's happy description of "the amusements of the lower orders of society."[3] In 1803 Anne Grant was reminded of Smelfungus by a fellow traveler in a stagecoach, just as some thirty years earlier another chance acquaintance had made her believe that she was "certainly haunted by the ghost of Smelfungus, of whom Sterne gives such an amusing account."[4] Another ghost, one "of taste and discernment," was said at one time to inhabit the rooms in York where Sterne had supposedly written part of *Tristram Shandy,* although this ghost, far from proving to be that of Yorick, was later explained by natural causes. Charles Mathews, the famous comedian, was persuaded by his wife to take these rooms, however, since she was entranced by

8. Ibid., *3,* 39–40. I have amended the punctuation. The "Chief Baron" was Robert Dundas of Arniston, Chief Baron of the Exchequer in Scotland. For other early letters of Scott with references to Sterne, see *1,* 170; *12,* 192. Also, in a letter of 1813, Scott found "some touches" in Washington Irving which reminded him of Sterne; *3,* 250.

9. See *Diary, Reminiscences, and Correspondence of Henry Crabb Robinson,* ed. Thomas Sadler (3 vols. London, 1869), *1,* 73.

1. See *Life of William Hutton Written by Himself* (London, 1816), p. 131 and *A Trip to Coatham* (London, 1810), pp. 151–2.

2. *Posthumous Works,* ed. William Godwin (4 vols. London, 1798), *3,* 3, 169.

3. *Annual Register,* 1802 (London, 1803), p. 169.

4. *Letters from the Mountains,* *1,* 16; *3,* 155. Mrs. Grant was the friend of Scott.

"the very idea of sitting where Sterne sat, of writing where he wrote." [5]

The frequent references to Sterne by the reviewers in the periodicals likewise show that they expected *Tristram Shandy* and the *Sentimental Journey* to be part of most people's reading backgrounds. The character of Smelfungus and Sterne's classification of travelers are often referred to; and allusions to many different parts of *Tristram Shandy* are even more frequent throughout the period. Scarcely a year went by without several references to Sterne in the pages of the *Critical,* and statements about Sterne or allusions to his work were made by about a third of the seventy-odd reviewers who were principal contributors to the second series of the *Monthly.* Yorick was indeed the "old friend" of the reviewers for this latter periodical, as William Enfield had called him in 1794.[6] References in the *Edinburgh* and the *Quarterly,* both founded during this period, are less frequent, but the early issues of the *Quarterly* contain several mentions of Sterne,[7] and Jeffrey comments on him, though unfavorably, in the *Edinburgh* in 1812.[8]

Reviewers were also quick to point out resemblances to Sterne in the flood of imitations by would-be Yoricks which continued, seemingly unchecked.[9] As late as 1814 the *Critical* could say: "The sentimental traveller wanders toward the fascinations of Italian scenery, and dreams, in vain, to feel and to describe like Sterne." [1] Very few of the imitators could approach the excellences of their master, however, and the re-

5. *Memoirs of Charles Mathews, Comedian, by Mrs. Mathews* (4 vols. London, 1838–9), *1,* 247–56.

6. *Monthly Review,* 2d Ser. *15* (Nov. 1794), 358. I have arbitrarily counted as principal contributors to the *Monthly* all reviewers who during the years 1790–1815 contributed more than ten main articles apiece. Christopher Moody, who wrote almost twice as many main articles as any other contributor, frequently mentions Sterne, and an inspection of both the *Monthly* and the *Critical* during these years shows numerous references to Sterne.

7. In addition to the reference below, p. 102, see the following, with reviewers as indicated: *Quarterly Review, 3* (May 1810), 456, probably Southey; *6* (Aug. 1811), 35, probably Macvey Napier, possibly William Rowe Lyall; *8* (Dec. 1812), 409, John Barrow, and 444, William Stewart Rose; *12* (Oct. 1814), 190, Southey. Attributions are based on Hill Shine and Helen Chadwick Shine, *The Quarterly Review under Gifford,* Chapel Hill, Univ. of North Carolina Press, 1949.

8. Jeffrey refers to the "paltry flippancy and disgusting affectation of Sterne," in dissenting from the high opinion of Yorick in a book by Madame de Staël (*Contributions to the Edinburgh Review by Francis Jeffrey,* 2d ed. 3 vols. London, 1846, *1,* 131). Madame de Staël had cited Sterne as the best example of the most original type of English humor (*De la Littérature considérée dans ses rapports avec les institutions sociales,* 2 vols. Paris and London, 1812, *1,* 299–300). In a letter written in 1792, however, Jeffrey had singled out Addison and Sterne as the only two writers since Shakespeare who had achieved "a charm in simplicity and naturality of expression" (Lord Cockburn, *Life of Lord Jeffrey,* 2 vols. Edinburgh, 1852, *2,* 9). For Jeffrey's later more favorable comment on Sterne see below, p. 131.

9. Translations and importations of the foreign imitators of Sterne vied with the domestic product, particularly through the works of August von Kotzebue and August Lafontaine.

1. *Critical Review,* 4th Ser. *6* (Aug. 1814), 124.

viewers were unanimously harsh in condemning most of these productions. The *Critical* even censured the imitations by the popular Samuel Jackson Pratt and Isaac D'Israeli, and felt that "no danger is to be dreaded from the imitations of Mr. Yorick, because on a comparison with their great prototype, they sink into insignificance, pitied and unread." [2]

Among the very few imitations to win any degree of critical acclaim was William Combe's *Fragments: In the Manner of Sterne,* first published in 1797.[3] After an appreciative "Address to the Shade of Yorick," Combe brings the characters at Shandy Hall to life again to discuss various topics of the day. Their speech rings fairly true as they condemn the British exploitation in India, castigate those who foment wars, deplore the social conditions of Great Britain, and enlarge upon the evils of slavery. It is interesting that Sterne's manner, as well as the popularity of his name, should be utilized in this plea for social justice.[4] The volume closes with the story of Anna, a tale which combines elements from the earlier stories of Le Fever and Maria. The *Critical* and the *Monthly* were in agreement that the work bore "as great a resemblance to the original as any that we have yet seen," [5] the latter praising especially the "benevolent sentimentality, the exquisite pathos, the happy abruptness of transition, and the peculiar felicity of expression, which gave to the *whimsical romances* of Sterne such a pleasing air of originality." [6]

The praise accorded to Combe's book was the exception rather than the rule for the imitations of Sterne; but although the critics had never been very enthusiastic about most of the writers of the sentimental school, some of the public obviously must have bought these productions, probably for the reason assigned by Dugald Stewart. The "peculiarities" of an author like Sterne, he says, "are consecrated by the connexion in which we see them, and even please to a certain degree, when detached from the excellencies of his composition, by recalling to us the agreeable impressions with which they have been formerly associated." Thus imitations of Sterne's defects "produce at first some effect on readers of sensibility, but of uncultivated taste, in consequence of the exquisite strokes of the pathetic, and the singular vein of humour with which they are united in the original." Stewart also concludes

2. See ibid., 3d Ser. *4* (Feb. 1805), 155; *5* (June 1805), 198; *7* (Jan. 1806), 22; *10* (March 1807), 250.

3. Curtis' evidence for Combe's authorship seems incontestable; see "Forged Letters of Laurence Sterne," pp. 1104–5. I have used the second edition (London, 1798) of *Fragments.*

4. Mrs. Barbauld also commended Sterne for awakening "the attention of his readers to the wrongs of the poor negroes." "Origin and Progress of Novel-Writing," p. 41.

5. *Critical Review,* 2d Ser. *23* (July 1798), 353.

6. Ralph Griffiths, *Monthly Review,* 2d Ser. *24* (Nov. 1797), 271.

that "great refinement of taste" automatically degenerates when authors "begin to gratify their love of variety, by adding superfluous circumstances to the finished models exhibited by their predecessors," just as the imitators of Sterne have done.[7]

The inept imitations of Sterne's sentimental side were becoming so hackneyed during this period that they were helping to call forth burlesques and parodies of the *Sentimental Journey* as well as of the "peculiarities" of *Tristram Shandy*. In a periodical which he edited a few years after publishing his *Fragments*, Combe himself inserted some "Rules for Tour Writing, in the true Modern Manner," ridiculing the vogue which had been initiated by the *Sentimental Journey*. "The tour-writer must have strong feelings," this essay says, but "it does not signify what they are employed upon—whether a dead jack-ass, a monk, a nun, a grey-bearded peasant, or a lame soldier . . . the more contemptible and unaffecting the subject is, the better." [8] In his *Modern Novel Writing,* published in 1796, William Beckford had likewise given a parody of the tale of Maria.[9]

Maria also figures in Eaton Stannard Barrett's *The Heroine,* first published in 1813. The heroine, Cherubina, who like Don Quixote has read so many novels that they have turned her head, tries to befriend a girl named Maria whom she meets on the street. From the girl's attitude of dejection, Cherubina thinks she will be "a congenial outcast" and therefore "should she but have a Madona face, and a name ending in a, we will live, we will die together," she says. When the "fair unfortunate" and "interesting unknown" proposes that they go to a gin shop to "moisten" their grief, however, Cherubina is shocked; and after her refusal, Maria tries unsuccessfully to steal her purse and runs away. Caught by a watchman, Maria attempts to turn the tables and maintains that the purse has been stolen from her by Cherubina. The pair are taken before a magistrate the next morning, when Maria again lies about the whole incident. Barrett describes her treachery in a parody of one of Sterne's most famous passages: "The accusing witness who insulted the magistrate's bench with the oath, leered as she gave it in; and the recording clerk, as he wrote it down, drew a line

7. *Elements of the Philosophy of the Human Mind,* in *Collected Works,* ed. Sir William Hamilton (11 vols. Edinburgh, 1854–55), *2,* 324–5. First published in 1792, this treatise had reached a fourth edition by 1811. Stewart, professor of moral philosophy at the University of Edinburgh, quoted Sterne favorably in lectures and essays, thus giving the sanction of a well-known moralist to his works. See ibid., *2,* 452–3; *4,* 198; *5,* 417; *7,* 222–3.

8. *Pic Nic* (2d ed. [i.e. 2d repr.], 2 vols. London, 1806), *2,* 132. The essay, which first appeared in 1803, is unsigned. Cf. *Christian Observer, 4* (Sept. 1805), 547, in which a correspondent gives a similar characterization of the "sentimental writer."

9. *Modern Novel Writing, or the Elegant Enthusiast* (2 vols. London, 1796), *1,* 219–22. This work was published under a pseudonym.

under the words, and pointed them out for ever." Finally Maria is caught in her own trickery and Cherubina is released, sadder, but unfortunately no wiser.[1]

Readers of an earlier day would not have been amused by Barrett's satire; but *The Heroine* went through three editions in as many years. The public was beginning to join the reviewers in tiring of the excesses of the sentimental school of writing and to take it less seriously. Francis Hodgson noted this change in public taste in a review for the *Monthly* in 1811. "Sensibility," he says, "falsely so called, has been laughed down from the parlour into the housekeeper's room," although it still lingers there, "shedding maudlin tears over the private bottle of that lady and the butler." It may still be found "in the back-parlours also of smaller grocers' shops," and among school boys and girls in country towns, while "indigenous waiters at hotels in watering-places, when the season is over, hire their two-penny-worth of sensibility from the circulating library." Hodgson went on to state that the subject of sensibility had been "too much hackneyed and too much degraded of late years" for the educated reader to avoid being prejudiced against it, and concluded that "good feelings suffer greatly by the hypocrisy which imitates them." [2]

Some critics were even beginning to tire of Sterne's own manner in the sentimental side of his works. In a letter to Wordsworth written in 1801, Charles Lamb criticized the former's "Cumberland Beggar" because "the instructions in it are too direct and like a lecture," and continued: "They don't slide into the mind of the reader, while he is imagining no such matter. An intelligent reader finds a sort of insult in being told, I will teach you how to think upon this subject. This fault, if I am right, is in a ten-thousandth worse degree to be found in Sterne and many many novelists & modern poets, who continually put a sign post up to shew where you are to feel." [3] Though Sterne's sensibility had often been criticized on moral grounds, and Dr. Johnson, to be sure, had found nothing pathetic in his work, Lamb is the forerunner of a general attitude among a large group of critics of the early nineteenth century who were to find the sentimental side of Sterne much less attractive on aesthetic grounds than most of their predecessors had.[4]

1. *The Heroine* (London, Oxford Univ. Press, 1927), pp. 57–65. The text of this edition is taken from the third edition of 1815, in which Barrett listed in his notes a total of seven passages from the *Sentimental Journey* and three from *Tristram Shandy* which he had echoed or parodied.

2. *Monthly Review*, 2d Ser. 64 (March 1811), 317. Cf. Reginald Heber's similar remarks in the *Quarterly Review* three years later, 10 (Jan. 1814), 389.

3. *Letters of Charles Lamb, 1*, 239. Lamb mentions *Robinson Crusoe, The Vicar of Wakefield,* and *Roderick Random* as examples of "beautiful bare narratives" which are free of this fault.

4. Although a reviewer in the *Westminster Magazine, 6* (March 1778), 158, had accused Sterne of "bad *Generalship*" in the *Sentimental Journey,* since he had too

The turn of the century and the years immediately following also saw a change in the moral standards which were demanded of contemporary writers, as the evangelical movement swept the country.[5] The results of this change in taste may be seen in the contemporary reception of Byron's *Don Juan*, which was attacked on much the same grounds that critics used in censuring Sterne.[6] Francis Hodgson summarized this change in standards in a review for the *Monthly* in 1812, when he condemned the "ludicrous liberties" of George Colman's *Poetical Vagaries*. Although in a previous book Colman had "pleaded the example of Swift and Sterne," it would be "as effectual to appeal to the authority of Boccaccio, or of Rabelais, in the present decorous times, as to that of our departed English humourists," Hodgson says. Now, "the wings of fancy are clipped; whether, in some respects, they are not clipped too closely, some persons may doubt: but whether or not the age, which so clips them, be virtuous enough *in action* to clip them with sincerity, we think that no person can doubt." [7] The new age thought of itself as more "refined," and tended to group together all the writers of the eighteenth century, and particularly the four great novelists, as representatives of a ruder and less moral age. In reviewing Richardson's *Correspondence* when it was published in 1804, the *Critical* could see little difference in point of morality between his work and that of Fielding and Sterne. The reviewer quotes Richardson's remark that *Tom Jones* was "a dissolute book," and goes on to say that "the inimitable pathos of Sterne could not, in our author's opinion, compensate for slight indelicacies." But Richardson *"should* have recollected," he concludes, "that he ought not to have cast a stone on that account." [8]

Though the liberties taken by the great eighteenth-century novelists would no longer have been tolerated in contemporary productions, there was at the same time a growing respect for the novel as a genre, and with it an acceptance of the earlier novelists. Their excellences could be applauded, while whatever defects they might have, from the point of

---

openly "declared the *fort* he meant to attack," few other critics had made the same objection.

5. For the unfavorable remarks on Sterne by two of the leaders in the movement, Wilberforce and Hannah More, see above, pp. 92–3. Scott faced the problem of this change in public taste in editing the works of Dryden. Though he had at first stated he would not "castrate" Dryden, he later decided that if he did not leave out "some of the more obnoxious lines" he would have "the Bishop of London and the whole corps of Methodists" about his ears. *Letters of Sir Walter Scott, 1,* 264, 284.

6. See Edward D. H. Johnson's unpubl. diss., "Lord Byron in *Don Juan*. A Study in Digression" (Yale, 1939), pp. 79–87, 210–26, and passim.

7. *Monthly Review,* 2d Ser. *68* (Aug. 1812), 388–9.

8. *Critical Review,* 3d Ser. *3* (Nov. 1804), 285. The reviewer has perhaps forgotten that Richardson's death in 1761 occurred before most of Sterne's "pathetic" work had appeared.

view of the new age, could be excused on historical grounds. In a note to his *Pursuits of Literature,* which was so popular at the turn of the century, T. J. Mathias reflects this new respect for the novel. "No man of genius or judgment ever despised or neglected the great masters of this useful and alluring species of writing," he says. "No works can be read with more delight and advantage, when they are selected with discrimination; they animate and improve the mind." Praise of *Don Quixote, Gil Blas,* and *Tom Jones* follows, with the statement that these are, perhaps, "all which it is *necessary* to read" since "they afford illustration to every event of life." But Smollett is credited with "much penetration, though he is frequently too vulgar to please," and of Sterne and Rousseau he says "it is impossible to deny the praise of wit and *originality* to Yorick, or of captivating eloquence to the philosopher of vanity." [9]

Respect for the eighteenth-century novelists may also have been increased by the fact that the quality of contemporary novels had sunk to a new low, with the extremes of the Gothic and sentimental schools dominating the scene. The very future of the novel form appeared to be in doubt, as the *Critical* remarked in 1814. In a review of Fanny Burney's *Wanderer,* the unknown writer said: "The era of the novel, as distinguished in common language from the romance, like that of legitimate comedy, is rapidly passing away." The reviewer attributed the decline of the novel to the changes which were taking place in society, for "the natural result of increased inquiry and communication, is a kind of melting of the individual into the species, every way beneficial to mankind collectively, but insensibly destructive of that eccentricity and diversity, which are essential to every amusing delineation of life and manners." Prototypes of the characters of Fielding, Smollett, and Sterne no longer existed and the genre which they had helped to found appeared to be at low ebb indeed.[1]

It is against this background of an age of transition in taste and attitude that the extended comments on Sterne by critics of the younger generation should be considered. Since they have a good deal in common, they will be considered together. The first critic of the group in point of time is Jeremiah Newman, the miscellaneous writer whose *Lounger's Common-Place Book* was first published serially during the nineties and had reached a third edition in 1805.[2] That same year Hugh Mur-

9. *Pursuits of Literature,* p. 57. The passage quoted above on p. 88 appears as a footnote to the present quotation, which was first added to the poem in 1798. The book reached a sixteenth edition in 1812.

1. *Critical Review,* 4th Ser. 5 (April 1814), 405–6.

2. *Lounger's Common-Place Book* (3d ed. 3 vols. London, 1805), *3,* 234–6. The first volume of the series appeared in 1792, followed by a second in 1793 and a third in 1794. A revised edition was issued in two volumes in 1796. Comments on Sterne appear in this edition of 1796 (a copy of which may be found in the Lewis Walpole Library, Farmington, Conn.) apparently for the first time. The text of the 1796 edition differs

ray's *Morality of Fiction* appeared.[3] In 1807 an essay written by one of
the Reynells was used as a preface to a group of selections from Sterne in
Classic Tales, published under the general editorship of Leigh Hunt.[4]
William Mudford likewise wrote an introductory essay for his edition
of Sterne in *British Novelists* in 1811.[5] Finally, in 1814 Edward
Mangin, a clergyman prominent in the literary circles of Bath, discussed
Sterne in his *View of the Pleasures Arising from a Love of Books.*[6]

These critics place varying emphasis on Sterne's plagiarisms and on
the supposed failings of his moral character. Murray, Reynell, and
Mangin all state that Sterne's humor is frequently "purloined"; but
both Murray and Newman recognize Sterne as the founder of the new
school of sentimental writing, and Reynell implies that Sterne did not
need "to stoop to this obligation" of borrowing. Mangin finds Sterne's
claim to originality chiefly in his "power of awakening emotions of
tenderness." Mudford gives the strongest censures of Sterne's borrowing, for he feels that there is no "plagiary more shameless than Sterne"
in the annals of literature; but the question of Sterne's literary honesty
at least vaguely troubles all of the group.

All these critics include strictures on Sterne's indecency. Reynell and
Mudford especially deplore the degradation of Sterne's clerical character
which they feel his books imply. Newman censures the "dangerously
inflammatory, if not grossly lewd" passages which came "steaming from
the hotbed of a lascivious imagination"; and Reynell deplores Sterne's
"inbred and incorrigible pruriency of imagination" which would have
been more appropriate to "a woman of pleasure, a comedian, or buffoon."
Mangin regrets the "impurities of all kinds" which render Sterne's
works "repulsive to every admirer of *moral* propriety." Mudford is
somewhat more perfunctory in his strictures and Murray feels that
Sterne's indecency arises "chiefly in those parts where he aims at wit"
and that the main danger of his work lies in its overemphasis on intui-
tion and feeling at the expense of reason and action. At the same time
both Reynell and Mudford appreciate the moral inspiration to be derived from Sterne's "benevolence" and "good humour." Reynell believes

from that of 1805 in being more sympathetic to Sterne and more noncommittal in regard
to his moral lapses. The quotations below are from the third edition.

3. *Morality of Fiction* (Edinburgh, 1805), pp. 129-45, esp. 142-4.

4. "Sterne," *Classic Tales,* (5 vols. London, 1806-7), 5, 264-82. Edmund Blunden
(*Leigh Hunt. A Biography,* London, Cobden-Sanderson, 1930, p. 41) attributes the
article to one of the Reynells, though he does not say whether it was Carew Reynell,
printer of *Classic Tales,* or one of his relatives associated in the business with him.

5. "Critical Observations upon Tristram Shandy and the Sentimental Journey,"
British Novelists, (5 vols. London, 1810-16?), 3, i-viii. There is a copy of this collection
in the New York Public Library.

6. *A View of the Pleasures Arising from a Love of Books* (London, 1814), pp. 81-
105. The *Critical* took exception to many of Mangin's strictures on Sterne, 4th Ser. 5
(June 1814), 602-3.

that Sterne has shown "the value of honest and ardent feeling," while Mudford praises the character of Uncle Toby, in which "virtue is taught by example, rather than by precept, and robbed of all her austerity."

The group are not uniformly enthusiastic about Sterne's characters, however, for Reynell feels that even the characters of Trim and Uncle Toby in their "moodiness and incoherence . . . frequently resemble too strongly the prattling and waywardness of childhood, or the wanderings and tearfulness of dotage." Mangin, in even more extreme vein, says that Sterne's characters in *Tristram Shandy* are inconsistent, for they "are goblins, not human beings : not individuals selected from the mass of mankind, but formations of his own which he chooses to call men, yet to which he has assigned qualities never found united in any one of our race." Mangin treats the characters in the *Sentimental Journey* in much kindlier fashion, however, comparing Sterne's power in "the art of painting with his *pen*" to that of great artists like Van Dyck, Teniers, and Hogarth.[7]

These younger critics are unanimous in preferring the *Sentimental Journey* to *Tristram Shandy,* largely because it exhibits Sterne's special skill in the pathetic and has less indecency and more regularity of plan. In *Tristram Shandy,* Mudford says, there is no "artful intricacy of plot." "All is studied confusion and perplexing abruptness, and the occasional gleams of fancy, wit, and humour, which diversify and adorn this dreary continuity of ruggedness, are like those glimpses of a smiling and beauteous landscape which a traveller sometimes catches as he journies over lonely hills or gloomy desarts of interminable extent." Thus Sterne's is "a brief excellence, for ever spoiled by some weakness. Affectation was, to Sterne, what a quibble was to Shakespeare : 'the fatal *Cleopatra,* for which he lost the world, and was content to lose it.' " Though the *Sentimental Journey* is "a more equal performance," even Sterne's "sentimental touches become, at last, irksome," Mudford says, because "they betray their origin, which was certainly from the head, and not from the heart." Sterne is "a sort of knight-errant, who sets forth in quest of adventures, and makes or finds them on all occasions. The emotions which he describes must either have been artificial, or must have sprung from a morbid delicacy of feeling : but the accounts which I have heard of his private life lead me to conclude the former." Like Mudford, Reynell feels that *Tristram Shandy* "must be acknowledged often to fail in interest" and though he too prefers Yorick's travels, in both of Sterne's books he finds a strange mixture of "bagatelle, obscenity, and sentiment." Newman also speaks of Sterne's "strange compound of wit and absurdity, goodness and indecorum, excellence and inanity, delicacy and grossness."

Murray thinks of Sterne as a "great and irregular" genius who is inferior to Henry Mackenzie "in point of taste and selection," but he

7. Reynell also compares Sterne's powers to those of a painter. See also below, p. 108.

finds somewhat less formlessness in Sterne than these other critics, for he believes that in writers of the sentimental school, the "ideas are connected, not indeed in the ordinary manner, but by certain secret links, not discernible by common readers. Of these links the most general seem to be, either the resemblance, or the contrast, of the sentiments which they tend to inspire." Mangin also feels that the comic and the pathetic are skillfully blended in Sterne, for, like Burns, he introduces "moral reflections" into humorous passages and the force of the moralizing "is increased by the reader's surprize on perceiving himself allured . . . from light and joyous topics, into meditations the most solemn and awful." It is unfortunate, Mangin adds, that Sterne and Burns also share coarseness and indecorum, which render "complete" copies of their works "inadmissible into any society where good breeding and innocence are cultivated." The result is that "two thirds of [Sterne's] admirers are laudably ashamed of their idol, and accordingly his works are read by numbers who *dare* not praise them."

This last statement is the key to these evaluations of Sterne by minor critics. They dare not praise Sterne without also including the strongest censures of his supposed indecency. Nor, on the whole, do they understand Sterne's artistry well enough to see beyond the seeming incoherence and affectation of *Tristram Shandy*. It is largely for these two reasons that they are unanimous in placing the *Sentimental Journey* first, with its greater apparent regularity of plan and its fewer lapses against decorum. Unlike the enthusiastic readers of *Beauties of Sterne*, however, they do not always whole-heartedly approve of Sterne's sentimental side; and if this trend of criticism had continued unchecked, Sterne's reputation would have eventually sunk to a very low level indeed.

Meanwhile other critics during the period, especially those who had stronger ties with the previous age, displayed more diversity in their positions. Perhaps the most enthusiastic of these other commentators was William Godwin, who included remarks on Sterne in his *Enquirer*, a series of essays published in 1797. Godwin is not greatly bothered by Sterne's alleged indecency, for he feels that the censure "against loose conversation, has probably been carried too far," since it is usually "more remarkable for ordure and a repulsive grossness, than for voluptuousness." There is no reason, he says, "why knowledge should not as unreservedly be communicated on the topic here alluded to, as on any other affair of human life." In judging people like Sterne, who "may have chosen this subject as the theme of a wit, pleasant, elegant and sportive, it is not easy to decide the exact degree of reprimand that is to be awarded against them." [8] Godwin also comments enthusiastically on Sterne's style, which he finds preferable to Fielding's, even though he had given the highest praise to the structure of *Tom Jones*. Fielding's

8. *The Enquirer* (London, 1797), Pt. II, p. 271.

style is "feeble, costive and slow" and his irony is "hard, pedantic and unnatural." If one compares "the hide-bound sportiveness of Fielding, with the flowing and graceful hilarity of Sterne," he will "be struck with the degree in which the national taste was improved, before the latter author could have made his appearance." [9]

Mary Berry, the friend of Horace Walpole, also judged Sterne quite candidly, though she found him much less to her liking than did Godwin and declared her preference for Rousseau. Writing in 1798, she admitted that *Tristram Shandy* was diverting, but compared it with "a Dutch portrait, in which we admire the accurate representation of all the little disgusting blemishes—the warts, moles, and hairs—of the human form. Even when he affects us," she continues, "it is by a minute detail of little circumstances which all lead to the weaknesses, and are often connected with the ridicules, that belong to our nature." Rousseau, on the other hand, "gives grace and dignity to every character he brings forward" and never loses sight of "decent grace," or presents "anything disgusting to the imagination. The one degrades worth," she concludes, "by a thousand little mean circumstances that destroy the respect which it *ought* to inspire; while the other consoles frail human nature with the idea that even great failings are redeemable by virtuous exertion." [1]

Finally, there are the statements by Richard Cumberland and Mrs. Barbauld, the only two major critics during this period who were old enough to remember the days when *Tristram Shandy* was first being published. When writing his *Memoirs,* which appeared in 1806, Cumberland recalled with pleasure John Henderson's readings from *Tristram Shandy* during the seventies, although his comments on the book itself are brief and somewhat disappointing. He repeats the clichés about Sterne's eccentricity, his "unpardonable" want of delicacy, and his strength in the pathetic, and finds that Sterne's "real merit lies not only in his general conception of characters, but in the address, with which he marks them by those minute, yet striking, touches of his pencil, that make his descriptions pictures, and his pictures life." [2]

Mrs. Barbauld agreed with this estimate of Sterne's merit. In her essay on "The Origin and Progress of Novel-Writing," published in 1810, she says Sterne's "peculiar characteristic" is "that he affects the heart, not by long drawn tales of distress, but by light electric touches which thrill the nerves of the reader who possesses a correspondent sensibility of frame. His characters, in like manner, are struck out by

9. Ibid., Pt. II, p. 462.

1. *Extracts from the Journals and Correspondence of Miss Berry,* ed. Lady Theresa Lewis (2d ed. 3 vols. London, 1866), 2, 80. The editor does not specify the exact source of the quotation. The metaphor of the Dutch painting was current. Mrs. Barbauld speaks of turning away "with disgust" from a scene of wretchedness, unless we are pleased with it, "as we are with a Dutch painting, from its exact imitation of nature." *Works of Barbauld,* 2, 222.

2. *Memoirs of Richard Cumberland* (London, 1806), pp. 453–4, 506–7.

a few masterly touches," she continues. "He resembles those painters who can give expression to a figure by two or three strokes of bold outline, leaving the imagination to fill up the sketch; the feelings are awakened as really by the story of *Le Fevre,* as by the narrative of *Clarissa.*" At the same time she feels called upon to condemn Sterne's personal character and the indelicacies of his volumes, which are "very reprehensible, and indeed in a clergyman scandalous"; although she admits that *Tristram Shandy* has "the richest vein of humour" in spite of the fact that it is more indecent than the *Sentimental Journey.* She credits Sterne with "much originality, wit, and beautiful strokes of pathos," although she deprecates his "total want of plan." [3] On the whole, her comments are fairly well balanced, for though she repeats some of the clichés about Sterne's moral character and the indelicacy of his work, she can nevertheless appreciate the humor of *Tristram Shandy,* and her favorable comparison of the story of Le Fever with Richardson's *Clarissa* was indeed high praise from a critic whose idol was Richardson.

During this period, as throughout previous ones, critics were still in disagreement as to just what Sterne's excellences were and just how his work should be taken. In general, however, the younger generation of critics, often under the influence of the evangelical movement, were tending to be more unanimous in their verdicts, at least in their condemnation of Sterne's immorality and their preference for the pathetic side of his work and for the *Sentimental Journey.* The one point on which there was practically unanimous agreement was the fact of Sterne's continuing popularity; and the few dissenting opinions were speedily contradicted. Thus, when George Gregory's *Letters on Literature,* published posthumously in 1809, attacked Sterne and insisted that his popularity had "so far passed away, that it seems like insulting the ashes of the dead to criticize him with severity," [4] the *Monthly* was quick in its defense. "Sterne is professedly a loose, rambling, desultory author," Francis Hodgson wrote in his review of Gregory's book, "a sort of after-dinner-companion, who moralizes without method, and laughs when he can." It is impossible to argue "on matters of feeling and humour," Hodgson continues, but he believes that few readers could have perused the story of Le Fever "without sympathy," or read of Uncle Toby's exploits "without a smile." [5]

3. "Origin and Progress of Novel-Writing," pp. 40–1. Mrs. Barbauld's collection of reprints does not contain any of Sterne's work.
4. *Letters on Literature, Taste, and Composition* (Philadelphia, 1809), pp. 16, 215. Copies of this book may be found in the New York and Boston Public Libraries. Gregory has previously praised Fielding highly, although with some reservations as to his morality; has commended Smollett's "most excellent vein of humour"; and has confessed his unfamiliarity with Richardson, whom he attempted to read in his youth but found full of "trite sentiment." For Gregory's other remarks see above, pp. 76–8.
5. *Monthly Review,* 2d Ser. 52 (March 1810), 256.

In two reviews which had appeared a few years earlier, the *Critical* had defended Sterne as "one of our greatest humourists," [6] and had expressed the conviction that his reputation was definitely established. "Whoever hears in these days of the idle calumnies that were scattered around Pope, or Sterne, or the numerous boasts of British genius?" the reviewer asks. "The criticisms have passed away like vapours on the winds of heaven," he says, but "the works will remain for ever." [7] A writer in the *Ladies' Monthly Museum* agreed, asking the question, "Can that man's education be said to be finished,—can he be considered a man of general knowledge who is unacquainted with the novels of Fielding, Sterne, or Smollett?" [8] Even the moralists were forced to admit that Sterne had become a classic; and a correspondent of the *Christian Observer* conceded that "Shakespeare and Congreve on the one part, and Swift and Sterne on the other, have gained the public suffrage; and are, therefore, likely to form . . . parts of every liberal and popular education." [9]

Sterne was indeed becoming a part "of every liberal and popular education." For confirmation of this fact, one need look no further than the important figures of the younger literary generation, who were beginning to dominate the age and were to continue to set the tone for several years to come. Lamb, Jane Austen, Byron, Southey, Scott, Hazlitt, and Coleridge were all familiar with Sterne; in fact, there is scarcely a major figure who does not mention him.

At the same time, the extended critical treatments of Sterne during this period of transition in taste and attitude reflected the effects of both the revelations of Ferriar and the attacks on his character by the moralists and the enthusiasts of the evangelical movement. Although the vast majority of the critics preferred the *Sentimental Journey* to *Tristram Shandy,* they no longer always praised the sentimental side of Sterne unreservedly, for they sometimes questioned its aesthetic merit as well as its sincerity and its moral tendency. His humorous side they usually rated even lower, believing that Ferriar had stripped this part of Sterne's work of most of its claim to notice. It remained for the major figures of the Romantic Period to restore the balance, as they made their important contributions toward a revaluation of Sterne in the years immediately following.

6. *Critical Review,* 3d Ser. *10* (March 1807), 250.
7. Ibid., 3d Ser. *8* (Aug. 1806), 447.
8. *Ladies' Monthly Museum,* New [2d] Ser., *16* (1814), 27.
9. *Christian Observer, 3* (April 1804), 215. The correspondent, who signs himself "C.F.," has previously lamented that "those authors, who are generally referred to as standards of sound composition, should be liable to so much objection on points of decorum and virtue."

5

The Rediscovery of Tristram Shandy *(1815–50)*

WHEN Leigh Hunt edited *Classic Tales* in 1807, he included an essay on Sterne by another writer which denounced the pages "stained with references and descriptions which modesty must ever blush to meet with, and language scarcely to be heard within the walls of a bordello." In both *Tristram Shandy* and the *Sentimental Journey* this critic found only an odd mixture of "bagatelle, obscenity, and sentiment." [1] When Hunt came to set down his own opinion of Sterne in his "Essay on Wit and Humour" in 1846, the remarks were in quite a different key. Asserting that Sterne was "the wisest man since the days of Shakespeare," he added that even Shakespeare himself "never arrived at a character" like that of Uncle Toby.[2] In the forty years which had elapsed between the two essays, there had been many additions to the criticism of Sterne which were both keen and appreciative. It would be exaggerating to say that both essays reflect universally accepted opinions of their respective times, but it is undeniable that each mirrored a prominent segment of opinion in its own era.

Before the nineteenth century there had been few extended discussions of Sterne's work by major critics, but among the literary generation which came into prominence during the Romantic Period most of the leading critics made more careful analyses. While Johnson, Walpole, and Gray had merely offered random comments on Sterne and his work, Hazlitt, Coleridge, and Scott left extended treatments. As these later critics came to look at Sterne more closely, they rejected many of the clichés which had been bandied about ever since the initial appearance of *Tristram Shandy* and came to appreciate him even more, in certain respects, than most of his original readers had.

The first of these significant contributions to the criticism of Sterne came in an article by Hazlitt in the *Edinburgh Review* in 1815. While reviewing Frances Burney D'Arblay's *Wanderer,* he comments on the greatest names in the English novel up to that time, insisting that the novel is a completely respectable genre, as worthy of study and attention as other supposedly more serious literature. "The most moral writers," he believes, "are those who do not pretend to inculcate any

1. See above, pp. 105–6.
2. *Wit and Humour* (London, 1846), p. 69. Hunt's comments are discussed in detail below, pp. 141–2.

moral," but rather give "the facts of human nature" and leave the reader to draw his own conclusions. Thus, Richardson, Fielding, Smollett, and Sterne are among the "first-rate" writers in the novel class, who "take their rank by the side of reality, and are appealed to as evidence on all questions concerning human nature." [3]

When he comes to speak of Sterne at greater length, Hazlitt regrets that there is a good deal of "*mannerism* and affectation in him," but believes that "his excellences, where he is excellent, are of the first order." Sterne's characters "are intellectual and inventive, like Richardson's—but totally opposite in the execution. The one are made out by continuity, and patient repetition of touches; the others, by rapid and masterly strokes, and graceful apposition. His style is equally different from Richardson's:—it is at times the most rapid,—the most happy,— the most idiomatic of any of our novel writers. It is the pure essence of English conversational style." [4] Hazlitt also makes the pronouncement that was to become so famous, that "Uncle Toby is one of the finest compliments ever paid to human nature."

The remarks on Sterne are fairly brief, however, compared to those on the other great novelists. Hazlitt does not see any overall pattern in his work, merely contenting himself with the observation that it "consists only of *morceaux,*—of brilliant passages," and noting without explaining, the seeming paradox of the two elements in Sterne of "a vein of dry, sarcastic humour" and another of "extreme tenderness of feeling." No attempt is made to relate these two elements to each other.[5]

These remarks in the *Edinburgh Review* were taken over, with slight variations, into the sixth of the series of *Lectures on the English Comic Writers,* which Hazlitt delivered at the Surrey Institution during the winter of 1818–19. Although the comments on Sterne were not materially augmented, they were repeated in a context which shows that he held a place in Hazlitt's theory of humor, since there are other brief references to him here and there in the *Lectures.* In the first lecture "On Wit and Humour," Hazlitt elaborates his theory. Laughter, he says, is a "convulsive and involuntary movement," occasioned by "surprise or contrast" before the mind "has time to reconcile its belief to contradictory appearances." Hence the "essence" of the laughable is "the incongruous, the disconnecting one idea from another, or the jostling of one feeling against another."

3. *Works of Hazlitt, 16,* 6–7.
4. Cf. Hazlitt's similar later remarks, ibid., *12,* 40–1.
5. Ibid., *16,* 18–19. In another review for the *Edinburgh* the same year Hazlitt admitted that in *Tristram Shandy* "the progress of the narrative is interrupted by some incident, in a dramatic or humorous shape"; ibid., *16,* 50. See also his statement in 1827 that "Sterne (thank God!) has neither hero nor heroine, and he does very well without them"; ibid., *17,* 250.

When Hazlitt comes to specific cases, he cites Cervantes and Sterne among the masters in the humorous, since both handle the incongruities in the characters to produce the highest comic effects. "There is nothing more powerfully humorous than what is called *keeping* in comic character, as we see it very finely exemplified in Sancho Panza and Don Quixote. . . . The deep feeling of character strengthens the sense of the ludicrous." Thus the "consistency in absurdity" in the character of Don Quixote heightens the comic effect, since after the "multiplication of chances for a return to common sense," our expectations are ultimately baffled. This "truth of absurdity to itself" also softens the effect of the ridicule, because there is "a certain beauty and decorum . . . from the principle of similitude in dissimilitude." Finally, humor of this sort has an appeal ultimately both to the reader's sympathy and to his sense of morality, for although "we cannot suppress the smile on the lip . . . the tear should also stand ready to start from the eye. The history of hobby-horses," he continues, "is equally delightful"; and after Don Quixote and Sancho, "My Uncle Toby's is one of the best and gentlest that 'ever lifted leg!' The inconveniences, odd accidents, falls, and bruises, to which they expose their riders" both amuse us and have also "applied their healing influence to many a hurt mind." Although Hazlitt is thinking first of Cervantes throughout this section of his remarks, it is significant that he finds Sterne deserving of mention for the same excellences.

In the eighth and last lecture of the series "On the Comic Writers of the Last Century," Hazlitt defends the earlier writers from the charge that they lacked refinement, and cites Sterne to prove his thesis that refinement in style was just as great in the earlier age. Moreover, this earlier period was actually richer in comic materials, he believes, for the refinements of society have tended to take away much of the individuality of character which had furnished such excellent humorous material to writers like Sterne.[6]

It is significant that Hazlitt does not feel it necessary to comment upon the questions of plagiarism and morality during his discussion of Sterne in these lectures. What he thought about these matters is to be found in brief comments in other works. In 1818 he said that "the only real plagiarism" that Sterne had been guilty of was "in taking Tristram Shandy's father from Martin's, the elder Scriblerus"; and in a review written the year of his death he said: "Gross plagiarism may consist with great originality. Sterne was a notorious plagiarist but a true genius. His Corporal Trim, his Uncle Toby, and Mr. Shandy, are to be found no where else." Although "no one has a right to steal, who is not rich enough to be robbed by others," he continues, writers like

6. Ibid., *6*, 5–12, 151–2. Part of these latter remarks are copied from the letter quoted from above, p. 97. Cf. also above, p. 104.

Sterne can compensate amply for what they take.[7] Hazlitt's inclusion of Walter Shandy among Sterne's great characters shows that he felt that Sterne's originality lies mainly in his humorous characters, and not, as so many earlier critics had insisted, in his pathetic side.[8] Hazlitt also disagrees with earlier critics in his assessment of Sterne's personal character. He does not believe that Sterne should be accused of being unfeeling in his personal relationships, for authors inevitably mirror something of themselves in their works. Sterne may have worn out his passions "with constant over-excitement," so that he only knew how he formerly felt; but always "where a strong impression of truth and nature is conveyed to the minds of others, it must have previously existed in an equal or greater degree in the mind producing it." [9]

Hazlitt's only extended discussion of Sterne is to be found in the *Edinburgh Review* article and the *Lectures,* but much of his other work throughout his life is permeated with allusions to Sterne. He thought that no one could "feel much happier—a greater degree of heart's ease—than I used to feel in reading Tristram Shandy," since he was one of those who lived upon the book "as a sort of food that assimilated with our natural dispositions." He classed Sterne among the writers who "each left works superior to any thing of the kind before," and quoted approvingly the remark of his friend Joseph Fawcett, who used to say that anyone "should deserve to be hanged" if he didn't like Sterne.[1]

Less than a year before Hazlitt's lectures, Coleridge had also given a series of lectures on English literature at the room of the Philosophical Society in Fetter Lane. The ninth lecture of this series, delivered February 24, 1818, was devoted to the nature of wit and humor and to the three figures, Rabelais, Swift, and Sterne.[2] Like Hazlitt, Coleridge

7. Ibid., *5,* 104; *20,* 300. Cf. above, p. 84.

8. In the *Edinburgh Review* article, Hazlitt speaks of Sterne's "fine pathos" and calls the story of Le Fever "perhaps the finest in the English language," but he thinks there is "affectation" in the tale of Maria and the apostrophe to the Recording Angel; ibid., *16,* 11, 19. The overwhelming majority of casual references to Sterne throughout his works are to *Tristram Shandy,* rather than the *Sentimental Journey.*

9. Ibid., *12,* 297–8. See also *12,* 371.

1. Ibid., *12,* 233, 303; *16,* 215; *8,* 224.

2. No text of the lecture has survived. It must be reconstructed from the following sources: (1) a report by an auditor published many years later in the *Tatler* (May 24, 1831) pp. 897–8; (2) Hartley N. Coleridge's reconstruction from MS notes and reports of auditors, first printed in *Literary Remains* in 1836 and reprinted in *Complete Works of Coleridge,* ed. W. G. T. Shedd (7 vols. New York, 1853, repr. 1884), *4,* 275–85; and (3) the surviving part of Coleridge's MS notes, appearing in Thomas M. Raysor, *Coleridge's Miscellaneous Criticism* (Cambridge, Harvard Univ. Press, 1936), pp. 117–26, which were printed together with all of the *Tatler* report (pp. 111–17) and most of Hartley Coleridge's reconstruction (pp. 440–6). There are discrepancies between these various sources, and sometimes within a single source. Unfortunately Coleridge's own notes leave gaps which must be filled in from the other sources. I have taken all direct quotations from Coleridge's own notes, as printed by Raysor, unless I have specified otherwise. I have not attempted to follow Coleridge's original order of presentation, which appears to have been somewhat rambling and must remain at least partly conjectural.

builds his discussion of the specific figures upon a more generalized treatment of the nature of humor. For this section of the lecture, he draws heavily upon Jean Paul Richter's *Vorschule der Aesthetik,* and, to a lesser extent, upon Aristotle. Coleridge defines the "pure unmixed ludicrous or laughable" as belonging "exclusively to the understanding plus the senses of eye and ear" and hence to the fancy, and "not to the reason or the moral sense." It arises from things which are out of their proper time and place, yet do not have the possibility of danger attached to them. Thus in "the simply laughable, there is a mere disproportion between a definite act and a definite purpose or end, or a disproportion of the end itself to the rank of the definite person." The laughable "is its *own end,*" for when "serious satire commences . . . the free laughter ceases." Wit, on the other hand, arises from the perception of identities in dissimilar things, "always appeals to the understanding, and does not necessarily produce laughter." Wit, then, "consists in presenting thoughts or images in an unusual connection with each other, for the purpose of exciting pleasure by the surprise." [3]

Humor, however, is more complicated than either laughter or wit, for words, thoughts, and images cannot by themselves produce humor, unless they indicate "some peculiarity of individual temperament and character." Coleridge apparently believes that, unlike the different kinds of wit, which are impersonal, humor is not merely limited to the understanding and the senses in its appeal, but also appeals to the reason and the moral sense. The difference may be seen by comparing the wit in the comedies of Congreve with the humor in the characters of Trim, Uncle Toby, and Walter Shandy. [4] The very origin of the word in "the humoral pathology . . . excellently described by Ben Jonson" suggests the relationship between humor and character. [5] There is a "tender feeling connected with the *humors* or hobbyhorses of a man," because the reader respects the "absence of any [selfish] interest" in a character of this sort and also perceives an "acknowledgement of the hollowness and farce of the world, and its disproportion to the godlike within us." Humorous writers, like Sterne, often "delight to end in nothing, or a direct contradiction," since in true humor "the little is made great, and the great little, in order to destroy both, because all is equal in contrast with the infinite."

3. These last two sentences are based on Hartley Coleridge and the *Tatler* report.

4. These three sentences come from Hartley Coleridge. He also includes the character of Falstaff with the characters of Sterne, but I suspect that Coleridge meant to have Falstaff grouped with Congreve, since the *Tatler* says that he described Falstaff's character "as one of wit, rather than of humour" (Raysor, p. 111), and among Coleridge's marginalia is the statement that although Falstaff is "so often extolled as the masterpiece of humor," his character does not contain "any humor at all" (Raysor, p. 50).

5. Though not to be found in the surviving portion of Coleridge's own notes, this idea occurs in both Hartley Coleridge and the *Tatler*. The wording comes from Hartley Coleridge.

One of Sterne's chief excellences consists in his ability "to seize happily on those points in which every man is more or less a *humorist*," by "bringing forward into distinct consciousness those minutiae of thought and feeling which appear trifles," and have "the novelty of an individual peculiarity," as well as "the interest of a something that belongs to our common nature." Coleridge believes that "the propensity to notice these things" in itself constitutes a humorist, and "the super-added power of so presenting them to men in general gives us the man of humor." Hence the difference between the man of humor, "the effect of whose portraits does not depend on the felt presence of himself as a humorist," as in the cases of Cervantes, Shakespeare, and Rabelais; and the writer, like Sterne, "in whom the effect is in the humorist's own oddity." Sterne, in other words, has the same sort of comic view to be found in Cervantes, Shakespeare, and Rabelais, though he does not objectify this view of life in the same way, for his presence is always felt in his work through the mannerisms of his style.

At the same time, a kindred excellence in Sterne is to be found in his presentation of those traits of human nature "which so easily assume a particular cast and color from individual character." This ability, "and the pathos connected with it," often form the groundwork of Sterne's humor. Coleridge instances the famous passage about Uncle Toby and the fly as an example, praising the delicacy of presentation. In this incident "individual character [is] given by the . . . elevation in degree of a common good quality, humanity, which in itself would not be characteristic at all." [6] He also refers to the skill with which Walter Shandy's character has been drawn with his "craving for sympathy in exact proportion to the oddity and unsympathizability," and notes the happy comic effect of his frustrations, which arise when he can find no one to discuss intelligently with him the theories which are nearest his heart. The contrasts between the brothers Shandy are likewise praised, as well as other passages which show an acute understanding of human nature. He selects a passage in which Walter Shandy is discussing his theory of names [7] to illustrate Sterne's skill in adding "life" and "character" to a passage of ironic wit to make it "dramatic." He likewise praises Sterne's "happiest use of drapery and attitude, which at once gives the *reality* by individualizing, and the vividness, by unusual, yet probable combinations," and commends the "physiognomic tact" in the depiction of Dr. Slop.

Thus, Coleridge is the first critic to recognize so clearly the sharp distinction between the humor to be found in Sterne's characters, who display a thorough knowledge of human nature, and the more questionable humor to be found in Sterne's style and manner. He finds "more

6. The wording of this quotation is taken from Hartley Coleridge.
7. *Tristram Shandy, I*, ch. 19; Work, pp. 50-1.

humor in the single remark, 'Learned men, Brother Toby, do not write dialogues on long noses for nothing,' than in the whole Slawkenburghian tale that follows, which is oddity interspersed with drollery." [8] The true humor lies in the interplay and development of the characters rather than in the wit of Sterne's mode of expression. It is also in the characters that the unity of the work may be found, for each part "by right of humoristic universality" is a whole. "Hence the digressive spirit [is] not wantonness, but the *very form* of his genius. The connection is given by the continuity of the characters."

It is also in the characters that the "moral good" of Sterne is to be found, as instanced, for example, in the contrast between the sincerity of Trim, when he is mourning the death of his young master Bobby, and the "cold skepticism of motives which is the stamp of the Jacobin spirit." [9] This basic moral good in the characters is quite separate from the elements in Sterne which have been censured for their immorality. These latter he describes as consisting in

> a sort of *knowingness,* the wit of which depends, first on the modesty it gives pain to; or secondly, the innocence and innocent ignorance over which it triumphs; or thirdly, on a certain oscillation in the individual's own mind between the remaining good and the encroaching evil of his nature, a sort of dallying with the devil, a fluxionary act of combining courage and cowardice, as when a man snuffs a candle with his fingers for the first time, or better still, perhaps, that tremulous daring with which a child touches a hot tea urn, because it had been forbidden—so that the mind has in its own white and black angel the same or similar amusements as might be supposed to take place between an old debauchee and a prude—[her] resentment from the prudential anxiety to preserve appearances, and have a character, and an inward sympathy with the enemy. We have only to suppose society *innocent*—and [this sort of wit] is equal to a stone that falls in snow; it makes no sound because it excites no resistance. [This accounts] for nine tenths [of its effect]; the remainder rests on its being an offence against the good manners of human nature itself.[1]

Coleridge regrets "the *mésalliance*" of this questionable sort of wit with the true humor in Sterne, but points out that the two are quite distinct. We can assure ourselves of this fact "by abstracting in our imagination the *characters* of Mr. Shandy, my uncle Toby, and Trim,

8. In Hartley Coleridge's reconstruction, drollery is defined as arising "where the laughable is its own end, and neither inference, nor moral is intended." Raysor, p. 411.

9. The wording of the quotation in the last part of this sentence comes from Hartley Coleridge.

1. Later critics often quoted from this passage, which was printed with minor variations by Hartley Coleridge. The emendations are Raysor's.

which are all *antagonists* to this wit," and supposing in their place "two or three callous debauchees." The result, Coleridge says, "will be pure disgust." Hence, Sterne "cannot be too severely censured" for this tasteless side of his work, since "he makes the best dispositions of our nature the panders and condiments for the basest" by joining this undesirable kind of wit with the true humor of the characters.[2]

Coleridge apparently also mentioned the danger to be apprehended from the tendency of Sterne's philosophy, since "all follies *not selfish,* it pardons or palliates." Although it is impossible to determine exactly how much he said on this subject in the lecture, other passages in his works are quite explicit. In a section "On Sensibility," published in *Aids to Reflection* in 1825, he expressed strong disapproval of this side of Sterne's work. "All the evil achieved by Hobbes and the whole school of materialists," he asserts, "will appear inconsiderable if it be compared with the mischief effected and occasioned by the sentimental philosophy of Sterne, and his numerous imitators. The vilest appetites and the most remorseless inconstancy towards their objects," he continues, "acquired the titles of the *heart, the irresistible feelings, the too tender sensibility*: and if the frosts of prudence, the icy chains of human law thawed and vanished at the genial warmth of human nature, who could help it? It was an amiable weakness!"[3] For Coleridge, love was an act of the will rather than of "the irresistible feelings," and it is partly for this reason that he places the *Sentimental Journey* far below *Tristram Shandy.* "There is truth and reality in the one," he is reported to have said, "and little beyond a clever affectation in the other."[4] At the same time, there were some aspects of Sterne's sentimental side which he appreciated, for in a letter written in 1828 he refers to "polish of style and that sort of prose which is in fact only another kind of poetry, nay, of metrical composition, the metre *incognito* such as Sterne's Le Fevre, Maria, Monk, etc."[5]

Coleridge's last recorded comment on Sterne comes from a conversation which took place the year before his death. It does not differ materially from his earlier statements, although it shows, perhaps, a slightly greater concern with Sterne's indecency:

2. The *Tatler* report says that Coleridge censured Sterne "for his indecency, his degradation of the passion of Love, and his affected sensibility," and concluded that "the works of Sterne had been productive of much more evil than good." This has no authority in the MS notes or in Hartley Coleridge, but agrees in part with a similar passage in *Aids to Reflection* which had been published before the *Tatler* report appeared (see below).

3. *Works of Coleridge, 1,* 137. Cf. similar remarks in *Table Talk and Omniana of Samuel Taylor Coleridge* (London, Oxford Univ. Press, 1917), p. 388; and *Lectures and Notes on Shakspere,* ed. Thomas Ashe (London, G. Bell, 1908), p. 119.

4. *Works of Coleridge, 6,* 480. This remark appears in a note by Hartley Coleridge.

5. *Unpublished Letters of Samuel Taylor Coleridge,* ed. Earl Leslie Griggs (2 vols. New Haven, Yale Univ. Press, 1933), *2,* 420–1. Cf. a similar passage in ch. 18 of *Biographia Literaria, Works of Coleridge, 3,* 418.

I think highly of Sterne; that is, of the first part of Tristram Shandy; for as to the latter part, about the Widow Wadman, it is stupid and disgusting; and the Sentimental Journey is poor sickly stuff. There is a great deal of affectation in Sterne, to be sure; but still the characters of Trim and the two Shandies are most individual and delightful. Sterne's morals are bad, but I don't think they can do much harm to any one whom they would not find bad enough before. Besides, the oddity and erudite grimaces under which much of his dirt is hidden, take away the effect for the most part; although, to be sure, the book is scarcely readable by women.[6]

Like Hazlitt, Coleridge has not attached any importance to the question of plagiarism in Sterne, for he has nowhere thought it necessary to discuss it.[7] Also like Hazlitt, he has approached the question of morality from a fresh point of view, drawing sharp distinctions between the different elements in the humorous side of Sterne's work. Though he is as sweeping in his denunciation of Sterne's pruriency as any of the earlier critics, he realizes the difference between this questionable sort of wit and the genuine humor which arises from the characters.

The third major critic of Sterne during the period is, of course, Sir Walter Scott, whose prefatory essay in Ballantyne's series of standard novelists first appeared in 1823.[8] Allusions in Scott's letters, journals, and miscellaneous prose works show that he must have read Sterne as thoroughly and as appreciatively as had Hazlitt and Coleridge;[9] but when he comes to write about him, he does not display as much originality in his approach as do the other two. Though Scott had been thinking about the possibility of editing a collection of novelists as early as 1808,[1] he apparently found himself pressed for time when he finally came to execute the project. The lives, he wrote to Lady Louisa Stuart, were "rather flimsily written," since they were "done merely to

6. *Works of Coleridge, 6,* 480-1. Cf. similar remarks about the Widow Wadman in a letter in 1820 discussing changes in taste in fiction; *Table Talk and Omniana,* p. 415.

7. There is, however, a note among Coleridge's marginalia which alludes to this topic: "In Shakespeare and Cervantes it is wit so precious that it becomes wit even to quote or allude to it. Thus Sterne is a secondary wit of this order." Thomas M. Raysor, *Coleridge's Shakespearean Criticism* (2 vols. Cambridge, Harvard Univ. Press, 1930), *I,* 242.

8. *The Novels of Sterne, Goldsmith, Dr. Johnson, Mackenzie, Horace Walpole, and Clara Reeve* (London: printed in Edinburgh, 1823), pp. i-xxii. This was the fifth volume of Ballantyne's series, though not so numbered on the title-page.

9. In addition to the references above and below, see *Letters of Sir Walter Scott, 4,* 174, 224, 244, 303, 382; *9,* 173, 295, 434, 501; *10,* 107. See also *Journal of Sir Walter Scott,* ed. J. G. Tait and W. M. Parker (Edinburgh and London, Oliver and Boyd, 1950), pp. 69, 74, 239, 546; and *Miscellaneous Prose Works* (28 vols. Edinburgh, 1834-36), *18,* 333, 383; *19,* 327; *21,* 11, 17, 21, 111, 318.

1. See *Letters of Sir Walter Scott, 2,* 114.

oblige a friend. They were yoked to a great illconditiond and lubberly double-columnd book," he continued, "which they were as unfit to tug along as a set of fleas would be to draw a mail-coach." [2] This rather forbidding format may partially explain why the series was never very successful, although the prefatory essays were, of course, republished under the title of *Lives of the Novelists*.[3]

Scott's essay on Sterne is mainly a compilation, but it does show both sympathy and judgment in the use of his different sources. As he writes, he evidently has some half-dozen books open on the desk before him. First, there is some edition of Sterne's *Works* with one of the standard prefaces in supplement to Sterne's own "Memoir." Then there are Ferriar's *Illustrations* and the Medalle edition of the *Letters*. Boswell's *Life of Johnson* is once or twice laid under contribution. Scott also draws heavily on the rather unreliable account of Sterne, supposedly from the lips of La Fleur, which he had found in William Davis' *Olio*.[4] Finally, he probably had some other brief biography of Sterne, and perhaps a collection or two of anecdotes. In transcribing from these various sources, Scott occasionally shows signs of haste,[5] but in general his selection of materials represents a good deal of critical acumen.

The biographical treatment of Sterne is kind. Though Scott does not add any new material, his omissions are significant. He does not repeat any of the sensational stories about Sterne's friendless deathbed and the desecration of his corpse, nor does he relate the calumnies about Sterne's neglect and mistreatment of his wife and mother. He does admit that Yorick had "too little respect for his cloth and character, to maintain the formalities, not to say the decencies, of the clerical station" and that his "temper was variable and unequal." He concludes, however, that "we will not readily believe that the parent of uncle Toby could be a harsh or habitually a bad-humoured man," and states that "his resources, such as they were, seem to have been always at the command of those whom he loved." [6] In his prefatory essay to Smollett's novels,

2. Ibid., *10, 95*.

3. Scott's *Lives* were first extracted and published in a pirated edition at Paris in 1825. The bankruptcy of Constable prevented a projected republication in Britain (*Letters of Sir Walter Scott, 10, 95*), but the *Lives* were included in editions of Scott's prose works after his death. Apparently the original collection of novels with the lives prefixed was not very well known, for Lady Louisa Stuart said in 1826 that nobody "seems ever to have heard of the prefaces before, but all are eager to get it from France." (*Lady Louisa Stuart, Selections from Her Manuscripts,* ed. Hon. James Home, New York and London, 1899), p. 233.

4. *An Olio of Biographical and Literary Anecdotes and Memoranda* (London, 1814), pp. 25–32. Davis condensed the "interview" with La Fleur, which had appeared in the *European Magazine* in 1790; see above, pp. 66–7.

5. There are, for example, one or two errors in fact. Sterne's death is said to have taken place in February (*Novels of Sterne, Goldsmith . . . ,* p. xv) and Scott also states that four, rather than two additional volumes of *Sermons* were published in 1766 (p. xi). In most cases Scott makes specific acknowledgment of his sources.

6. Lockhart's review of the Paris edition of Scott's *Lives* for the *Quarterly* insinuated

published two years earlier, he had made the statement that "Sterne's writings shew much flourish concerning virtues of which his life is understood to have produced little fruit"; [7] but this censure is not repeated in the later essay.

When Scott comes to consider Sterne's critical reputation, he assumes that it rests chiefly on *Tristram Shandy* and hence that he is liable to the "two severe charges" of indecency and affectation. The first charge Scott disposes of by saying that "the licentious humour of *Tristram Shandy* is [not] of the kind which applies itself to the passions, or is calculated to corrupt society." It is, however, "a sin against taste, if allowed to be harmless as to morals. A handful of mud is neither a firebrand nor a stone; but to fling it about in sport, argues coarseness of taste, and want of common manners." The second charge he believes to be more valid, for even Sterne's greatest admirers must admit "that his style is affected, eminently, and in a degree which even his wit and pathos are inadequate to support." The affectation arises partly from his imitation of Rabelais, though there was no necessity in Sterne's case for "assuming the cap and bells of the ancient jester as an apology" for his satire. Sterne's manner appears to have been assumed "only as a mode of attracting attention, and of making the public stare; and, therefore, his extravagancies, like those of a feigned madman, are cold and forced, even in the midst of his most irregular flights." Hence Sterne's popularity "carries in it the seeds of decay; for eccentricity in composition, like fantastic modes of dress . . . is sure to be caricatured by stupid imitators, to become soon unfashionable, and of course to be neglected." [8]

In discussing the question of plagiarism, Scott states that although Sterne has been shown to be "the most unhesitating plagiarist who ever cribbed from his predecessors in order to garnish his own pages," at the same time he "selects the materials of his mosaic work with so much art, places them so well, and polishes them so highly" that we forgive the borrowing. The element of dishonesty appears to bother Scott, however; and he believes that it is the more censurable, since Sterne "had enough of original talent, had he chosen to exert it, to have dispensed with all such acts of literary petty larceny."

Sterne's real originality lies in his characters. "The passages which he borrowed from others were of little value, in comparison to those which are exclusively original," particularly those with Uncle Toby and Trim. These two characters, who are "the most delightful . . . in the

---

that Scott had been too lenient on Sterne's personal character. See *Quarterly Review, 34* (Sept. 1826), 370–1. The attribution is based on Margaret Clive Hildyard, *Lockhart's Literary Criticism,* Oxford, B. Blackwell, 1931.

　7. *Novels of Tobias Smollett* (London, 1821), p. xxviii.

　8. Cf. Johnson's statement, p. 60 above.

work, or perhaps in any other," more than make up for Sterne's faults
and allow him "to leave the court of criticism . . . applauded and re-
warded, as one who has exalted and honoured humanity" with "such
a lively picture of kindness and benevolence, blended with courage,
gallantry, and simplicity." At the same time, Walter Shandy must be
considered "the principal figure," if one views *Tristram Shandy* as
"no narrative, but a collection of scenes, dialogues, and portraits, humorous or affecting, intermixed with much wit, and with much learning,
original or borrowed." For it is mainly in Walter Shandy's character
that Sterne finds a convenient repository for "the great quantity of
extraordinary reading, and antiquated learning, which he had collected."
Unlike Coleridge, Scott fails to see an organic unity arising from the
characters in *Tristram Shandy,* but thinks that the book "resembles the
irregularities of a Gothic room, built by some fanciful collector, to
contain the miscellaneous remnants of antiquity which his pains have
accumulated, and bearing as little proportion in its parts, as the pieces
of rusty armour with which it is decorated."

Scott further developed this theme in his essay on Henry Mackenzie,
published in the same volume as that on Sterne. He contrasts the
"chaste, correct, almost studiously decorous manner and style" of
Mackenzie with the "wild wit, and intrepid contempt at once of decency,
and regularity of composition, which distinguish *Tristram Shandy*."
Even when the two authors aim at pathos, their methods are entirely
different. "The pathos of Sterne," Scott says, "resembles his humour,
and is seldom attained by simple means; a wild, fanciful, beautiful flight
of thought and expression is remarkable in the former, as an extravagant, burlesque, and ludicrous strain of thought and language
characterizes the latter." He uses the famous passage with the Recording Angel as illustration: "To attain his object—that is, to make us
thoroughly sympathize with the excited state of mind which betrays
Uncle Toby into the indecorous assertion which forms the groundwork of the whole—the author calls Heaven and Hell into the lists,
and represents, in a fine poetic frenzy, its effects on the accusing Spirit
and the registering Angel." Scott contrasts this passage with Mackenzie's tale of La Roche, in which the "sublime scene of the sorrows
and resignation of the deprived father" has been achieved with delicacy
and simplicity, concluding that "Mackenzie has given us a moral truth,
Sterne a beautiful trope." If Sterne is superior in "brilliancy of imagination," Mackenzie, nevertheless, surpasses him in "accuracy of human
feeling." [9] Sir Walter's loyalty to Scotland and his friendship for
Mackenzie may partially explain the high estimate of his fellow Scot,
but he was not alone in this judgment. Throughout the period in
question, other critics, perhaps following his lead, sometimes considered

9. *Novels of Sterne, Goldsmith* . . . , pp. lii–liii.

Mackenzie and Sterne on a par, or even placed the author of *The Man of Feeling* above Yorick.[1] Scott himself never seems to have gotten completely away from the idea that the "cap and bells" was "Tristram Shandy's vein," and that Sterne's purpose was "to make the world stare."[2]

Thus, Scott's concluding evaluation in his essay on Sterne does not rise very far above many of the clichés that had been repeated for some time. Sterne is at the same time "one of the most affected, and one of the most simple writers . . . one of the greatest plagiarists, and one of the most original geniuses, whom England has produced." In conclusion he quotes Ferriar's poem in which he believes that Sterne's "ingenious inquisitor makes the amende honourable to the shade of Yorick" by stressing the originality and excellence of Sterne's pathetic side.[3]

This conclusion, of course, is not entirely consistent with Scott's opinion that Sterne's reputation rests mainly on *Tristram Shandy*, since the *Sentimental Journey* is in many ways a better example of Sterne's powers in the pathetic than is the earlier book. The inconsistency may perhaps be explained, at least in part, by the haste with which Scott compiled the essay and the excessive reliance which he sometimes placed upon his sources. Actually, the amount of original material in the essay (and even the percentage of Scott's own words) is relatively small. In general, however, he displays perceptiveness in most of his choices from among the previous clichés about Sterne, lending the authority of his name to selections which were dictated by a sound critical judgment. His biographical treatment of Sterne was far kinder than that which was standard for the age; he placed Sterne's indecency in the realm of taste rather than that of morality; and he stressed the excellence of the characters in *Tristram Shandy*, even though he failed to see the same structural unity in it which Coleridge had. Although he did not open up the same kind of new insights into Sterne's work that Coleridge and Hazlitt had, he did his job of compilation skillfully and sympathetically.

While the dicta of Hazlitt, Coleridge, and Scott are of paramount interest, they are by no means at variance with the evaluations of other prominent critics of the age. De Quincey and Carlyle, both in discussions of Jean Paul Richter during the twenties, show their admiration for Sterne. De Quincey's essay, which first appeared in the *London Magazine* in 1821, contains a discussion of the "possibility of blending, or fusing, as it were, the elements of pathos and of humour,

1. See, among others, Sir Thomas Noon Talfourd's comparison of Sterne and Mackenzie in the *New Monthly Magazine, 13,* Pt. 1 (1820), 324–5; and Allan Cunningham, *Biographical and Critical History of the British Literature of the Last Fifty Years* (Paris, 1834), p. 134. There is a copy of the latter in the Boston Public Library.
2. *Journal of Sir Walter Scott,* p. 249.
3. See above, p. 85.

and composing out of their union a third metal *sui generis*." Since Shakespeare, De Quincey believes, Richter and Sterne are the two writers who have "pretensions . . . to the *spolia opima*" in this kind of writing. In both, the "interpenetration of the humorous and the pathetic" is excellently managed. De Quincey finally gives his preference to Richter, since he believes him to excel by "his faculty of catching at a glance all the relations of objects, both the grand, the lovely, the ludicrous, and the fantastic." This "inordinate agility of the understanding" is invaluable to a writer of "inordinate sensibility. The active faculty balances the passive," he continues, "and without such a balance there is great risk of falling into a sickly tone of maudlin sentimentality, —from which Sterne cannot be pronounced wholly free." [4] Even though De Quincey finally places Richter above Sterne, it is significant that he feels it necessary to treat Sterne's claim seriously and that he finds Sterne and Richter the only two writers who can be compared with Shakespeare in this kind of writing.

Carlyle is even more enthusiastic in his remarks on Sterne. In a review of Döring's *Life of Richter* for the *Edinburgh* in 1827, he discusses the affinity between humor and pathos, coming to a conclusion similar to De Quincey's. Though critics have sometimes marveled "that things so discordant should go together," the wonder "should rather be to see them divided; to find true genial humor dwelling in a mind that was coarse or callous. The essence of humor is sensibility," he says, and "unless seasoned and purified by humor, sensibility is apt to run wild; will readily corrupt into disease, falsehood, or, in one word, sentimentality." Thus, "true humor is sensibility" and "springs not more from the head than from the heart; it is not contempt, its essence is love; it issues not in laughter, but in still smiles, which lie far deeper. It is a sort of inverse sublimity; exalting, as it were, into our affections what is above us." It is the product of "a nature in harmony with itself, reconciled to the world and its stintedness and contradiction, nay finding in this very contradiction new elements of beauty as well as goodness." Carlyle next considers the various English writers who have claims to eminence in this kind of writing. Shakespeare is denied first place, since "his humor is heartfelt, exuberant, warm, but seldom the tenderest or most subtle." Swift often inclines to irony, although "he had genuine humor too, and of no unloving sort, though cased, like Ben Jonson's, in a most bitter and caustic rind." The last specimen of British humor, "and, with all his faults, our best; our finest, if not our strongest" is Sterne. Yorick, Corporal Trim, and Uncle Toby "have yet no brother but in *Don Quixote,* far as *he* lies above them." Cervantes is "the purest of all humorists," and Richter stands unsurpassed among

4. *Collected Writings of Thomas De Quincey,* ed. David Masson (14 vols. Edinburgh, 1890), *11,* 264-8.

the German writers for this quality; but Sterne is worthy to be compared with them.[5]

In essays on Burns and Voltaire written during the next two years, Carlyle again refers to Sterne as a master in the humorous. Burns is "brother and playmate to all Nature," and the "evanescent and beautiful touches," resulting from his tender "sportfulness," show "traits of a Humor as fine as that of Sterne." The wit of Voltaire, on the other hand, exhibits a "mere logical pleasantry; a gayety of the head, not of the heart," and there "is scarcely a twinkling of Humor in the whole of his numberless sallies." We look in vain "for one lineament of a *Quixote* or a *Shandy."* When Carlyle writes again on Richter in 1830, he refers to "the light kindly comic vein of Sterne in his *Trim* and *Uncle Toby."* [6]

Carlyle's acquaintance with the works of Sterne had begun during his college days [7] and continued thereafter for some time with unabated interest. His love letters to Jane Welsh, as well as her replies, contain references to Sterne.[8] When he was traveling to Paris in 1824 he felt that the *Sentimental Journey* "is alive in one from the first stage onwards," and half-expected to come upon the dead ass at Nampont.[9] He later used the alias "Smelfungus" for an article in 1832.[1] Meanwhile, his admiration for Sterne had played a part in the composition of *Sartor Resartus* during 1830 and 1831. The book contains several allusions to *Tristram Shandy,*[2] and Carlyle's friend, John Sterling, saw resemblances in style between the two books, characterizing *Sartor* as a "Rhapsodico-Reflective" composition which resembles the "masterworks of human invention" written by Rabelais, Montaigne, Swift, and Sterne.[3]

Although one of Carlyle's biographers states that in later years he thought that perhaps *Tristram Shandy* would have been a better subject than Richter "if the 'humorist' were to be his theme," [4] his early

5. *Critical and Miscellaneous Essays, 1,* 17–18, in *Complete Works,* Sterling Ed. (20 vols. Boston, [1885]).

6. Ibid., *1,* 279–80, 443; *2,* 127.

7. See R. S. Craig, *The Making of Carlyle* (New York, Lane, 1909), p. 64.

8. See *Love Letters of Thomas Carlyle and Jane Welsh,* ed. Alexander Carlyle (2 vols. London and New York, Lane, 1909), *1,* 184, 259; *2,* 204. See also *Early Letters of Jane Welsh Carlyle,* ed. David G. Ritchie (London, 1889), pp. 19, 291. Miss Welsh's dog was called "Shandy" (p. 69).

9. *Reminiscences of Thomas Carlyle,* ed. Charles Eliot Norton (2 vols. London, 1887), *2,* 156–7.

1. See David Alec Wilson, *Carlyle to "The French Revolution"* (London, K. Paul, Trench, Trubner, 1925), p. 286.

2. See *Sartor Resartus,* ed. Charles F. Harrold (New York, Doubleday, 1937), pp. 14, 62–4, 66, 87, 105, 131, 148, 170.

3. Ibid., pp. 308–9. Sterling pointed out that *Sartor* differed from Sterne, however, since it did not rely upon "obscene and sensual stimulants" and Sterne was "never obscure, and never moral; and the costume of his subjects is drawn from the familiar experience of his own time and country."

4. Craig, *Making of Carlyle,* p. 385.

enthusiasm for Sterne appears to have cooled somewhat.[5] When he came to deliver his *Lectures on the History of Literature* in 1838, his former ardor was lacking. The brief remarks on Sterne are preceded by a more extended discussion of Swift, with whom he is asserted to have much in common. In Swift's conduct there is "much that is sad and tragic, highly blameable," although he was the victim of misfortune in having entered the church early in his life without "having any vocation for it." He was "a kind of cultivated heathen, no Christianity in him." At the same time he often had "a sympathy . . . with the thing he satirises" and "great pity for his fellow-men." Sterne, Carlyle continues, was "another man of much the same way of thinking," for "in him also there was a great quantity of good struggling through the superficial evil." Though he "terribly failed in the discharge of his duties," we must admire him for "that sportive kind of geniality and affection, still a son of our common mother, not cased up in buckram formulas as the other writers were, clinging to forms, and not touching realities." Although much has been said against him, Carlyle concludes, "we cannot help feeling his immense love for things around him; so that we may say of him, as of Magdalen, 'much is forgiven him, because he loved much.' A good simple being after all." [6] Though Carlyle appreciates Sterne as a rebel in his style and a man with "love for things around him," he no longer compares him with Shakespeare. The change in his attitude is probably due to various factors. Perhaps the most important is that as he became more and more absorbed in the idea of the "hero" in history and literature, he found Sterne wanting in some of the personal qualities which he believed necessary for greatness. Johnson, Rousseau, and Burns, the three illustrations in "The Hero as Man of Letters," all had a certain strength which could not be ascribed to a man who was merely a "good simple being." Sterne's philanthropy was likewise in opposition to the ideas about society which Carlyle was developing. He never completely forgot Sterne, however, for in the *History of Frederick the Great,* which he was writing some twenty years later, he states that the only thing which renders the expedition against Vigo and the siege of Gibraltar memorable is the fact of Roger Sterne's participation in them. "History ought to remember," says Carlyle, "that he is 'Uncle Toby,' this poor Lieutenant, and take her measures!" [7]

5. See Francis Espinasse, *Literary Recollections and Sketches* (New York, 1893), p. 227. Espinasse says: "I never heard Carlyle speak of Pope, Swift, and the other Queen Anne men, nor of Fielding, nor even of Sterne, for whom he had an early love."
6. *Lectures on the History of Literature,* ed. J. Reay Greene (2d ed. London, Ellis and Elvey, 1892), pp. 169–71.
7. *Works: History of Frederick the Great, 1,* 454; *2,* 55–6. Carlyle was by no means the first critic to speculate that the character of Uncle Toby might have been taken from Sterne's father.

Other major figures of the age had read Sterne and his works appreciatively. The letters of Keats contain allusions to *Tristram Shandy*.[8] Shelley quotes from the *Sentimental Journey* in one of his early essays, which was published posthumously.[9] Byron may very well have reread Sterne about 1821, since there are references to *Tristram Shandy*, as well as to one of Sterne's letters in his private papers for that year.[1] It was during the same year that Canto iv of *Don Juan* was published, containing a reference to "Yorick's starling" in the *Sentimental Journey*.[2]

Southey continues to refer to Sterne in letters during the twenties and thirties, and occasionally copies into his commonplace book various passages from Sterne's *Sermons* and bits of information relative to him. Much of the material in the commonplace book found its way into *The Doctor,* the rambling collection of wit and erudition which served Southey as a hobby during most of his life. The germ of the idea for *The Doctor* had come to him during the nineties, when he had visualized a work "in a style compounded of those of Rabelais, Swift, Sterne, and Baron Munchausen." [3] When the first installment of the work was finally published in 1834, Lockhart immediately recognized *Tristram Shandy* as its "immediate prototype." He thought the later work fell far short, however, for Sterne's plan, "with all its wildness," contains much art, Lockhart wrote, and Sterne's diverse materials are "poured out dramatically" through the characters; while the author of *The Doctor* has taken "the office of showman openly into his own hands" and many of the eccentricities of the style are "but paltry imitations of the poorest sort of fun" in *Tristram Shandy*.[4] Southey seems to have found Sterne's stylistic and typographical oddities more amusing than most of his contemporaries did, since in *The Doctor* he imitated some of these devices which other major critics of the age dismissed as unfortunate "mannerisms" or "affectations." He shared their admiration for Sterne's characters, however, even though he was unequal to imitating them successfully, and included a graceful apostrophe in *The Doctor* to "our dear Uncle Toby." [5]

8. See *Letters of John Keats,* ed. Maurice Buxton Forman (4th ed. London, New York, Toronto, Oxford Univ. Press, 1952), pp. 18, 43, 399, 453.

9. *The Keepsake for 1829* (London, 1828), p. 49. Writing "On Love," Shelley quotes Sterne's statement that "if he were in a desert he would love some cypress" ("In the Street. Calais").

1. See *Works of Lord Byron: Prose, 5,* 183-4, 396, 462-3.

2. *Don Juan,* iv. 109.

3. *Life and Correspondence, 2,* 335. See also *5,* 187; *6,* 269. Regarding the book as a sort of hobby, Southey took delight in keeping its authorship secret.

4. *Quarterly Review, 51* (March 1834), 69-70. The attribution is based on Hildyard, *Lockhart's Literary Criticism.*

5. *The Doctor &c.,* ed. John Wood Warter (new ed. London, 1849), p. 385. For other references to Sterne see pp. 45, 77, 82, 122, 278, 341-2, 401, 413, 428, 505-6, 533, 583, 609, 659.

Macaulay was also a lifelong admirer of Sterne. On his yearly trips with members of his family during the forties he would read aloud in the evenings from Fielding, Smollett, or Sterne.[6] *Tristram Shandy* must surely have been among the favorite books which "he opened for the tenth or fifteenth time," since his biographer states that "there was no society in London so agreeable that Macaulay would have preferred it at breakfast or at dinner to the company of Sterne, or Fielding, or Horace Walpole, or Boswell." When he was reading these favorite authors, "his feeling was precisely that which we experience on meeting an old comrade, whom we like all the better because we know the exact lines on which his talk will run." [7]

Wordsworth is practically the only major figure of the period who does not refer to Sterne, although he surely must have read him.[8] He presumably did not share the opinion of one of his anonymous critics in the *Gentleman's Magazine,* who called Wordsworth "the Sterne of poetry" because he had "endeavoured to extract sentiment where nobody else ever dreamt of looking for it" and "often exalted trifles into a consequence which nature never intended them to occupy," thus lending his aid in implanting "a tone not always auspicious to true and genuine feeling." [9] Nor would the laureate have been pleased at the description which Francis Espinasse, who visited him during his school days, later penned of him. "Of his features," wrote Espinasse, "that which struck me most was his nose, one massive enough to have satisfied Mr. Walter Shandy himself." [1] Unlike Southey, his predecessor in the laureateship, Wordsworth had very little of the Shandean in his own temperament.

The roster of major critics who are favorable to Sterne during this period is indeed impressive. There is Hazlitt's statement that Sterne has "the pure essence of English conversational style." There is Coleridge's recognition of the fact that Sterne's "digressive spirit" is "the *very form* of his genius," with continuity supplied to the work by characters who display a deep knowledge of human nature. There is Scott's sym-

6. G. Otto Trevelyan, *Life and Letters of Lord Macaulay* (2 vols. New York, 1876), *2,* 189–90.

7. Ibid., *2,* 394. Though Macaulay "thought it probable that he could rewrite 'Sir Charles Grandison' from memory" (*1,* 129), he apparently didn't know Sterne quite so well (see *1,* 397–8).

8. In Christopher Wordsworth's *Memoirs of William Wordsworth,* 2 vols. London, 1851, Wordsworth is said to have read Fielding, Cervantes, *Gil Blas, Gulliver's Travels,* and *Clarissa* during his school days (*1,* 10, 48), but there is no mention of Sterne. Dorothy Wordsworth had read *Tristram Shandy* in 1796 (see above, p. 96), and in letters to Dorothy and Mary Wordsworth, Henry Crabb Robinson makes references to Sterne; *Correspondence of Henry Crabb Robinson with the Wordsworth Circle,* ed. Edith J. Morley (2 vols. Oxford, Clarendon Press, 1927), *1,* 293, 443.

9. "Some Speculations on Literary Pleasures," *Gentleman's Magazine, 98* (21st of new series), Pt. 1 (May 1828), 399–400. The essay is signed "Alciphron."

1. *Literary Recollections and Sketches,* p. 10.

pathetic assessment of Sterne's character and the tendency of his work, which is fairly well balanced if not as original as the pronouncements of Hazlitt and Coleridge. There is the recognition by De Quincey and Carlyle of the art with which Sterne has blended the comic and the pathetic. Finally, there are the references to Sterne by other major figures which show that they had read *Tristram Shandy* and the *Sentimental Journey* appreciatively. Charles Lamb may be allowed to speak for the entire group when he places Sterne among the classics of English literature: "In some respects the better a book is, the less it demands from binding. Fielding, Smollet, Sterne, and all that class of perpetually self-reproductive volumes—Great Nature's Stereotypes—we see them individually perish with less regret, because we know the copies to be 'eterne.' "[2]

The comments of these major critics, however, tell only half the story. Minor critics did not always completely agree with them, and furthermore many of the comments were not very widely known until several years after their original appearance. Hazlitt's essay, of course, had a wide circulation in the *Edinburgh,* but Scott's *Lives* were apparently not very generally read until their subsequent republication. Hartley Coleridge's reconstruction of his father's remarks on Sterne was not published until 1836. The essays of De Quincey and Carlyle must have had a wide circulation in their periodical form, but De Quincey's reputation was not fully established in 1821, and Carlyle remained a struggling, relatively unknown writer until late in the thirties. In any case, the essays were published anonymously. Though these pronouncements by major critics had an increasing influence as they became better known, the full impact was not felt at once.

Various kinds of evidence are available to round out the picture. Indications of Sterne's continuing popularity may be found in the steady demand for his works, the allusions to him in widely differing connections, and the imitations of both his pathetic and humorous sides. The statements of biographical compilers, minor critics, and literary historians likewise reflect some of the common attitudes of the time. Finally, there are the comments by members of the generation of younger writers who were to become the great names of the Victorian Period.

The demand for fairly frequent editions of Sterne's various works continued throughout the period.[3] The edition of *Tristram Shandy*

---

2. *Works of Charles and Mary Lamb,* ed. E. V. Lucas (7 vols. London, Methuen, 1904), *2,* 173. The remarks were first printed in 1822.

3. Reissues of Sterne's *Works* during the period include the following: 4 vols. 1815; 4 vols. 1819; 4 vols. 1823; 6 vols. 1823; 1829 [Lowndes]; 6 vols. 1833; 1839; 1843 [Chicago]; 1847; 1849 [New York]. In addition to the edition with Scott's preface there were the following reprints of *Tristram Shandy:* 1819, Walker's Classics [Lowndes]; 2 vols. 1823 [Allibone]; 2 vols. 1836, Roscoe's Novelist's Library

and the *Sentimental Journey* in 1832 with illustrations by Cruikshank is perhaps the most notable one of the period, outside of Ballantyne's edition with Scott's essay. The separate reprints of the *Sentimental Journey,* so numerous in the preceding period, almost ceased entirely as critics and public alike began to rediscover the excellences of *Tristram Shandy.*

Material about Yorick still found a place in the magazines. John Poole, the minor playwright, wrote an article for the *London Magazine* in 1825 on "Sterne at Calais and Montreuil," retracing the route of his "witty and philosophic predecessor." Poole found that Sterne was "minutely correct in his topography" and concluded that all the incidents in the *Sentimental Journey* had been founded on fact. He discovered, as did other travelers of the period, that French landlords still talked about Sterne and proudly exhibited rooms where he was said to have stayed,[4] though some of them were located in buildings which had not even been constructed until later. Sterne had always been one of Poole's favorite authors, "not for his *sentiment,*" which was "of a questionable character," but for "his wit, his pathos, his philosophy, and his acute and accurate perception and masterly sketching of character."[5]

Sterne must also have been a favorite with W. H. Pyne, who wrote under the pseudonym of Ephraim Hardcastle. In his *Wine and Walnuts,* a collection of literary chitchat published in 1823, the famous figures of the eighteenth century are brought to life again in imaginary conversations and adventures. Sterne figures prominently along with Garrick, Reynolds, Johnson, Hogarth, and many other luminaries both great and small. Pyne even contrives to put Sterne in company with Johnson. Yorick is pictured as "a wicked dog of a parson" and "a wily sinner," surrounded by "a knot of wits"; but he is also referred to as the "sensitive Sterne," the "fabricator of feeling." The character is presented with good humor and gusto and there is no hint of serious censure. Although exaggerated and not always complimentary, the portrait does show an insight into Sterne's temperament with his sudden transitions from sentimental musing to moments of mirth.[6]

[Lowndes] ; 1839, Smith's Standard Library [Lowndes]. The *Sentimental Journey* had the following editions: 1817, Walker's Classics [Lowndes] ; 1833 [Yale] ; 1839 [Lowndes] ; 1841 [Lowndes]. The two latter editions were illustrated with 100 wood-cuts. *Tristram Shandy* and the *Sentimental Journey* were issued together in a two-volume edition in 1823 [Allibone], and the travels were reprinted in a single volume together with *Letters from Yorick to Eliza* and Goethe's *Sorrows of Werter* in 1838 [Yale].

4. See Cyrus Redding, *Fifty Years' Recollections* (2d ed. 3 vols. London, 1858), *1,* 299–300.

5. *London Magazine,* NS, *1* (Jan.–April 1825), 38–46, 387–94.

6. *Wine and Walnuts; or, After Dinner Chit-Chat,* 2 vols. London, 1823. The phrases quoted come from *2,* 187; *1,* 209; *1,* 257; *1,* 88; *2,* 235, respectively. See also *1,* 183–6. It is interesting to note that this book antedates by a year the first volume of

Yorick apparently continued to be considered an old friend by reviewers for the *Monthly,* since casual references to him and to the characters in *Tristram Shandy* appear fairly frequently until nearly 1830.[7] References in the newer reviews, like the *Edinburgh* and the *Quarterly,* are not as common and are usually limited to contexts in which Sterne's work has a direct bearing on the discussion. Nor did the newer reviews demand the same degree of uniformity of opinion from their writers that had been required by the *Critical,* and even more by the *Monthly.* Hence, the comments on Sterne to be found in them are less homogeneous and represent the opinions of individual critics rather than the policy of the magazine.[8] A significant number of critics, however, make references to Sterne, especially during the earlier part of the period under discussion. Writers like Hazlitt and Scott, of course, often refer to Sterne in their essays and reviews for periodicals. In an article for the *Edinburgh* in 1823, Jeffrey praises the character of Uncle Toby, comparing him with Sir Roger de Coverley and the Vicar of Wakefield.[9] Three years later, Jeremy Bentham alludes to a passage in *Tristram Shandy* in an article for the *Westminster Review.*[1] The essays of Thomas Griffiths Wainewright, the grandson of the founder of the *Monthly* who was later to acquire notoriety as a forger and poisoner, also display a thorough acquaintance with Sterne.[2]

Imitations of Sterne by essayists, travelers, and novelists continued in fair numbers, although somewhat sporadically, until nearly 1830. Alexander Chalmers stated in 1816 that Sterne had been "the founder of a school of sentimental writers which may be said still to flourish,"[3] and three years later there appeared *A Sentimental Journey through Margate,* as direct an imitation of the *Sentimental Journey* as any of those of earlier travelers.[4] Pierce Egan also attempted to follow in the footsteps of Sterne and the other great novelists of the eighteenth

Landor's *Imaginary Conversations,* which it distantly resembles. Pyne was a minor painter as well as author.

7. See *Monthly Review,* passim. The *Monthly,* though it declined during this period, continued in publication until 1845. The *Critical* ceased in 1817.

8. Nangle discusses the uniformity of opinion imposed upon the *Monthly* reviewers. The same appears to have been true, though perhaps to a lesser extent, of the *Critical.* The new reviews, though they had broad, general policies, did not expect all their writers to express consistent views about a given author.

9. *Contributions by Jeffrey, 3,* 106. For Jeffrey's earlier remarks, see above, p. 99.

1. *Works of Jeremy Bentham,* ed. John Bowring (11 vols. Edinburgh, 1843), *5,* 416.

2. See *Essays and Criticisms by Thomas Griffiths Wainewright,* ed. W. Carew Hazlitt (London, 1880), pp. 115, 245, 265, 277, 279, 319. Hazlitt's introduction gives biographical details of this amazing critic, connoisseur, and criminal, whose essays were praised by Lamb and William Hazlitt.

3. *General Biographical Dictionary* (London, 1812-17), *28,* 393.

4. *A Sentimental Journey through Margate and Hastings,* London, 1819. Though the book, published by an unknown author under the pseudonym of Dr. Comparative, is a very close imitation of Sterne, there are no direct references to him.

century. In the introductory chapter of his *Life in London,* the story of Jerry Hawthorn and his friend Corinthian Tom which became tremendously popular after its publication in 1821, Egan invokes the shades of Fielding, Smollett, and Sterne, among others. Fielding is described as a "true delineator of HUMAN NATURE," and Smollett is praised for his "touching heartfelt qualities." It is Sterne, however, who is asked to lend Egan some of his "stock of SENSIBILITY," which Egan promises to use after Yorick's "rich felicity." [5]

Reviewers still deplored the inferior quality of most of the imitations of Sterne, the *Monthly* lamenting in 1823 what writers of "no conscience, but much feeling" do "when they get hold of a living dog or a dead jack-ass." [6] Despite the harshness of the reviewers, however, the vogue for sentimental travels was still sufficiently widespread in 1821 for Thomas Hood to consider it worthy of burlesquing in his "Sentimental Journey from Islington to Waterloo Bridge." He starts out resolved to "extract reflections out of a cabbage stump, like sun-beams squeezed out of cucumbers," although he refuses to vent his feelings upon "the first dead dog or lame chicken" he meets with. "I hate the weeping-willow set," he says, "who will cry over their pug dogs and canaries, till they have no tears to spare for the real children of misfortune and misery." He finally decides against being sentimental at all since it is "ridiculous," "useless," and "inconvenient," and he has just remembered that there's a large hole in his pocket handkerchief. [7]

A less playful attack on Sterne's sentimental philosophy came in John Wilson's "Noctes Ambrosianae" in *Blackwood's* in 1831. In one of the dialogues between Christopher North and the Ettrick Shepherd, the latter says:

> A puny, sickly sensibility there is, which is averse frae all the realities of life; and Byron or somebody else spoke well when he said that Sterne preferred whining owre a dead ass to relieving a living mother! But wha was Sterne? As shallow a sentimentalist as ever grat—or rather tried to greet. O, sir! but it's a degrawdin' sicht to humanity, yon—to see the shufflin' sinner tryin' to bring the tears intil his een, by rubbin' the lids wi' the pint o' his pen or wi' the feathers on the shank, and when it a' winna do, takin' refuge in a blank, sae – – – –, or hidin' his head amang a set o' asterisks, sae****; or boltin' aff the printed page a 'thegither, and disappearin' in ae black blotch!

When North tries to argue that "Sterne had genius," the Shepherd flatly denies this and calls the characters of Uncle Toby and Trim

5. *Life in London* (new ed. London, 1900), pp. 32–3.
6. *Monthly Review,* 2d Ser., *102* (Nov. 1823), 270.
7. *Works of Thomas Hood,* ed. "by his son and daughter" [Thomas Hood Jr. and F. F. Broderip] (10 vols. London, 1871), *4,* 354–72.

"fantastic phantoms." The Shepherd continues that his own theory of the social affections was never so refined as to prevent his practicing them, although it was in reality refined "far beyond the reach o' sic a meeserable deevil as Lowry Sterne." [8]

Many of the standard biographical dictionaries of the time painted a similar picture of Sterne as "a miserable devil," and this same impression was conveyed by various anecdotes which continued to be circulated during the period. Henry Fox, afterwards Lord Holland, entered in his journal in 1819 the notation that "Sterne has left a bad name behind him in Yorkshire"; [9] and in Northcote's *Life of Reynolds* Sterne is said to have met a lady at Sir Joshua's table who upbraided him so strenuously for his immorality "that his death was considerably hastened in consequence of it." [1]

Compilers of biographical dictionaries, often drawing upon anecdotes of this sort and upon the unfavorable accounts of Sterne in previous sources, continued to present unflattering pictures of his personal character and to lament the seeming disparity between his benevolent philosophy and his conduct. The calumnies about Sterne's mistreatment of his mother, which had been circulated at the turn of the century under the authority of Horace Walpole's name, received fresh impetus when Byron's *Journals* were published in 1830.[2] Other writers quoted the unfavorable estimates which had appeared in the essays of Vicesimus Knox and the *Encyclopaedia Britannica*.[3] The *Britannica* itself continued to print, unchanged, the disparaging remarks of 1797 in all subsequent editions until that of 1842; and then, in the seventh edition, even harsher censure was given. Sterne's plagiarisms from Burton and Swift are more strongly emphasized, although Sterne is said to differ from Swift in having "set up for a lover of his species" in order "to make room for his pathos." But since "his philanthropy did not extend so far as to his own mother," the writer concludes, his "sensibility is worthy only of ridicule." [4] As the biographical compilers continued to copy from previous sources and from each other, hardly one of them failed to include strong censures of Sterne's private character, and they

8. "Noctes Ambrosianae, No. 53," *Blackwood's Magazine, 29* (Jan. 1831), 19–22. The reprint of the *Noctes* in book form went through several editions.

9. *Journal of the Honourable Henry Edward Fox,* ed. Earl of Ilchester (London, T. Butterworth, 1923), p. 29.

1. James Northcote, *Life of Sir Joshua Reynolds* (2d ed. 2 vols. London, 1819), *1*, 105. (The first American edition, Philadelphia, 1817, does not contain this anecdote.) Allan Cunningham repeated the story in *Lives of the Most Eminent British Painters and Sculptors* (3 vols. New York, 1831), *1*, 223–4.

2. The *Journals* had several editions in the thirties.

3. See, e.g., James Harrison, *Biographical Cabinet,* 2 vols. London, 1823.

4. *Encyclopaedia Britannica* (7th ed. Edinburgh, 1842), *20*, 721–2. The article is unsigned but may have been written by Dr. James Browne who is said to have compiled many of the biographies for this edition (see its preface). For more favorable comments on Sterne in this same edition see below, p. 137.

often also included some of the clichés about the immorality of his work.[5]

Moralists took up the same tune. A writer in the *Christian Observer* in 1817 dismissed Sterne, along with Fielding and Smollett, "as registered in the *index expurgatorius* even of accommodating moralists, and to be found . . . in no decent family." [6] Other writers over the course of the next few years refer to *Tristram Shandy* as a "contemptible, nauseous, and obscene rhapsody" [7] and revive the charge that Sterne's work gives too many clues "to the inner shrine in the foul labyrinth" of human passions.[8] The *Sentimental Journey* is often thought of now as "more immoral in its tendencies" than *Tristram Shandy*. "At the gross incidents of the latter we laugh," a writer said in the *Retrospective Review,* "and the virgin would blush; and with the laugh and the blush the joke passes away; but the garnished looseness of principle, and refined impurity of the other, steal into the imagination, and endanger the moral principle in proportion as we neither blush nor laugh." [9] A reviewer in *Fraser's Magazine* probably also spoke for a fairly large portion of the public when he asserted that "Swift and Fielding, Smollett and Sterne, are not according to the refined notions of the present generation. They might have a partial sale," he continued, "if it were possible to emasculate the productions of those witty writers, as Mr. Bowdler has done for Shakespeare: but this is out of the question." [1]

These unsatisfactory accounts of Sterne by encyclopedists, compilers of biography, and moralists were at least partially counterbalanced by some of the minor critics and literary historians of the time. Whereas the former group, often no doubt reflecting the impetus of the evangelical movement, usually concentrated on biography and contented themselves with a few clichés of literary criticism, the latter

5. The following are typical in their strictures on Sterne's life and works: *Historic Gallery of Portraits and Paintings and Biographical Review,* London, 1819; *Biographical Cabinet,* ed. James Harrison, 2 vols. London, 1823; *General Biographical Dictionary,* ed. John Gorton, 2 vols. London, 1828; *Edinburgh Encyclopaedia,* ed. David Brewster, Edinburgh, 1830; *General Biographical Dictionary,* ed. E[dmund] Bellchambers, 4 vols. London, 1835 (a copy in New York Public Library); *Anecdotes of Books and Authors* (London, 1836), p. 170; *Universal Biography,* ed. William à Beckett, Jr., 3 vols. London, 1836; *Biographical Treasury,* ed. Samuel Maunder, London, 1851 (1st ed. 1838).

6. *Christian Observer, 16* (June 1817), 372.

7. John Taylor, *Records of My Life* (2 vols. London, 1832), *1,* 62–3. It is rather curious that Taylor, who is said to have "consorted with all the convivial spirits of the day" (*DNB*), should express such strong antipathy.

8. "Gallery of Illustrious Irishmen—No. 6, Lawrence Sterne," *Dublin University Magazine, 8* (Sept. 1836), 247–63. Mixed with the censures are some fairly perceptive comments on Sterne's genius by this unknown author.

9. *Retrospective Review, 9,* Pt. I (1824), 205. Cf. *Gentleman's Magazine, 97* (20th of new series), Pt. II (Sup. July–Dec. 1827), 601–2.

1. *Fraser's Magazine, 4* (Aug. 1831), 11.

usually looked first at Sterne's work, and at his private character second, if at all. The result was a much more favorable picture of Yorick, especially during the latter part of the period in question, when the dicta of the great critics of the Romantic Age became more generally known.

The "history of literature," practically unknown before this time, began to achieve popularity and to take its place as an accepted authority beside the biographical dictionaries and encyclopedias. Among the earliest of the books of this type is John Dunlop's *History of Fiction,* first published in 1814. Though it contains no extended discussion of Sterne, a casual reference to *Tristram Shandy* shows Dunlop's appreciation of the book. While nothing can be "more irregular," he says, a man of genius may "produce an interesting composition in defiance of the laws of criticism, while one without talent will compose a work by rule" which is "lifeless and insignificant." [2] John Duncan, whose *Essay on Genius* was published six years later, also admitted that "the admirers of irregularity will find disorder and minuteness in sufficiency" in Sterne, but insisted that he also shows "considerable judgment" and gives many general principles "with accuracy." In the pathetic, he says, "Sterne is excelled by no writer, ancient or modern." [3]

Though Duncan had not done much more than repeat the cliché about Sterne's mastery in the pathetic, critics during the thirties more often leavened their clichés with some of the new insights of Hazlitt, Scott, and Coleridge. Though they might feel called upon to deplore Sterne's private conduct, they nevertheless placed more importance on the distinctive elements of Sterne's genius. An unidentified reviewer, writing in *Blackwood's* in 1835 is typical:

> Sterne was a man of genius, but a sad sinner. Strange that nature should sometimes be so kind to men who have no hearts! But let us not say he had no heart; he had a heart, and a good one—though no man save himself knew how he had corrupted it. Not otherwise could he have imagined my Father—and my Uncle Toby—and Corporal Trim. They had all hearts, and how have they touched ours! No phantoms they—flesh and blood like ourselves—but we pass away—they endure for ever—we are the phantoms. Peace then be with Lawrence—and may all his sins have been forgiven —as may ours be who had not his genius to consecrate or profane. [4]

2. *History of Fiction* (2d ed. 3 vols. Edinburgh, 1816), *1,* 21–2.
3. *An Essay on Genius, or the Philosophy of Literature* (London, 1820), pp. 78–80. There is a copy of this book in the University of Michigan Library. Duncan continues by censuring Dr. Johnson as "a man of no ability" in telling a story, since "he possessed so much judgment as to leave no room in his mind for what is called genius" (p. 81).
4. *Blackwood's Magazine, 38* (Aug. 1835), 271.

Praise of the same sort is given by Robert Chambers, another of the literary historians, who published his *History of the English Language and Literature* the same year, and expanded this work into a *Cyclopaedia of English Literature,* which appeared in 1844. In the earlier book he quotes the praise of his friend Sir Walter Scott in regard to the characters of Uncle Toby and Trim; [5] while in the later one he quotes Coleridge's remarks on the characters in *Tristram Shandy,* asserting that they "will go down to posterity with the kindred creations of Cervantes." He believes that Sterne is still read mainly for "passages of pure sentiment," however, since his indecencies "startle the prudish and correct." [6]

Isaac D'Israeli, a more random literary historian whose ties were further in the past, included an essay on Sterne in his *Miscellanies of Literature,* which appeared in 1840. He begins the essay with the assertion that "CERVANTES is immortal," while "RABELAIS and STERNE have passed away to the curious," although he admits that the latter two "were not perhaps inferior in genius." Recalling the popularity of *Tristram Shandy* during his youth, he says that "forty years ago, young men, in their most facetious humours, never failed to find the archetype of society in the Shandy family—every good-natured soul was uncle Toby, every humourist was old Shandy, every child of nature was Corporal Trim! It may now be doubted," he continues, "whether Sterne's natural dispositions were the humorous or the pathetic: the pathetic has survived." [7] D'Israeli then repeats some unreliable anecdotes which are to Sterne's discredit, but elsewhere in his *Miscellanies* he praises the charm of his work, since "he interests us in his minutest emotions, for he tells us all he feels." [8]

Few among these minor critics were more enthusiastic admirers of Sterne than David L. Richardson, whose *Literary Leaves,* published the same year that D'Israeli's *Miscellanies* appeared, contained an essay comparing the four great humorous characters of Falstaff, Don Quixote, Sir Roger de Coverley, and Uncle Toby. These characters are no mere "shadowy shapes" but "as distinct to our apprehension as living

---

5. *History of the English Language and Literature* (Hartford, 1837; 1st ed. London, 1835), p. 165.

6. *Cyclopaedia of English Literature* (2 vols. Edinburgh, 1844), *2,* 171.

7. D'Israeli's comment is somewhat misleading, since at the turn of the century *Beauties of Sterne* and Ferriar's *Illustrations* had both helped to put Sterne's pathetic side in the ascendancy with the critics, although writers like Hazlitt, Scott, and Southey grew up preferring *Tristram Shandy.* In 1840 *Tristram Shandy* was widely preferred to the *Sentimental Journey,* although it may have been the pathetic rather than the humorous parts of *Shandy* which had the widest appeal. D'Israeli's comment is most significant in indicating the decline in the number of Sterne's audience.

8. *Miscellanies of Literature* (new rev. ed. London, 1840), pp. 4, 25–8. D'Israeli's essay served as introduction to five of Yorick's letters to Miss Fourmantel which he was publishing for the first time. There is a copy of this edition in the University of Michigan Library.

creatures, and have an individuality founded upon general nature that renders them equally intelligible and pleasing to all times and nations." He quotes Hazlitt's apostrophe to Uncle Toby as "one of the finest compliments ever paid to human nature," and concludes that had Uncle Toby's "head been equal to his heart, he would have been almost like a god; but it is by no means certain that we should have loved him better." [9]

The discussion of Sterne in the article on "Romance" by George Moir in the 1842 edition of the *Britannica* also praises Sterne's characters. "The clue which Sterne chiefly follows through the mazes of character, is humour," he says, and like Fielding he preferred the humour which arises from bringing out "the secrets of character" by "light and happy touches." In Sterne, however, "the humour is steeped in sensibility," and hence "humour and feeling heighten and set off each other; the pathetic rises in gentle relief out of the background of the comic, and sinks gracefully and imperceptibly back into it again." [1] William Benton Clulow likewise praises Sterne's "not unfrequent mixture of gaiety and penetration" in his *Aphorisms and Reflections,* published the next year. He also defends Yorick from the charges of the moralists, saying that "a heart capable of *conceiving* such a character as Uncle Toby . . . could not have been without stamina essentially estimable." [2]

George L. Craik, the best known of the literary historians of the time, gives even stronger praise. Sterne is to be compared only with Shakespeare and Cervantes in his mastery of humor, for "it would be difficult to name any writer but one of these two who could have drawn Uncle Toby or Trim." Craik continues by correcting a common mistake among those critics who assert "that the mass of what he has written consists of little better than nonsense or rubbish—that his beauties are but grains of gold glittering here and there in a heap of sand." Craik believes that "of no writer could this be said with less correctness," since Sterne's language, descriptions, and characters are "wrought with the utmost care, and to the highest polish and perfection." The "immortal author" of *Tristram Shandy,* he concludes, possesses "the finest spirit of whim" among all the novelists.[3]

9. *Literary Leaves* (2d ed. 2 vols. London, 1840), *2*, 211–33. This essay appeared for the first time in the second edition. Elsewhere Richardson refers to Sterne's supposed neglect of his mother (*2*, 93), but it has not at all affected his estimate of Sterne's work.

1. *Encyclopaedia Britannica* (1842), *19*, 339–40. Moir also quotes Coleridge and Scott on Sterne.

2. *Aphorisms and Reflections* (London, 1843), p. 71. Clulow, a dissenting minister in Devonshire, also refers to Sterne on pp. 2, 35, 189, 256, 284, 410, 461.

3. *Sketches of the History of Literature and Learning in England* (6 vols. in 3, London, 1844–45), *5*, 158–60. The discussion of Sterne is reprinted without change in Craik's *Compendious History of English Literature* (2 vols. London, 1861), *2*, 281–2. Craik was professor of history and English literature at Queen's College, Belfast,

Craik's literary associate, Charles Knight, was more reserved in his praise, although the *Penny Cyclopaedia,* printed under his supervision, was one of the few books of its class to take a fairly favorable view of Sterne's character. It likewise praises his literary abilities, comparing his characters to those of Shakespeare and stating that "the art of arts, the *ars celare artem,* never was possessed in a higher degree by any writer than by Sterne." [4] In a prefatory essay in one of Knight's own anthologies, published in 1847, similar excellences are allowed to Sterne, although he believes that his licentiousness has condemned him "to comparative neglect." If the pruriences could be "weeded" from *Tristram Shandy,* he concludes, "there are few creations of original talent more capable of calling forth the highest and best feelings of our nature." [5]

If these statements by minor critics and literary historians are placed beside the comments of the minor critics during the early years of the century, several significant differences become apparent. Though many of the later writers continue to deplore Sterne's personal character, they are less apt to let this influence their estimates of his work. Often they even take the tenderness to be found in Sterne's handling of character and incident as proof of his essential goodness of heart. As the judgments of Hazlitt, Coleridge, and Scott come to have more and more influence, less is said about Sterne's plagiarism, and the preference for *Tristram Shandy* over the *Sentimental Journey* becomes almost as universal as the opposite preference for Yorick's travels had been during the early part of the century. Finally, the numerous remarks on Sterne show that critics still considered him an important figure.

Hence, it is not surprising to find that Bulwer, Dickens, and Thackeray, the three most prominent novelists of the new literary generation which appeared on the scene during the thirties and forties, all knew Sterne's work thoroughly. As early as 1832, Bulwer defends Sterne's character in his series of essays which was published under the title of *The Student.* In the tender parts of his work, Bulwer says, Sterne was not "belying his real nature," but "truthfully expressing the gentlest part of it." If a contrast "between act and sentiment" did exist, we should lament it rather than scoff at it, since "the dark caverns of the human heart" are infinitely complex. In another essay in the same series he classes Sterne among the great poets, men who have expressed

and the friend of Carlyle, John Forster, and Leigh Hunt. The *Compendious History* had reached a ninth edition by 1883.

4. *Penny Cyclopaedia of the Society for the Diffusion of Useful Knowledge* (London, 1842), *23,* 44–6. The article concludes with the statement that *Tristram Shandy* is Sterne's greatest work, although the *Sentimental Journey* is more popular among foreigners and also "among some English women."

5. *Half-Hours with the Best Authors* (4 vols. New York, 1848; 1st ed. London, 1847), *2,* 347.

"truth through fiction, by the creation of images which never existed, or the narrative of events which never happened," sometimes dispensing "with the mechanism of verse." [6] A few years later in his essay "On Art in Fiction," he praises the mixture of humor and sentiment in the characters of Uncle Toby and Don Quixote.[7]

Dickens counted Sterne, together with Fielding and Smollett, among his lifelong favorite authors. No one "read them younger," he said; and he continued to read them, for he "gradually grew up into a different knowledge of them." [8] If we may believe that the narrator in one of Dickens' later stories is speaking for the author, he knew "every word" of the *Sentimental Journey*.[9] Reviews of Dickens' early work sometimes called attention to his resemblance to the three eighteenth-century novelists who were his favorites,[1] and both the *Sketches by Boz* and *Pickwick Papers* contain allusions to Sterne. In the latter work, Sam Weller elaborates one of his delightful theories: "No man never see a dead donkey, 'cept the gen'l'm'n in the black silk smalls as know'd the young 'ooman as kep a goat; and that wos a French donkey, so wery likely he warn't wun o' the reg'lar breed." [2] Dickens may also very well have had Sterne in mind when he penned the preface to the first edition of *Pickwick* in 1837 and said that if it was objected that his book was "a mere series of adventures, in which the scenes are ever changing, and the characters come and go like the men and women we encounter in the real world," he could only reply that "the same objection has been made to the works of some of the greatest novelists in the English language." [3] Nearly ten years later Dickens carried *Tristram Shandy* with him on his trip to Europe. When he was at Lausanne and

6. *Miscellaneous Prose Works* (3 vols. London, 1868), *2*, 6–7, 316–7. For Bulwer's later more extended discussion see below, pp. 169–70.

7. *Monthly Chronicle, 1* (March 1838), 51.

8. *Works of Charles Dickens: Letters,* ed. Walter Dexter (3 vols. Bloomsbury, Nonesuch Press, 1938), *2*, 52. (The Nonesuch Press edition of Dickens' *Works* was issued in twenty-three unnumbered volumes, 1937–38. Subsequent references are to this edition under the individual titles.) Another prominent novelist of this period also read Sterne early in life. See John Coleman, *Charles Reade As I Knew Him* (London, Treherne, 1903), p. 37.

9. "The Holly-Tree," in *Mystery of Edwin Drood. Christmas Stories,* p. 315. "The Holly-Tree" appeared originally in 1855.

1. In reviewing *Pickwick,* the *Monthly, 1* (Feb. 1837), 153, said that Dickens was sometimes compared with Smollett, Sterne, and Fielding. William Carleton, the minor Irish novelist, said many years later that "the character of Pickwick is a compound of Uncle Toby and the Vicar of Wakefield." David J. O'Donoghue, *Life of William Carleton,* ed. Mrs. Cashel Hoey (2 vols. London, 1896), *2*, 158.

2. *Pickwick Papers,* p. 712 (ch. 51). As Percy Fitzgerald points out in *Pickwickian Dictionary and Cyclopaedia* (London, P. Fitzgerald and W. H. Spencer, [1900]), p. 274, Sam "was not likely to have read the work, but the incidents were the subject of popular stippled prints of oval shape by Wheatley, and he must have often seen them in shop windows." For another allusion see *Sketches by Boz and Early Minor Works,* p. 61.

3. *Pickwick Papers,* p. xv.

about to begin *Dombey and Son,* he picked the book at random, looking for an omen, and opened to Sterne's words, "What a work it is likely to turn out! Let us begin it!" [4]

Thackeray, too, must have read Sterne in his youth. There is an allusion to *Tristram Shandy* in the *Irish Sketch Book,* written during 1842; [5] and the same year he made a reference in one of his magazine articles which shows that he even knew the background of the French translation of the *Sentimental Journey.*[6] Thackeray also seems to have felt that Sterne's theory of humor agreed with his own. In a review in 1847 which partially echoed the earlier remarks of Carlyle, he wrote: "Love is the humourist's best characteristic, and gives that charming ring to their laughter in which all the good-natured world joins in chorus," and cited as illustrations "the tender Jean Paul, Sterne, and Scott." [7] Two years later he imitated Sterne's manner in a letter to Mrs. Jane Brookfield written from Paris: "I fancy the old streetsweeper at the corner is holding the cab, I take my hat and stick. I say Goodbye again—the door bangs finally. Here's a shilling for you old street- sweeper— The cab trots solitary into the Park—Je fais de la littérature ma parole d'honneur—du style—du Sterne tout pur— O vanitas van- itatum!" [8] The hint of affectation is significant, for though he might speak of "the tender Sterne," Thackeray appears to have always had a low opinion of Sterne's sincerity. As early as 1842 he wrote: "Look what a sentimental man Sterne was, ditto Coleridge who would have sent his children to the poor house—by Jove, they are a contemptible, impracticable selfish race, Titmarsh included and without any affecta- tion: Depend upon it," he continues, "a good honest kindly man not cursed by a genius, that doesn't prate about his affections, and cries very little, & loves his home—he is the real man to go through the world with." [9] Like Byron, who considered himself "as bad as that dog Sterne," [1] Thackeray tended to identify his own faults with those he supposed to be Sterne's, for Titmarsh himself was included in the "contemptible, impracticable selfish race" of false sentimentalists. The results of this penchant may be seen in the pronouncements on Sterne

4. *Letters, 1,* 760.

5. *Paris Sketch Book and Irish Sketch Book* in *Works of Thackeray,* Harry Furniss Centenary Ed. (London, Macmillan, 1911), p. 492. (This edition of Thackeray's *Works,* to which subsequent references are made under individual titles, was issued in twenty unnumbered volumes.)

6. *Critical Papers in Literature,* pp. 222–3.

7. Ibid., p. 388.

8. *Letters and Private Papers of William Makepeace Thackeray,* ed. Gordon N. Ray (4 vols. Cambridge, Harvard Univ. Press, 1945–46), *2,* 583–4. For a discussion of Thackeray's relationship with Mrs. Brookfield, which parallels that of Sterne with Eliza in some ways, see J. Y. T. Greig, *Thackeray: A Reconsideration* (London, Ox- ford Univ. Press, 1950), pp. 141–53.

9. *Letters and Private Papers, 2,* 53.

1. See above, p. 90.

in Thackeray's famous lecture (to be considered in the next chapter), which even today tends to obscure the attitude both of Thackeray and of his age toward Sterne.

During the thirties and forties, however, the interest in Sterne among the early Victorians seemed to bode well for his future reputation; and the famous statements by the leading figures among the Romantics had raised him to a higher place among serious critics than he had ever held before. In the thirty-five years from 1780 to 1815, Sterne had been appreciated mainly for the *Sentimental Journey* and for his sentimental side; but the excesses of his imitators, the suspicions of insincerity and affectation in Yorick's own work, the charges of plagiarism, and the strictures on his personal character were gradually lowering his reputation in the early years of the nineteenth century, at the same time that the evangelical movement was helping to bring about a sharp change in public taste. The thirty-five years between 1815 and 1850 saw the balance restored, with the rediscovery of the excellences of *Tristram Shandy*. Hazlitt, Coleridge, and Scott had helped to place Sterne in a more prominent position with the critics than he had previously held; and as their pronouncements became famous, they had an influence on subsequent critics of lesser stature, who often tempered the old clichés about Sterne with some of the fresh insights afforded by these three major writers. Among the lesser writers of the period, some see conscious artistry, rather than merely disorder and irregularity in Sterne; and most make distinctions between his work and his private character. Though they may censure his indecency, they are also able to see the true humor of the characters in *Tristram Shandy* and to appreciate Sterne's knowledge of human nature.

At the same time, it must be admitted that Sterne probably had fewer readers in 1850 than he had had in 1815, for one need look no further than the record of the editions of his work to see that the public in general were not buying it as eagerly as they once had. This is, in part, a natural historical process, and one which the other great novelists of the eighteenth century were also experiencing, in general to a more marked degree than Sterne.[2] But many readers still found delight in his pages; and the critics had placed him among the classics of English literature, a position which he was never really to lose.

Thus Leigh Hunt's favorable estimate of Sterne in 1846 is not an isolated phenomenon, but rather an indication of the critical sentiment of the time; for the remarks in his "Essay on Wit and Humour" are truly representative of the high position that Sterne had achieved with

2. See Blanchard, pp. 368–407, *passim*, and Boege, pp. 95–110, *passim*, esp. p. 106, in which he states that "the number of Smollett's admirers thinned out rapidly during these years." See also *CBEL* for editions of the works of Richardson, Fielding, and Smollett during this period. Of the three, Smollett appears to have had the most editions, though no more than Sterne.

the critics during this period. Hunt defines humor in the way that Coleridge and Hazlitt had, as the result of incongruities of character and circumstance. "Exquisite Uncle Toby" is "the prince of them all" when it comes to characters of this type. He is the "quintessence of the milk of human kindness," and the "high and only final Christian gentleman," [3] unrivaled in the characters of Shakespeare himself. "As long as the character of Toby Shandy finds an echo in the heart of man," Hunt continues, "the heart of man is noble."

Hunt goes on to quote passages from *Tristram Shandy* illustrating Sterne's moral value and his deep knowledge of human nature. He is described as "Rabelais, reborn at a riper period of the world, and gifted with sentiment." To accuse him of "cant and sentimentality," Hunt continues, "is itself a cant or an ignorance," or in any case "but to misjudge him from an excess of manner here and there. The matter always contains the solidest substance of truth and duty." Though Sterne's occasional coarseness is to be regretted, even among some of the passages "which are supposed to be connected with that coarseness, but really are not so, are some which are yet destined to be of important service to mankind; and if I were requested to name the book of all others, which combined Wit and Humour under their highest appearance of levity with the profoundest wisdom," Hunt concludes, "it would be *Tristram Shandy.*" [4] The revaluations by Hazlitt, Coleridge, Scott, and the other leading figures of their age had indeed borne fruit, and had set the tone for almost unanimous acceptance of Sterne as a classic by serious critics.

3. Cf. Charles R. Leslie's statement: "Uncle Toby is the most perfect specimen of a Christian gentleman that ever existed, for I don't like to doubt that he existed. Sir Charles Grandison is not to be compared to him." *Autobiographical Recollections,* ed. Tom Taylor (Boston, 1860), p. 318. Leslie, a minor artist, did two illustrations for Sterne's work; see pp. 289, 293, 297.

4. *Wit and Humour,* pp. 11–12, 68–72. Hunt also praises Sterne in his *Men, Women and Books* (new ed. London, 1870; 1st ed. 1847), pp. 57–61; and mentions him in his *Autobiography,* ed. Roger Ingpen (2 vols. Westminster, A. Constable, 1903; 1st ed. 1850), *2,* 21, 88, 158, 163.

6

Mountebank or Genius? (1851–68)

WHEN Henry Crabb Robinson picked up his copy of the *Edinburgh Review* in 1815 and read Hazlitt's article on the great novelists, he commented that the "strictures on Sterne are less pointed" than those on the other novelists.[1] More than thirty-five years later when he heard Thackeray's lecture on Sterne and Goldsmith, he was even less enthusiastic, for he described the lecture in these words: "Sterne in rather a canting style abused for his impurity, and Goldsmith [praised] for his goodness. . . . On the whole the matter not sterling, but the form graceful."[2] Robinson's comments are not particularly noteworthy in themselves; but they do point up the fact that within a single generation the attitudes of the age toward Sterne changed twice. Just as Hazlitt had been the forerunner of a new sympathy and understanding in the approach of critics during the Romantic Age, Thackeray likewise set in motion a new train of critical comments from the Victorians. Though the pronouncements of Thackeray have not had the lasting effect that those of Hazlitt, Coleridge, and Scott have had, they nevertheless have had to be reckoned with by subsequent critics, and their violently unfavorable tone has often tended to obscure the real attitude of the age toward Sterne.

Thackeray's *Lectures on the English Humourists,* first delivered in 1851, were quite different from the earlier lectures of Hazlitt and Coleridge, or those of Carlyle. In the first place, they were important social events, which were attended by the élite and rivaled even the Great Exhibition in interest. They were given in the fashionable Willis' Rooms, an impressive setting with its gilded walls and blue damask sofas. "Duchesses were there by the score," as Charlotte Brontë wrote after attending the first lecture.[3] So were such literary notables as Dickens, Carlyle, and Harriet Martineau; and neither Macaulay

---

1. *Diary, Reminiscences, and Correspondence,* ed. Thomas Sadler (3 vols. London, 1869), *1,* 480. Robinson's own opinion of Sterne was that "posterity will rank Lamb with Sterne in genius & taste," though "in moral worth [Lamb] rises infinitely above." *Letters of Charles Lamb, 3,* 346.

2. *Henry Crabb Robinson on Books and their Writers,* ed. Edith J. Morley (3 vols. London, J. M. Dent, 1938), *2,* 715.

3. *The Brontës. Their Lives, Friendships and Correspondence,* ed. T. J. Wise and J. A. Symington, Shakespeare Head Ed. (4 vols. Oxford, Blackwell, 1932), *3,* 239.

nor Hallam missed a single lecture.[4] Thackeray indeed "took the town by storm" and became the literary lion of the season just as Sterne had done some ninety years earlier.[5] But the town had changed and it is not surprising that Thackeray was somewhat carried away by his audience and decided, as Blanchard says, that "there would be no harm . . . in deepening the lights and shadows of the portraits in his Humourists."[6] As he must have known, the audience had come as much out of an interest in Thackeray himself as in his subject. James Hannay said a few years later: "Everybody was delighted to see the great masters of English of a past age brought to life again in their habits as they lived, and endowed with the warm human reality of the lecturer's Dobbins, and Warringtons, and Pendennises. It was this power, and not the literary criticism, which constituted the value of Thackeray's lectures."[7] Thackeray doubtless sensed that this sort of performance was expected of him, and in the very first sentence of his first lecture he says that he will speak "of the men and of their lives, rather than of their books."[8]

This plan for the lectures led to especially unfortunate results in the case of Sterne, who was treated, along with Goldsmith, in the last of the series on July 3, 1851. Partly through inaccurate biographical data, partly through misinterpretation of the facts which he had, and partly through a lack of personal sympathy with the supposed shortcomings of his subject, Thackeray denounced Sterne's personal character more sweepingly than any of his previous critics had. Having arrived at this unfavorable estimate of Sterne the man, he then went against his avowed intention and applied it to Sterne the author as well.

Thackeray has two main charges to make against Sterne's character: hypocrisy and licentiousness. Concentrating mainly on the last few years of Yorick's life, he censures his philanderings and accuses him of neglecting his wife merely because he had become bored with her. He then goes on to charge him with being insincere even in his avowal of admiration for Mrs. Draper. While writing affectionately to Eliza, "the wretched worn-out old scamp was paying his addresses" to other women.[9] The next year, Thackeray continues, "having come back to

4. *Works: English Humourists of the Eighteenth Century*, p. vii. The *Lectures on the Humourists* were first published in 1853 and reprinted in 1858 and 1866.

5. See George Barnett Smith, *Poets and Novelists* (London, 1875), p. 36.

6. Blanchard, p. 408.

7. *Characters and Criticisms* (Edinburgh, 1865), p. 55.

8. "Swift," *Humourists*, p. 1.

9. Thackeray's scorn was probably intensified by the fact that he had seen the unpublished manuscript of the *Journal to Eliza,* which seemed to prove that Sterne had written a pathetic passage to Eliza, claiming that he was "dying," the same day that he also wrote to Lady Percy, requesting an assignation. See *Letters and Private Papers, 2,* 799–800. Actually he was mistaken as to the date of the letter to Lady Percy, as Cross has demonstrated in *Works: Letters and Miscellanies, 2,* 82n. Thackeray did not refer

his lodgings in Bond-street, with his *Sentimental Journey* to launch upon the town, eager as ever for praise and pleasure; as vain, as wicked, as witty, as false as he had ever been, death at length seized the feeble wretch." Throughout a life in which he showed himself "as genuine as . . . Joseph Surface," his sole redeeming trait was his real affection for his daughter. The impurity of his mind is evidenced by his works, for "there is not a page in Sterne's writing but has something that were better away, a latent corruption—a hint, as of an impure presence."

The insincerity, hypocrisy, and immorality which Thackeray believes to be the fundamental traits of Sterne's personal character likewise become his main basis for judging his work. In "a hundred pages" of Sterne's books Thackeray finds beauty, "genuine love and kindness"; but the rest is false. It is difficult, he admits, to separate the two: "How much was deliberate calculation and imposture—how much was false sensibility—and how much true feeling—where did the lie begin, and did he know where? and where did the truth end in the art and scheme of this man of genius, this actor, this quack?" In partial answer to these questions, he speculates that Sterne "used to blubber perpetually in his study," and finding his tears brought him popularity, "he exercised the lucrative gift of weeping" on every occasion. But Thackeray doesn't "value or respect much the cheap dribble of those fountains," for he feels that Sterne is constantly posturing. "The humour of Swift and Rabelais," he says, "poured from them as naturally as song does from a bird," but Sterne "never lets his reader alone." To rouse the reader he "turns over head and heels, or sidles up and whispers a nasty story. The man is a great jester, not a great humourist," Thackeray concludes.

Not all of Sterne is false, however, for Thackeray draws sharp distinctions between various of the scenes in his works. He differentiates between the episode with the donkey in the *Sentimental Journey*, which he characterizes as the trick of a literary mountebank, and the episode of the ass and the artichoke in *Tristram Shandy*, which he believes to be a "charming description" with "wit, humour, pathos, a kind nature speaking, and a real sentiment." [1] The country dance at Languedoc is likewise worthy of praise. Nevertheless, he weights the scales heavily on the side of Sterne's faults, and it is the picture of the mountebank and the "impure presence" which remains uppermost. He is especially shocked, as he says in a letter written a few months after the lecture, at Sterne's "blasphemy" and "scornful unbelief." Any man *"except a parson"* is welcome to his own beliefs, but Sterne and Swift are "a

---

to the *Journal to Eliza* in the lecture, but later mentioned it in "A Roundabout Journey" in 1860.

1. Contrasts of this same kind are developed in the lecture on "Charity and Humour," which he gave in 1853 during his American tour, when he repeated the lectures on the *Humourists*. See pp. 195-6.

couple of traitors and renegades." [2] Nor may Sterne be excused on the plea that he was merely reflecting his age, for "some of that dreary *double entendre* may be attributed to freer times and manners than ours, but not all. The foul Satyr's eyes leer out of the leaves constantly," Thackeray says. When he thinks of writers like Sterne he is "grateful for the innocent laughter and the sweet and unsullied page which the author of David Copperfield gives to my children." [3] Drama and contrast indeed played an outstanding part in the lecture, to the exclusion of truth and candor.

Thackeray's censures of Sterne's immorality were probably to be expected from his own nature and that of his audience, but the virulence of his attack needs further explanation. Later critics often thought it strange that he should have so roundly abused an author to whom he was indebted for some elements in his own literary style,[4] and many of them pointed out resemblances between the two writers in their personalities as well as in their literary qualities. Carlyle is reported to have said that Thackeray had "a dash of Sterne" among his "many gifts and qualities." [5] Harriet Martineau noted an element in his character which he had censured Sterne for, when she spoke of "his frittered life, and his obedience to the call of the great." [6] William Roscoe may well have come close to the mark when he said that Thackeray's "hatred and contempt for Sterne [are] all the greater because he is conscious of a concealed thread of this same sentimentality running through his own nature." [7] Thackeray's own statements show that he sometimes identified himself with Sterne. Two years after the lectures, when he was traveling in France, he stayed in "Sterne's Room" at Dessein's Hotel. Writing to his friends, the George Baxters, he says: "Sterne's picture is looking down on me from the chimney piece at w^h he warmed his lean old shanks ninety years ago. He seems to say 'You are right. I *was* a humbug: and you, my lad, are you not as great?' Come, come Mr Sterne none of these tu quoques." [8] Many years earlier he had written in the flyleaf of his copy of the *Sentimental Journey*:

2. *Letters and Private Papers, 2,* 800.

3. *Humourists,* pp. 160–73.

4. At the time of Thackeray's death, the *Saturday Review* commented on the harshness of his view of the eighteenth century, expressing surprise that he had substituted "irrelevant criticism on the faulty life of Sterne" for "due recognition" of a genius which he might have been expected to appreciate and which was "even higher than his own"; *17* (Jan. 2, 1864), 10. For Thackeray's relations with the *Saturday Review,* see below, pp. 147–8.

5. *Table Talk* (Liverpool, 1890), p. 33.

6. *Harriet Martineau's Autobiography,* ed. Maria W. Chapman (2 vols. Boston, 1877), *2,* 61.

7. *Poems and Essays,* ed. Richard H. Hutton (2 vols. London, 1860), *2,* 275. The remarks appeared originally in Roscoe's review of the *Lectures on the English Humourists* in *The Inquirer.*

8. *Letters and Private Papers, 3,* 281. For similar instances see *3,* 153, 165, 284.

Sterne! thou great man of Genius, why wert thou so great a fool?
Why so dissipated?
My dear Willie
      You should take warning but [sic] this man's latter life, and
end. He was a great man. You have the stuff in you, to make
yourself great. Think over these words, my Lad,—think over
them.

W M Thackeray [9]

In dealing out the harsh censures to Sterne, he apparently felt that
he was fighting an undesirable trait in his own nature at the same time.
      The personal involvement in Thackeray's antipathy to Sterne is even
more apparent in his remarks a decade later in *Roundabout Papers*.
The first mention of Yorick in this series of essays was precipitated by
an unflattering comment on Thackeray in an article on "Sentimental
Writing" in the *Saturday Review*. The unknown writer contrasts
modern sentimentalism with that of "those great sentimental humourists" of past ages, condemning Dickens and Thackeray for not respecting
the individuality and isolation of the reader. A true sentimentalist, he
continues, is "a true gentleman. He does not presume upon his opportunity." There is "no objectionable familiarity" in Shakespeare or
in Sterne, since we are not called upon to "be on intimate terms" with
their characters. "But when Mr. Dickens is pert, or Mr. Thackeray
arch," he continues, we think "that we have some cause to be indignant.
The great cause why modern humour and modern sentimentalism repel
us is, that both are unwarrantably familiar." [1] The charge was extremely
galling to Thackeray. It was more than he could bear to have the man
whom he had characterized as a hypocrite and a mountebank called
"a true gentleman," with the implication that he himself was not. He
replies sarcastically that we should "be thankful for having an elegant
moralist watching over us, and learn, if not too old, to imitate his
high-bred politeness and catch his unobtrusive grace. If we are unwarrantably familiar," he continues, "we know who is not. If we repel
by pertness, we know who never does. If our language offends, we
know whose is always modest." [2] Thackeray continues this strain the
next month in "A Roundabout Journey." Referring to the Dutens
incident,[3] he says sneeringly: "Ah, dear Lawrence! You are lucky in

      9. This book is in the Rare Book Room of the Yale University Library. The note
is undated, but obviously must have been written fairly early.
      1. *Saturday Review, 10* (Aug. 25, 1860), 235–6. For an account of Thackeray's con-
troversies with this periodical, see Merle M. Bevington, *The Saturday Review 1855–
1868* (New York, Columbia Univ. Press, 1941), pp. 167–75. Unfortunately Bevington
does not identify the author of the article in question.
      2. "De Juventute," *Roundabout Papers,* p. 60.
      3. See above, p. 89.

having such a true gentleman as my friend [4] to appreciate you. You see he was lying, but then he was amusing the whole company. When Lawrence found they were amused, he told more lies. Your true gentlemen always do. Even to get the laugh of the company at a strange table, perhaps you and I would not tell lies; but then we are not true gentlemen." He continues with an example of Sterne's deception of Mrs. Draper, which he believes to be revealed in the *Journal to Eliza* and the *Letters,* as further proof of Sterne's mendacity.[5] He exhorts the *Saturday* reviewer, the next time he goes out of his way "to sneer at living, and bepraise dead gentlemen," to "pick a better specimen than this wretched old sinner." [6]

Thackeray continues to take pot shots at Sterne's character in subsequent essays of the *Roundabout* series. He censures Yorick for making love "to his neighbours' wives," and accuses him of "leering after the housemaids" as a school boy. He speaks ironically of his "manly stoicism," and hints that he was guilty of drunkenness.[7] In another of the series, on Dessein's Hotel, he calls up Yorick's ghost and engages him in conversation, giving a picture of affectation and false sentiment. The ghost appears after Thackeray has gone to sleep in "Sterne's Chamber," thinking "how I admire, dislike, and have abused him." [8]

The use of the word "admire" is no slip of the pen. Bitterly as Thackeray denounced Sterne's personal character in *Roundabout Papers,* he nevertheless had high praise for some parts of his work, and particularly for the character of Uncle Toby. In one essay he refers to the pictures of the Vicar of Wakefield and Uncle Toby as among "the masterpieces of our English school," which "still form the wonder and delight of the lovers of English art." [9] In other passages he mentions the Captain among the "dear old friends" of fiction who have given him many pleasant hours, and places him in company with Leatherstocking, Sir Roger de Coverley, and Falstaff, who are all heroic figures, "the great prize-men of fiction." [1] Even when remarking upon the fact that he doesn't remember having seen Sterne's books in the library during his school days, "no doubt because the works of that divine were not considered decent for young people," he hastens to add: "Ah! not against thy genius, O father of Uncle Toby and Trim, would I say a word in disrespect. But I am thankful to live in times when men

4. Thackeray is referring to the author of the essay on "Sentimental Writing" in the *Saturday Review.*
5. See above, p. 144.
6. "A Roundabout Journey," *Roundabout Papers,* pp. 264–6.
7. *Roundabout Papers:* p. 80, "On a Joke I once Heard from the Late Thomas Hood"; p. 201, "On a Peal of Bells"; p. 136, "On Two Roundabout Papers which I Intended to Write"; p. 225, "On Some Carp at Sans Souci."
8. "Dessein's," *Roundabout Papers,* pp. 213–22.
9. "A Roundabout Journey," *Roundabout Papers,* pp. 267–8.
1. *Roundabout Papers:* p. 195, "De Finibus"; p. 200 "On a Peal of Bells."

no longer have the temptation to write so as to call blushes on women's cheeks, and would shame to whisper wicked allusions to honest boys." [2] None of Sterne's faults, as Thackeray wrote to the Reverend Whitwell Elwin in 1863, "prevent the scamp from being a great man." [3] But it was the picture of the scamp rather than that of the great man which Thackeray had placed before the public in the *Humourists* and *Roundabout Papers.*

Thackeray's judgments, as expressed in the lecture on Sterne, called forth mixed critical comment. Posterity has tended to feel that he was speaking for his age, but such is by no means the case, for the comments on the lectures vary from complete agreement to violent opposition. *The Times* and the *Literary Gazette* merely presented summaries. [4] The *Athenaeum,* in a review by Henry F. Chorley at the time of the publication of the *Humourists* in 1853, pointed to Thackeray's estimate of Sterne "with entire approval. 'Yorick' was, indeed, a fair subject for a denunciatory sermon, addressed to the sentimentalists of Vanity Fair," Chorley says, "and its morals, and his want of morals, are not spared by our preacher." [5] Two of the great novelists of the age likewise expressed their approval. Charlotte Brontë thought that the lecture on Sterne was Thackeray's best and that "what he says about Sterne is true." [6] Anthony Trollope also agreed whole-heartedly with the estimate of Sterne's "meanness and littleness." In his biography of Thackeray, published some years later, he says that although Thackeray had made "some half excuse for him because of the greater freedom of the times," this was not to be allowed, since the age also produced Goldsmith. Sterne has been relegated "to some distant and high corner" of the bookshelves, Trollope concludes, and "the less often that he is taken down the better." [7]

Some critics even carried Thackeray's denunciation several steps further. An unknown writer in *Sharpe's London Magazine* in 1854 censured Sterne's "cool-blooded neglect and contumely" in his relations

2. "De Juventute," *Roundabout Papers*, pp. 66–7.
3. *Letters and Private Papers*, 4, 282. For Elwin's article on Sterne, see below, pp. 152–3.
4. See *The Times*, July 4, 1851, p. 3; and *Literary Gazette*, July 5, 1851, p. 468. Though neither article contains any direct critical comments on Thackeray's remarks, *The Times* seems moderately surprised that Sterne "is evidently less a favourite with the lecturer than William Congreve," while the *Gazette* appears to thoroughly approve the remarks.
5. *Athenaeum, 26* (June 25, 1853), 764. The attribution to Chorley is based on Leslie A. Marchand, *The Athenaeum* (Chapel Hill, Univ. of North Carolina Press, 1941), p. 318.
6. *The Brontës, 3,* 259.
7. *Thackeray,* English Men of Letters Series (London, 1882), pp. 166–7. In a manuscript copy of one of Trollope's lectures, first delivered in 1870, there is a cancelled passage which refers to *Tristram Shandy,* in which "the undoubted wit, and doubtful pathos, offer no adequate compensations for the obscenity." *Four Lectures,* ed. Morris L. Parrish (London, Constable, 1938), p. 136.

with his wife, stating that he "paraded his incessant and ever-changing *liaisons* before her, and indulged in a grossness of conversation which would have disgraced a tinker or coal-porter." Sterne had married "to the permanent misery of an amiable woman," and the writer even contrives to have him die "attended, with faithful and affectionate care, by the wife and daughter of whom he was wholly unworthy." [8] Of Yorick's relationship with Eliza he says, "The corruption of this woman he endeavoured to compass by every art of atrocious falsehood and deceit." While Fielding was "a man of strong, manly, practical benevolence and generosity," Sterne was "not only a profligate, but gloried in the avowal of his profligacy, and was never more in his element than when setting snares to corrupt others." His works contain "a concatenation of impurities such as nothing but a mind the most perverted" and "principles deliberately wicked and diabolically malicious" could imagine or put before the public. The writer does admit that part of Sterne's faults may be attributed to the moral corruption of his age, and he is forced to praise the "elaborate polish and refinement" of the style in *Tristram Shandy,* which he places well above *Don Quixote* in literary excellence. Although Cervantes' plot would "crumble into atoms" without the madness of the Don, the "eccentricities" of Toby and Walter Shandy are "not absolutely essential, but incidentally ancillary" to Sterne's plan. His ultimate praise of Sterne, however, comes in the ironic statement that he deserves the thanks of posterity mainly for unintentionally rendering "the mawkish order of sentimentalism as ridiculous as Cervantes, with set design, made the dreams of obsolete knight-errantry in Spain." [9]

The onslaught of John Cordy Jeaffreson a few years later was fully as severe. In his *Novels and Novelists,* published in 1858, he characterizes Sterne as "the buffoon of the *beau monde,*" who was "flattered and petted by all the most vicious nobles of the kingdom." He is "the hero of a hundred love affairs," "the adroit teller of nasty stories," "the vain, wicked, sensual old dandy." Like Thackeray, Jeaffreson concentrates mainly on the closing years of Sterne's life. When he went to London in 1767, Jeaffreson says, he immersed him-

8. The writer must have made this story up out of whole cloth. It is significant in showing the extent of ignorance about even the barest outlines of Sterne's biography and the ease with which writers could invent details to fit their own preconceptions. For a similar example, see *Quarterly Review, 106* (July 1859), 223, in which Sterne is accused of having been one of the "roystering wits" of Medmenham Abbey.

9. *Sharpe's London Magazine,* NS, *5* ([1854]), 8–13. The comparison with Fielding was made by other critics during this period, often taking their cue from Thackeray, whose lecture on Fielding had been uncomplimentary enough, though he had treated him far more kindly than he did Sterne. Though Fielding might be a man of low tastes and a prodigal, he nevertheless had a certain manliness about him and was a foe to hypocrisy, qualities which Thackeray denied specifically to Sterne. See Blanchard, pp. 408–45, for a discussion of Thackeray's influence on Fielding's literary reputation.

self in society, "making love to twenty ladies at the same time, intri-
guing, jesting, and *lying*." Then the "worn-out, jaded old debauchee
. . . fell violently in love" with Mrs. Draper and "his poor foolish wife,
who would persist in loving him, heard a story of her angel that gave her
a fresh though not an untried wound." Later, in his letters to Eliza he
acted "the hypocrite of the prayer book school to perfection." He
returned to Coxwold for the summer, "exhausted by pulmonary disease,
and also a loathsome affection (the consequence of vicious pleasures)." [1]
But early in 1768 he was again "in Bond Street, as witty, as false, as
heartless as ever." [2] Jeaffreson continues with an account of the close
of "Yorick's garish triumphs," repeating the stories of the anatomization of his corpse. It is not important whether the reports are true or
not, he continues, for "it is enough to know that English society under-
went such a revulsion of horror at the death of the brilliant man they
had petted and adored, that they were ready to believe, and even craved
for, any particulars that tended to make his fate appear sad and
strangely dreadful." [3]

When he comes to speak of Sterne's works, Jeaffreson is scarcely more
lenient. Though Sterne has plagiarized extensively from Burton and
Rabelais, he has not appreciated the worth of either. If he had been a
true humorist, he "would not have made Mr. Shandy a simple-hearted,
contemptible old twaddle, but would have drawn him heroic as well as
child-like, such as Augustine Caxton." [4] He was, in the words of
Thackeray, "a great jester, not a great humourist," since his acquaintance with both books and men was superficial and he could not see
"into his fellow creatures . . . an inch till his eyes were dimmed with
tears."

On the positive side of the ledger Jeaffreson admits, somewhat paradoxically, that Sterne "was that which it was his boast to be—a man
of feeling," and that "all his actions were regulated by that 'good taste'
which is the appropriate costume of fashionable society." He has the
ability "of *perceiving,* if not of *creating* the humourous," and though

---

1. Jeaffreson is practically the only critic to allude directly to Sterne's account of
suffering from a "venereal case." Sterne had described his conversation with his doctors
in a letter in May 1767, which had been published in 1775 by Mrs. Medalle. He protested
that he had "had no commerce whatever with the sex . . . these fifteen years," and the
doctors replied that "these taints of the blood laid dormant twenty years." *Letters,* p.
343; the incident is also recounted in the *Journal to Eliza,* ibid., pp. 329–30. Though
critics had not alluded to this passage, it is quite possible that this was one factor which
made them call Sterne "sensual" in his personal life. Whatever the facts of Sterne's
previous medical history, he seems to be sincere when he complains that he is
innocent though being compelled to suffer "the chastisement of the grossest sensualist."
2. Cf. above, p. 145.
3. This last statement is certainly more true of Jeaffreson's own time than of Sterne's,
for critics like Jeaffreson far outdo Sterne's contemporaries in their relish of the
"sensational" aspects of his death and burial.
4. See below, pp. 168–9.

he knew "only the superficial of human nature, he can still touch the very centre of our affections." No previous writer was "so skilful a narrator," for Sterne has shown us "how to tell stories gracefully." Though we find "no original forms of architecture," there is "a rare variety of tracery and ornament with which every later builder has decorated his structures." [5]

Though a few critics like Jeaffreson were in substantial agreement with Thackeray, the majority were inclined to think that the picture of Sterne in the *Humourists* had been unfair. Among the ablest of these was the Reverend Whitwell Elwin, whose lengthy article on Sterne appeared in the *Quarterly Review* in March 1854. In the "hasty sketch" which Thackeray has given in his lecture, Elwin says, he has remembered "little else than his profligacy, and has passed too lightly over the mental gifts which alone entitled him to a place in the gallery of 'English Humourists.'" Though he agrees with Thackeray that Sterne was "beyond all question a profane and profligate man," Elwin thinks of him more as a "hair-brained, light-hearted" Epicurean, than as a cold-blooded hypocrite or an abandoned wretch. Sterne's faults lie in the fact that he "was prouder of his cap and bells than of his gown," and that he "followed the impulse of the moment." [6]

When he comes to discuss Sterne's literary qualities, he does not confuse biography and literary criticism as Thackeray had done. He disposes of the question of plagiarism with the statement that "the whole of the pretended parallel passages would barely suffice to fill a dozen pages." He is much harsher on Sterne's indecency, however, for he feels that "too much of his wit is the phosphoric light emitted by corruption," and his "licentious imagination" shows the "incurable depravity of his taste." He is the more to be blamed for his licentiousness, because "it is interwoven with beauties which will not suffer it to die."

Elwin speaks at length of these beauties, displaying an especially keen insight into the characters of *Tristram Shandy*. Though Sterne avowed that Cervantes was his model, he has not attempted merely "a feeble copy of an inimitable original," but has "borrowed the conception of a man mastered by a fantastic passion" and given it "an application thoroughly novel." While Don Quixote's madness "is beyond the limits of nature," the character of Uncle Toby is "evolved naturally out of the circumstances in which he is placed, and has the merits so hard to unite of being as original as any monstrosity of the imagination,

<hr/>

5. *Novels and Novelists, from Elizabeth to Victoria* (2 vols. London, 1858), *1*, 180–222. Jeaffreson also quotes Coleridge's famous pronouncement on Sterne's indecencies. See above, p. 117.

6. Elwin commends Sterne's generosity to his wife, but finds "damning evidence of the utter worthlessness of poor Yorick's character" in the letters to Eliza. His treatment is much more restrained than Thackeray's, however, and shows more pity than scorn.

and as truthful as any transcript from commonplace life," for he "acts according to verified laws of the mind." Sterne has displayed the same skill which Cervantes has in dignifying "the ludicrous element by noble traits without breaking in upon the consistency of the character." Praise of Trim and Walter Shandy follows. The action of the brothers upon each other "is managed with wonderful address," and "the strokes with which the portraits are drawn are altogether so deep and yet so delicate . . . that we question if, out of Shakspeare, there is a single character in English fiction depicted with greater or even equal power." Sterne is also compared to Shakespeare in another of his excellences, for though his descriptions are vivid, "yet, next to Shakspeare, he is the author who leaves the most to the imagination of the reader," allowing "the subtlest traits to produce their own effect. His work is full of interior meanings which escape the mind on a rapid perusal," Elwin continues, "and the interest is sustained, and the admiration increased, by the innumerable beauties which keep rising into view the longer we linger over it. It is a kindred merit that he excels in painting by single strokes. 'I have left Trim my bowling-green, cried my Uncle Toby,' to give one instance in a hundred. 'My father smiled. I have left him, moreover a pension, continued my Uncle Toby. My father looked grave.' "

It is unfortunate, however, that "whatever rare quality Sterne possesses, he is sure to be conspicuous for the opposite defect." With all his "abstinence from explanatory comment at one time, he indulges in it to excess at another. He constantly takes upon himself to act the part of a showman, and disagreeably reminds us that the characters are his puppets." His style, too, is "frequently deformed by insufferable affectation," although at other times it is "remarkable for its purity, its ease, its simplicity, and its elegance." *Tristram Shandy* is without question Sterne's masterpiece, for the *Sentimental Journey,* though it has "some beautiful passages which are familiar to everybody," is pervaded by "a capital defect," which "is embodied in the fact that it has brought the word *sentimental* into discredit, and made it the standard epithet for feelings that are sickly and superficial." The travels leave the impression of being "affected, morbid, and hollow," since artistic skill cannot "compensate with healthy minds for this want of nature." Of Sterne's earlier work, however, Elwin says that "the entire library of fiction contains no more delightful pages, and none which bear a more palpable impress of genius, than many which are to be found in 'Tristram Shandy.' " [7]

This well-balanced picture of Sterne's excellences and his defects, together with an assessment of his personal character which, though

7. *Quarterly Review,* 94 (March 1854), 303–53. The essay was later reprinted in Elwin's *Some Eighteenth Century Men of Letters,* London, J. Murray, 1902.

harsh, is sympathetic compared to Thackeray's, is far more typical of the enlightened criticism of the age than are the distortions of critics like Jeaffreson. David Masson, another prominent critic, whose *British Novelists and Their Styles* was published in 1859, admits that Thackeray may not have been "a whit more severe than the evidence warrants" in regard to Sterne's life, but he also suggests that further research might enable us to "find the man, after all, as good as his genius." For his genius is of the first rank. "There is scarcely anything more intellectually exquisite than the humor of Sterne," [8] and "Shakespeare himself, as one fancies, would have read Sterne with admiration and pleasure." The great characters of *Tristram Shandy* are "creations of a fine fancy working in an ideal element, and not mere copies or caricatures of individualities actually observed." As Coleridge has pointed out, they exhibit a "faith in moral good" and display the "art of minute observation." Sterne succeeded admirably in "representing and diffusing" sensibility through his writings; and "the grace, the insinuating delicacy, the light lucidity, the diamond-like sparkle of Sterne's style make reading him a peculiar literary pleasure." [9]

Other critics during the period in question were equally appreciative of Sterne's literary merits. Among the most enthusiastic of these was Thomas Purnell, the editor of Lamb's works and the friend of Swinburne. In his *Literature and its Professors,* published in 1867, he distinguishes two types among "the great masters of humour." One treats of fashions, foibles, and manners and hence "is concerned with what is transient"; while the other is "the humourist of nature," who "deals by choice with the old Adam that leavens us." Sterne belongs to the latter class. While "other writers concoct their situations" and then "ingeniously adapt their puppets to the predetermined scheme, as if there were a regularly constructed plot in every Shandy family," Sterne worked with a different method. "He had furniture of quaint but rarest fashion," Purnell says, "and was indifferent as to where he should house it so long as he was able to fix it somewhere in the edifice. A set of gentler human creatures was never before collected under one roof," he continues. "Nothing, it is true, was well hung; the creaking door, always unswung, was never repaired; the dispute begun was never ended. It was a queer family . . . but every member of it becomes an especial favourite with all who have passed an hour under

---

8. Masson believes that Sterne's humor is "unique" and that he "was himself a humorist by nature," even though he may "remind" us of Rabelais.

9. *British Novelists and Their Styles* (Boston, 1859), pp. 151–5. Masson was professor of English literature at University College, London, at this time. The review of the book in the *British Quarterly Review* stated that Sterne had been rated too high, but commended his characters, style, and narrative method; *30* (Oct. 1859), 455–6.

their roof." Though the characters "all are Shandean," each one never-theless possesses "a well-defined individuality by which he is rec-ognized." Uncle Toby has been compared to Sir Roger de Coverley and to Parson Adams, but the comparison is not valid, for their creators "deliberately station themselves on a moral elevation which necessarily prevents them from exhibiting that complete sympathy" which Sterne always shows. We also feel sympathy for Don Quixote and Falstaff, but it, likewise, is of a different sort, because "our pity is largely inter-fused with a sense of our own superiority." In the presence of Uncle Toby, however, "you yourself become Shandean." Sterne "does not excite emotions in us"; but, rather, "we suffer them in company with him; we feel merely because he himself feels. Although his literary merits in other directions are great, in this particular excellence he has no equal."

Thackeray's inability to appreciate or understand Sterne arose from a "cardinal defect" in his own powers as a novelist, Purnell believes. He lacked "tolerance for what is beyond the area of his own experience and customary horizon." He has charged Sterne with insincerity, asserting that he utilized his emotions to gain money; but there is actually "no reason why a man should not utilize his sensations as well as his reflections, and publish 'Sentimental Journies' as well as 'Snob Papers.'" The censures of Sterne's life have likewise arisen from a failure to understand his character and realize that it was natural for him to "suffer acutely and resent warmly the want of a sympathetic and conciliatory spirit in a cold-hearted wife." Though Sterne was "indiscreet" in his relationships with women, even if we "judge him by strictest canons of morality, he will not be found guilty of active wrong." He must have known that his writings were "improper," but at the same time he knew "that nothing he wrote was capable of exciting unhallowed passion in the other sex." His "most subtle innuendoes are for men," and "his books are essentially men's books." Though his life "was not in strict keeping with the character of a clergyman as we now conceive it to be," it was not unusual for the eighteenth century and should be judged leniently in view of the many mitigating circum-stances.[1]

If Purnell had written his essay a few years earlier, he probably would not have been able to give such a sympathetic picture of Sterne's life and character, for most of the critics who opposed Thackeray during the decade after his lecture disagreed with him more on his low estimate of Sterne's genius than on the correctness of his biographical facts. In 1864, however, an important literary event had taken place

1. *Literature and its Professors* (London, 1867), pp. 205-30.

with the publication of Percy Fitzgerald's *Life of Laurence Sterne.*[2] In this first full-length biography of Sterne, Fitzgerald corrected many of the distortions of Thackeray in regard to the facts of Sterne's life and the interpretation of them.

The "gross and odious character" which Thackeray held up to scorn, Fitzgerald says, seemed "almost out of nature" and came upon the world as a surprise. This unfair picture has led to "the popular view" of Sterne as

> an abandoned clergyman, free of manners, gross in speech and writings; a Joseph Surface in orders; a false, whining, and canting parson, who sold his sentiment to the booksellers; a cold, unfeeling, heartless "mountebank," that whimpered over a dead donkey but left his mother to starve; a cruel and neglectful husband, a cold father, and a hollow friend; one that corrupted his age with a foul stream of written impurity, and poured out his corruption upon a spotless and reluctant generation;—in short, "the foul satyr," "the coward," "the wretched worn-out old scamp," "the feeble wretch," and "mountebank"; as, indeed, he has been painted in the vigorous language of one of the best masters of English of our day.

In correcting the distortions of this view, Fitzgerald has tried to show the sincerity of Sterne's sentiment and the kindliness and generosity of his nature, though he has not "ventured to pass any very decided judgment" on Sterne's morals, manners, and writings.[3] He has attempted an impartial review of the facts rather than "an extravagance of panegyric" or a "wholesale extenuation, or universal scouring-down

---

2. Much of the material in Fitzgerald's *Life* had appeared in his series of articles on "Sterne and his Day" in the *Dublin University Magazine* during 1862 and 1863. These were unsigned, except for the last one, which bore his initials. There were also two other articles, one unsigned but unmistakably Fitzgerald's ("Sterne in the Stereoscope," *Dublin University Magazine, 55,* May 1860, 542–60), and one which bore his initials ("An Odd Preacher," *Temple Bar, 7,* March 1863, 579–88). In these earlier articles, perhaps because they were for the most part unsigned, Fitzgerald writes in a less cautious style than he does in the *Life* and is not as guarded in his opposition to the judgments of Thackeray and other earlier writers. A single set of parallel passages will serve to illustrate this:

There is the theatrical, and, it must be said, cruelly-savage sketch of the author of "Esmond," full of stagey devices and Adelphi effects, to reach which but too many other things have been unhappily sacrificed. . . . There is an article very much fairer, yet still severe, to be seen in the *Quarterly Review.* ("Sterne and his Day," *Dublin University Magazine, 60,* Aug. 1862, 180.)	There is the vigorous and, it must be said, cruel sketch of the author of "Esmond," full of scathing satire and dramatic effects, to reach which but too many other things have been unhappily sacrificed; with which may be contrasted an admirable *Quarterly Review* article, written in a true spirit of genial appreciation, yet not without a calm critical severity. (*Life of Laurence Sterne,* 2 vols. London, 1864, *I,* 4.)

3. *Life of Sterne, I,* 2–3.

of an old figure, much grimed and soiled by long exposure. An honest sympathy is indeed essential," he continues, "together with a certain warmth and generous advocacy"; and he has undertaken a review of "the delicate story" of Sterne's life in the same spirit which "Sterne himself applied to the case of the old *remise*—'Something might be said for it, but not much.' " [4]

In spite of the somewhat timid nature of this purpose and in spite of some errors in fact,[5] Fitzgerald did nevertheless clear up many biographical questions which had led to previous misinterpretations. He disposes of the story of the "dead ass and the living mother" once and for all, by showing the absence of factual background for it, and characterizes Sterne's mother as "little more" than a "poor genteel tramp." He also contradicts Thackeray's description of Sterne as a schoolboy, "leering at the housemaids," since "this grim portrait of youthful depravity has no more historical basis than one of the pleasant rambling humours of Mr. Roundabout." The Dutens anecdote is put in a favorable light. Though Sterne may have tired of his wife, his original passion for her was sincere, and he always remained a "kind, careful, *thoughtful* husband," providing generously for her wants. Although "the nuptial garment, as well as the ecclesiastical cassock, may have been equally unsuited to his shoulders," it is "a nice office to determine with whom rests the balance of fault." In his relationship with Kitty Fourmantel, he "recklessly puts himself in so suspicious a situation" that he should not complain if posterity "naturally judged him by the presumption of ordinary evidence"; but, at the same time, the affair seems to have been innocent. Sterne's relationship with Eliza is even more questionable and requires "a confidence almost chivalrous to exculpate him," but he made no secret of the attachment, Mrs. James seems to have accepted the situation "as perfectly harmless," and he probably had the model of Swift and Stella in his mind. Even so, the incident is "the most questionable of his many weaknesses," and his lack of discretion has fairly placed him open to the charges the world has made.

Fitzgerald's ultimate view of Sterne's character is that of a man who "had so many weaknesses but so many more redeeming features." Though he was "too 'gay' for one of his cloth," and gave in to "fashionable temptation," he was sincere, "a sentimentalist by constitution." He was "more or less weak, vain, careless, idle, and given to pleasure," Fitzgerald says, and these were "his natural faults." He was also "free of pen and speech—profane sometimes—and did not honour the

4. Ibid., *1*, 231-2. The quotation comes from "Calais," *Sentimental Journey.*
5. Perhaps the most glaring of these are an error as to the date of publication of Vols. 3 and 4 of the *Sermons* (*2*, 327), and the attribution of a review in the *Monthly* to Smollett (*2*, 264). Cross has corrected various other errors.

gown he wore," but "these were the general scandals of his time." He had "redeeming gifts of generous sympathy and warmth, kind fatherly affection," a care "for the pecuniary interests of those for whom it was his duty to provide, a genial humour, and, strange as it may seem, a tone of natural piety." His faults, "as he said over and over again so pathetically, [were] follies of heart and not of the head." When we "would anticipate the task of the Recording Angel," Fitzgerald concludes, we should not "blot out the entry for ever," but rather "set down a gentle and a charitable judgment."

There is not much literary criticism in Fitzgerald's *Life,* although he does go into the question of plagiarism quite extensively. He concludes that the borrowings from Burton are not important since Sterne has "absorbed" them "into his humorous system." His final opinion on the plagiarisms in the sermons seems to be in doubt, for he excuses them in one passage, while stating in another that Sterne "seems to have cast away all notions of literary morality." The originality of *Tristram Shandy* "is in the main secure," for "the humour, the gaiety, the farce" and "the clear distinct gallery of Shandean men and women, who live and breathe and walk before our eyes" are Sterne's own. Uncle Toby, especially, is of "the immortal company to which Sir Roger and Parson Adams belong."

Fitzgerald also makes various other random statements which have a bearing upon Sterne's literary character. He thinks that Thackeray's statement that Sterne was "a great jester, not a great humourist," is all the more startling and unjust, since it came "from one who was himself a great humourist, and not a great jester." Sterne's indecency may be partially excused from the manners of his time, although there are some passages which display "a coarse licence utterly inexcusable." Fitzgerald made his greatest contribution to an understanding of Sterne's literary qualities, however, in disposing once and for all of the concept of the "careless" writer. With a corrected manuscript copy of the *Sentimental Journey* before him, he gives several examples of Sterne's revisions and "careful elaboration" which show him "a master of the elegances of English." [6]

The defects of Fitzgerald's biography become obvious if one places it beside Cross's later definitive work, but in its own age it did much to counteract the distortions of Thackeray's prejudiced picture. Fitzgerald is occasionally carried away by the Shandean possibilities of his subject,[7] and he is sometimes handicapped by inadequate or faulty informa-

6. See *Life of Sterne,* *1,* x, 7, 77, 83, 87, 133, 156–7, 211, 235, 289–90, 323, 332, 338; *2,* 32–3, 40, 182–3 (see above, pp. 89 and 147), 238, 245, 334–59, 409, 418, 420, 425, 432–4, 443. Though Fitzgerald is somewhat cautious in contradicting Thackeray, he lists in an appendix several factual errors in *Humourists.*

7. In his preface, Fitzgerald says that Sterne's "character is so strange, and [his] history so odd, so dramatic, and so truly Shandean, that both together seem to work

tion; but he attempts to present his material impartially and does manage to correct many of the previous clichés which, as he says, "the new dictionary has filched from the old encyclopaedia, and which the newer encyclopaedia has helped itself to from the older dictionary." [8] Though his portrait of Sterne as a man of amiable weaknesses is not the whole truth, it is certainly much closer to it than Thackeray's picture of vice and unmitigated depravity.

The *Life* met with a favorable reception. Little more than a year after its appearance Fitzgerald wrote that "curiosity to know something about Sterne has nearly exhausted the first edition" and that he was already preparing a new revised edition.[9] While he had been engaged in his research for the *Life* and for an article on William Dodd, Fitzgerald later said, Dickens had been "infinitely merry on what he called 'my *two* disreputable parsons,'" [1] and Boz had requested a copy of the *Life* as soon as it came out.[2] Dickens' own periodical, *All the Year Round*, later gave a favorable review of the book.[3]

Other periodicals were in agreement that Fitzgerald had produced a well-written biography which showed candor and justice in correcting Thackeray's overly harsh view. The *Dublin University Magazine* spoke of Thackeray's "unaccountable prejudices," which "approached almost to a 'phobia'" so that "the name of Sterne seemed to have the effect of infuriating him like a piece of scarlet cloth" and he "tossed and gored the unhappy Yorick." Fitzgerald, on the other hand, has shown tact and judgment in correcting this unfair view and not even Thackeray's most ardent friends could "object to the calm and even tender fashion in which what we may call the monstrous image he set up of the great Shandean has been cast down." [4]

Even the reviewers who were not quite so sympathetic to Sterne felt that he could be at least partially excused for his failings on historical grounds, in the light of Fitzgerald's new evidence. An unknown critic

---

out one of the most curious biographical stories in English literature" (*1*, vii) ; and at times he stresses the "dramatic" and the "Shandean" at the expense of a more sober discussion of the facts.

8. Ibid., *1, 3.*

9. *Notes and Queries*, 3d Ser. 6 (July 2, 1864), 7. The new edition, in which Fitzgerald modified some of his earlier favorable opinions, did not actually appear until 1896. In addition to the reviews of Fitzgerald's book to be quoted below, see *Athenaeum*, April 2, 1864, pp. 463–6; *The Reader, 3* (April 16, 1864), 486–7. The latter contains one of the few relatively unenthusiastic reviews of the *Life*.

1. *Memories of Charles Dickens* (Bristol and London, 1913), p. 95. Dodd, who was hanged as a forger, had written an "admonitory epistle" to Sterne (see above, p. 26).

2. *Works of Dickens: Letters, 3,* 356. Dickens' *Uncommercial Traveller* also shows evidence of his continuing interest in Sterne. He may have derived something of the style for this work from the *Sentimental Journey* and he also refers to Sterne. *Reprinted Pieces. The Uncommercial Traveller and Other Stories*, pp. 345, 596.

3. *All the Year Round, 11* (July 2, 1864), 489–95.

4. *Dublin University Magazine, 63* (March 1864), 328–38.

wrote in the *British Quarterly Review* that if Sterne is tried "by the high standard of morality and decency to which we happily have become accustomed in the reign of Victoria, we shall be unable to acquit him," but that "when we remember that he had the misfortune to live amidst the unhealthy atmosphere, the riot, vice and irreligion" of his time, "we shall feel justified in dismissing him with a lenient sentence." Though Sterne is "a maze of inconsistencies and contradictions," he was "weak" rather than "wicked," "neither a hero nor a rogue." [5] A writer in the *Eclectic Review* agreed, deploring the low moral tone of the eighteenth century but stating that Sterne was by no means the worst clergyman of his age. Times have changed so much, he says, that "we could scarcely tolerate now the pure and healthful Dickens in that profession." [6] Both critics include favorable comments on Sterne's works, the writer in the *Eclectic Review* asserting that Sterne's books "will hold an immortal place in the history, and among the treasures and conquests of our language." The writer in the *British Quarterly* particularly praises the characters of *Tristram Shandy,* stating that a lesser artist would have made them "mere caricatures," while Sterne has given them "whimsical qualities" which are "only accidental and not essential." Even Dickens "will not stand this test," for "to delineate eccentricity, and yet to keep it subordinate, almost requires the delicate touch of a Shakspeare."

The same themes were taken up by other periodicals. Alexander H. Grant, who reviewed the book nearly two years later in *London Society,* stated that in an age "when the life of the Church was the galvanism of intrigue, we owe it to the memory of the Reverend Laurence Sterne to believe that there were hundreds of clergy before whom he stood out in the bold relief of an apostle." Thackeray has painted his false picture "with a wildness approaching hysteria," while Fitzgerald "has come to the rescue in a couple of warm-hearted but not overreaching volumes, that offer the first clearly-defined full-length portrait of one of the great masters of English humour." [7]

Though neither the *Edinburgh* nor the *Quarterly* reviewed the *Life, Blackwood's* carried an appreciative article in May 1865. Fitzgerald is commended for having given a "just, candid" estimate, though it is "by no means overstrained in its charity" and "many will think him but a timid advocate" since he "might have shown more zeal in the defence of his client without any departure from truth." Sterne's

5. *British Quarterly Review,* 40 (July 1864), 152–74.

6. *Eclectic Review,* NS, 7 (July [1864]), 1–20.

7. *London Society,* 9 (March 1866), 206–22. (The ascription to Grant is based on William Cushing, *Dictionary of Literary Disguises,* New York, 1885. I have been unable to identify Grant further.) Grant also praised Fitzgerald's method, comparing it to "a cobweb in the sunlight," in which "every shining thread of interest that radiates, interlacing the concentric circles, is joined with every other fitly and artistically."

"manifest, inexcusable fault" is his lack of decorum, for "his was a case of vitiated taste, not of corrupt life." The writer goes on to speak of Sterne's work, minimizing the importance of his borrowings and drawing an interesting comparison between Sterne and Goldsmith. Both men have "a clear, beautiful, idiomatic style," and both have "humour and refined observation." Goldsmith, however, aims "to harmonise and complete; his was the *classic* type of composition." Sterne, on the other hand, "was an extreme instance of what has in later days been called the *romantic* school, where incongruities are sought, not shunned. Sterne dared all things. It was his very aim to startle, and disappoint, and produce a sort of dazzling chaos." The reviewer finds Thackeray's attack on Sterne hard to explain, for "if there was a living man who had apparently absorbed into his own style and manner all that is indisputably excellent in the writings of Sterne, it was Thackeray himself." He must also have profited from his study of Fielding and Smollett,

> but Sterne is the only one of his predecessors who could have unconsciously taught him how to write. Fielding and Smollett write like carpenters: they cut and hammer and nail you up a box, with fit partitions, that holds well enough what they have to stow away in it. Sterne alone is the artist in language, and carves where the others cut. It seemed a little ungracious that a kindred artist, whose plots and stories derive all their charm from those strains of reflection, often very subtle, which, in fact, constitute what we call the style of the man, should have been so very bitter to that only one amongst his predecessors who also treated his story as the mere field or stage on which to disport himself.[8]

Though Sterne had to wait nearly a hundred years for a biographer, Thackeray found one the year after his death. John Camden Hotten's *Thackeray the Humourist and the Man of Letters* appeared the same year that Fitzgerald's *Life of Sterne* did, and Walter Bagehot reviewed the two books in a single article for the *National Review* in April 1864. Although Yorick's career has been "well commented on" by Thackeray, he says, he will discuss Sterne's life and works because his "artistic character presented one fundamental resemblance and many superficial contrasts" to Thackeray's. His interpretation of Sterne's personal character is much more sympathetic than Thackeray's, however, and comes closer to Fitzgerald's treatment. He credits Sterne with being sincere in his early love for his wife, and believes his later lack of sympathy for her is to be explained by the fact that she did not "comprehend or appreciate the new thoughts and feelings which a new and great experience had awakened in her husband's mind" after he became

8. *Blackwood's Magazine*, 97 (May 1865), 540–55.

famous. Of Sterne's relationships with other women, Bagehot says: "Sterne was 'an old flirt.' These are short and expressive words, and they tell the whole truth. There is no good reason to suspect his morals, but he dawdled about pretty women."

Sterne's biggest mistake, Bagehot asserts, was in entering the church, since Sterne was a man who was guided by taste, rather than by morality and conscience. He is among those "gentlemen" who shun vice because it is ugly. "These are the men whom it is hardest to make Christian," he says, because "paganism is sufficient for them. Their pride of the eye is a good pride; their love of the flesh is a delicate and directing love. They keep 'within the pathways,' because they dislike the gross, the uncultured and the untrodden," although they reject the idea of repentance and the force of conscience. This pagan philosophy was adequate to sustain Sterne in his youth, Bagehot believes, but toward the close of his life when "much of the gloss and delicacy of Sterne's pagan instinct had faded away," there was "a diffused texture of general laxity," even though he committed no grave offenses or misdeeds. Thus, Bagehot thinks that the people of Sterne's own time found him amusing, but did not respect this man who "looked like a scarecrow with bright eyes," for "mere amusers are never respected. It would be harsh to call Sterne a mere amuser," Bagehot hastens to add; "he is much more; but so the contemporary world regarded him. They laughed at his jests, disregarded his death-bed, and neglected his grave."

Perhaps this picture of Sterne is not so very much closer to the truth than Thackeray's; but it is certainly more attractive, and, more important, it did not prevent Bagehot from approaching Sterne's works in a more impartial manner than Thackeray had. Bagehot sees both great virtues and great defects in *Tristram Shandy* and the *Sentimental Journey*. In the earlier work Sterne displays three major defects. First, there is the "fantastic disorder of the form." A great writer "should not blunder upon a beauty, nor, after a great imaginative creation, should he at once fall back to bare prose." But Sterne "shies in a beauty suddenly; and just when you are affected he turns round and grins at it." Sterne's "best" things, Bagehot continues, "read best out of his books— in Enfield's *Speaker* and other places—and you can say no worse of any one as a continuous artist."

The second major defect of *Tristram Shandy,* one which is "especially palpable now-a-days," is its indecency. Some allowances must be made for the changes in taste which have come about, for "a large part of old novels may very fairly be called club-books; they speak out plainly and simply the notorious facts of the world, as men speak of them to men." This lack of reticence in novels designed mainly for men is desirable, for "a young ladies' literature must be a limited and truncated literature." Unfortunately, however, in *Tristram Shandy* there is not merely lack of reticence but also "indecency for indecency's sake" which becomes "an offence against taste, because of its ugliness." It is not the kind of offense against morals which describes "the refined, witty, elegant immorality of an idle aristocracy," but rather "consists in allusions to certain inseparable accompaniments of actual life which are not beautiful, which can never be made interesting, which would, if they were decent, be dull and uninteresting."

The third major defect in *Tristram Shandy* is that "it contains eccentric characters only." This may in part be explained by the difference in the age, since in Sterne's time English country life had "a motley picturesqueness" which is no longer to be found "when London ideas shoot out every morning, and carry on the wings of the railroad a uniform creed to each cranny of the kingdom." Sterne's descriptions of the vanished species of rural eccentrics is excellent, however, for he showed the relation of eccentricity "to our common human nature." Although "monstrous" characters and "ugly unintelligibilities" are not fit subjects for art, "as soon as they are shown in their union with, in their outgrowth from, common human nature, they are the best subjects for great art—for they are new subjects." Characters of this sort, like Hamlet and like Sterne's creations, enlarge "our conceptions of human nature" and take us "out of the bounds of the commonplace." But Sterne has failed to add a leavening element to these characters. "Though each individual character is shaded off into human nature," Bagehot says, "the whole is not shaded off into the world." There are no "half-commonplace personages" to set off and explain the "central group of singular persons." Thus *Tristram Shandy* "is a great work of art, but of barbarous art," for its characters form "an incongruous group of singular persons utterly dissimilar to, and irreconcilable with, the world in which we live."

The *Sentimental Journey* is an improvement upon *Tristram Shandy* in two respects. In the first place, the style "is simpler and better; it is far more connected; it does not jump about, or leave a topic *because* it is interesting." It is, in a sense, an artificial style, but a certain amount of artificiality was necessary because language "used in its natural and common mode" was not adequate to portray "the passing moods of human nature" and "the impressions which a sensitive nature receives from the world without." The *Sentimental Journey* "is not the true France of the old monarchy, but it is exactly what an observant quick-eyed Englishman might fancy that France to be." It is true not "to the outward nature of real life," but "to the reflected image of that life in an imaginative and sensitive man."

Just as contact with the French world led Sterne to "abandon the

arbitrary and fantastic structure of *Tristram Shandy*" for a more delicate, refined style, it also impelled him to discard the "ugly indecency"
of the earlier work. Though certain scenes in Sterne's travels may not
be moral, "there is nothing displeasing to the natural man in them."
They have "a dangerous prettiness, which may easily incite to practical
evil, but in itself, and separated from its censurable consequences, such
prettiness is an artistic perfection."

While the defects of Sterne "are numberless and complicated," his
real excellence "is single and simple." He excels "in mere simple description of common sensitive human action" and "places before you in their
simplest form the elemental facts of human life; he does not view them
through the intellect, he scarcely views them through the imagination;
he does but reflect the unimpaired impression that the facts of life . . .
make on the deep basis of human feeling." His best passages are "the
portrait painting of the heart," as pure reflections "of mere natural feeling as literature has ever given." Sterne's mind was "like a pure lake of
delicate water," Bagehot continues, for it reflects the things in the ordinary landscape around it "with a charm and fascination that they have
not in themselves. This is the highest attainment of art," he concludes,
"to be at the same time nature and something more than nature." Sterne
is a great author "because he felt acutely" and transferred this feeling
to the pages of his books.

The "fundamental and ineradicable resemblance" which Thackeray
bears to Sterne is that he, too, "looked at everything—at nature, at life,
at art—from a *sensitive* aspect." Impressions "burnt in upon his brain"
and "he acutely felt every possible passing fact—every trivial interlude
in society." From "this stern and humble realism" and the "ever-painful
sense of himself" have arisen most of the censures upon him "both as he
seemed to be in society and as he was in his writings," for he was "uneasy in the common and general world" and censured the follies and
snobbishness of mankind too severely. Although he has been compared
to Fielding, the comparison is not warranted; for Fielding was "a reck-
less enjoyer," while Thackeray had a "musing fancifulness" rather than
"a joyful energy" which accepts the world as it is. Hence, Thackeray is
similar to Sterne, for "this sensibility" is common to both, although in
Sterne's case "it did not make him irritable. He was not hurried away,
like Fielding, by buoyant delight; he stayed and mused on painful scenes.
But they did not make him angry," nor did he "amass petty details to
prove that tenth-rate people were ever striving to be ninth-rate people.
He had no tendency to rub the bloom off life." While Thackeray "was
pained by things, and exaggerated their imperfections; Sterne brooded
over things with joy or sorrow, and he idealised their sentiment." Thus,
Thackeray is "an uncomfortable writer," and there is a "peculiar and
characteristic scepticism" in him, which is not to be found in Sterne.

Perhaps in "a sceptical and inquisitive age like this," Bagehot concludes, it may no longer be possible to "accept simply the pains and pleasures, the sorrows and the joys of the world" as Sterne did.[9]

Thus, although they might not agree on Sterne's particular excellences, most discerning critics had rejected Thackeray's low estimate of his genius; and the uncomplimentary picture of Yorick's character in the *Humourists* had been considerably softened by Fitzgerald's *Life*. Long before Thackeray's lecture, however, there had been a gradual falling off in the number of Sterne's readers, and he was never again to be read as universally as he had been in his own age and in the earlier years of the nineteenth century. Charles Knight lamented in 1864 that "there are some works of imagination that are almost unknown to the present race of readers," and that, among these, "Tom Jones, and Roderick Random, and Tristram Shandy are utterly gone out of the popular view." [1] This is not altogether accurate, however, for there were several editions of Sterne's works during the period in question,[2] and Fitzgerald reported that there was "a steady regular annual demand of so many thousand copies" for Bohn's stereotyped edition of *Tristram Shandy*.[3] Fitzgerald's biography undoubtedly helped to renew interest in Sterne, as Thackeray's lecture itself also appears to have done.[4]

Tristram Shandy probably found few except male readers now, however, for it had come to be considered " a man's book," not fit reading for women or for the young.[5] This ban, indeed, seems to have been fairly generally applied to all the eighteenth-century novelists. William Spalding reflected a common attitude of the times when he wrote in his

9. *Works of Walter Bagehot*, ed. Mrs. Russell Barrington (10 vols. London, Longmans Green, 1915), *4, 229–66.*

1. *Passages of a Working Life* (3 vols. London, 1864), *3,* 12.

2. There were editions of Sterne's *Works* in 1853 [Allibone], 1854 [Lowndes], 2 vols. 1857, 1860 [New York], and 1868. The *Sentimental Journey* was issued separately in 1851 [Allibone], 1857 [Lowndes], and 2 eds. 1867 [Allibone]. *Tristram Shandy* was included in the Universal Library Series in 1853 [New York], and also reprinted in 1856 [Allibone] and 1858 [Allibone]. An edition of *Tristram Shandy* which was to be published serially in 1864, however, was given up after the first two numbers, since it was not selling well; *Notes and Queries*, 3d Ser. 6 (Nov. 26, 1864), 446.

3. *Life of Sterne, 2,* 76.

4. See John Camden Hotten's account of the effect of Thackeray's lectures in America: Theodore Taylor (pseud.), *Thackeray the Humourist and the Man of Letters* (London, 1864), p. 127. Presumably the lectures aroused a similar interest in England.

5. See above, pp. 155 and 162–3. James Hannay believed, however, that "the great humorists, free as they may be now and then, are not the corrupting men. If I wanted to corrupt a youth (which God forbid), I would not give him *Juvenal,* or *Tristram Shandy,* or *Don Juan;* the intellectual exhibition would delight him, and check the mischief to his feelings; no, I would hand him a Jesuit text-book on moral questions!"; *Satire and Satirists* (New York, 1855, pref. dated 1854), p. 215. Hannay had a high regard for Sterne. When asked to contribute an article for a periodical "in the style of Swift, with a dash of Sterne," he replied that he would expect "a cheque of corresponding value—something in the style of Rothschild, with a dash of Baring." George Hodder, *Memories of My Time* (London, 1870), p. 407.

textbook on English literature: "When we pass from Johnson to the Novelists of his time, we seem as if leaving the aisles of an august cathedral, to descend into the galleries of a productive but ill-ventilated mine. Around us clings a foul and heavy air," he continues, "which youthful travellers in the realm of literature cannot safely breathe. We must emerge as speedily as possible to the light of day." Richardson has "a virtuous aim" but his books "err chiefly by the plainness with which they describe vice." Fielding has a "greater knowledge of the world, pregnant wit, much power of thinking, and remarkable ease and idiomatic strength of style," but "his living pictures of familiar life, the whimsical caricature of Smollett, and the humorous fantasies of Sterne, are alike polluted by faults." The least of these defects are the "coarseness of language" and the "unscrupulous bareness of licentious description." More serious is the fact that not only "their standard of morality is low," but also they "display indifference to the essential distinctions between right and wrong, in regard to some of the cardinal relations of society," and their heroes are not true gentlemen.[6] Men might venture into the "ill-ventilated mine" in the privacy of their club rooms, but "youthful travellers"—and especially those of the fair sex—were kept away from the "foul and heavy air."

Sterne still had enthusiastic readers, however—among them the brother of a Miss Ross who was one of Samuel Butler's fellow art students. Butler's biographer recounts a story about this Sterne enthusiast which is certainly as Shandean as Sterne himself could have wished:

> [Ross] was an engineer making a railway somewhere in Central America in sole command of about 500 black men, only half-civilized. One of the men announced that he was going to marry the cook, who was one of the few women in the camp. Ross thought that it would tend to preserve decency and order if the union were not allowed to take place without a ceremony of some kind; and he, of course, would have to perform it, as there was no parson. He had but one book, which happened to be *Tristram Shandy*. The people, however, only spoke Spanish, so that it did not much matter; at any rate he determined to marry them out of it. A Sunday was fixed for the wedding, and proclaimed a high holiday. Ross put an old, but clean, night-shirt over all his clothes, and, looking as solemn as he could, read to the assembled people, and to the bride and bridegroom in particular, a chapter of *Tristram Shandy*; after which he declared them, and they were considered to be, duly married.[7]

6. *History of English Literature* (New York, 1863; 1st ed. 1853), p. 337. Spalding was professor of logic, rhetoric, and metaphysics at the University of Saint Andrews.
7. Henry Festing Jones, *Samuel Butler* (2 vols. London, Macmillan, 1919), *I*, 136-7.

Francis Espinasse describes a group of similar devotees who founded a literary club, called "the Shandeans," at Manchester during the fifties. Espinasse himself had suggested the name "from an old affection for Sterne." Tennyson was an honored guest of the group for an evening's visit in 1857. The laureate stayed until "two or three in the morning before he departed, declaring that he had never in his life met with such an odd set of fellows. This, of course, the Shandeans took as a compliment to their powers as entertainers." [8] The meetings of the club were probably less boisterous than those of John Henderson's similar group eighty years earlier, but both shared an admiration for Sterne.

Though Thackeray would have had little or no influence on devotees like these who admired Sterne's humorous side, his picture of false sentiment and insincerity in the *Humourists* probably helped to lower respect among a number of readers for Sterne's pathetic side. Some critics at this time were also voicing opposition to all sentimentality in literature. In an essay published a few weeks after Thackeray's lecture in 1851, a writer in the *North British Review* condemned sentimentality as "an indulgence of feeling for feeling's sake" which is "a caricature of really strong deep feeling" and "collapses instantaneously, if brought into contact with the actual." The jealousy of Othello, "founded though it be on trifles, is not sentimental," he says, "for the emotion penetrates his whole nature, it absorbs him—*it necessitates action.* On the other hand, for an instance of what is really sentimental, no one can be at a loss who has ever read a page of Sterne." [9] A few years later Fitzjames Stephen also censured "sentimental" literature and included the description of Le Fever's death among his examples, "because it is impossible to read it without feeling that it is introduced in order to set off Uncle Toby's generosity and Lefevre's affection for his son." [1] When the Reverend William Henry Brookfield read the story of Le Fever in 1860 to a group of friends, including the Carlyles and the Monckton Milnes, he recorded in his diary that it had fallen "flat as a plate, no one seemed to like it." [2]

8. *Literary Recollections and Sketches,* pp. 358–9. Tennyson appears to have recorded no comment of his own on Sterne, though he might well have applied the comment on his hosts to their patron saint since, like Wordsworth, his predecessor in the laureateship, he didn't have much Shandeism in his make-up.

9. *North British Review,* 15 (Aug. 1851), 419–20.

1. "The Relation of Novels to Life," *Cambridge Essays* (London, 1855), p. 173.

2. Charles and Frances Brookfield, *Mrs. Brookfield and Her Circle* (New York and London, Scribner's, 1906), p. 486. On a previous occasion, however, one of his hearers had complimented Brookfield on his reading of the story (p. 483). Some critics admitted Sterne's power in the pathetic even though they felt it to be the result of artifice. See John Skelton, *Nugae Criticae* (Edinburgh, 1862), p. 9. (Skelton was a miscellaneous writer who later had a long association with *Blackwood's.*) See also the remarks of John Addington Symonds who compared Sterne, somewhat unfavorably, with Oliver Wendell Holmes; *Letters and Papers,* ed. Horatio F. Brown (London, Scribner's, 1923), pp. 13–14.

Nevertheless, most of the famous literary figures among the Victorians read Sterne, although their critical comments on his work do not always show agreement. In his memoir of Rossetti, the poet's brother says that Dante Gabriel read *Tristram Shandy* "with keen enjoyment" during his youth.[3] Swinburne must also have read Sterne early in life.[4] Edward Dowden grew up knowing "Richardson and Fielding and Sterne pretty well, but Dickens and Thackeray very ill." [5] Newman also knew Sterne, for he uses a quotation from one of Yorick's sermons as a springboard for a discussion of literature in a lecture given in 1858.[6] Ruskin, in a lecture delivered five years earlier, had referred to Sterne, citing him as a "striking" example of the failure of eighteenth-century authors to appreciate the sublime in nature, since in the *Sentimental Journey* there is a "total absence of sentiment on any subject but humanity" and an "entire want of notice of anything at Geneva, which might not as well have been seen at Coxwold." [7] George Eliot quotes from *Tristram Shandy* in a letter written in 1858,[8] and she had compared Heine and Sterne in an article for the *Westminster Review* two years earlier. Heine "falls below Sterne in raciness of humour," she says, although "he is far above him in poetic sensibility and in reach and variety of thought." [9] The fact that these important literary figures, representing such varied backgrounds and interests, all knew Sterne shows that he was still pretty much a part of the education of those who were most interested in literature.

Though none of the writers mentioned above was influenced by Sterne, Bulwer, who was even considered the foremost novelist of his day by some critics,[1] imitated *Tristram Shandy* during one portion of

3. *Dante Gabriel Rossetti. His Family-Letters with a Memoir by William Michael Rossetti* (2 vols. London, 1895), *1*, 101.

4. Swinburne's biographer tells us that the poet "was indifferent" to *Tristram Shandy* during his college days (Edmund Gosse, *Life of Swinburne*, in *Complete Works of Swinburne*, Bonchurch Ed. 20 vols. London, Heinemann, 1925–27, *19*, 47) ; but many years later Swinburne wrote that he enjoyed reading it aloud (*Complete Works: Letters, 18*, 441). His sonnet on "Dickens," published in *Tristram of Lyonesse* in 1882, speaks of "the soft bright soul of Sterne."

5. *Letters of Edward Dowden and his Correspondents*, ed. Elizabeth D. and Hilda M. Dowden (London, J. M. Dent, 1914), p. 320.

6. See "Literature," *The Idea of a University*, ed. Charles F. Harrold (New York, London, Toronto, Longmans Green, 1947), pp. 235–7. Newman finds "a mixture of truth and falsehood" in the quotation from Sterne, though it is "eloquently written."

7. *Works of John Ruskin*, ed. E. T. Cook and Alexander Wedderburn, Library Ed. (39 vols. London, Longmans Green, 1903–12), *12*, 119.

8. *The George Eliot Letters,* ed. Gordon S. Haight (7 vols. New Haven and London, Yale Univ. Press, 1954–55), *2*, 493.

9. *Essays and Leaves from a Note-Book* (2nd ed. Edinburgh and London, 1884), p. 140. In a note written during the seventies, she was later partially to defend Sterne's irregular method of composition, stating that "the objections to Sterne's wild way of telling 'Tristram Shandy' lie more solidly in the quality of the interrupting matter than in the fact of interruption." Ibid., p. 371.

1. Blanchard points out that Bulwer was the "most popular writer of the day" in the

his career. Particularly in his *Caxtons,* which was first published in
1849 and became a best seller during the early fifties, there are many
very evident traces of *Tristram Shandy.* Although Bulwer's novel
was widely read, the extent of his reliance upon Sterne was apparently
not generally recognized at first. In a discussion of the two novels, an
unknown critic wrote in *Fraser's Magazine* in 1856 that Bulwer's novel
"has probably been now read by nearly every educated man in this country," and continued that only "the supposition that the splendid conception of Sterne has become nearly a dead letter in our own age" can
account for "the extraordinary fact that *The Caxtons* should have
maintained, as we believe it generally has maintained, the character of
an original fiction." He points out numerous parallelisms between the
two novels and regrets that though "there is scarcely anything which
can be deemed immoral in the tendencies of *Tristram Shandy,* it has
"a style of writing wholly antagonistic" to the "polished taste and the
stricter delicacy of the nineteenth century." The remarks of this critic
are significant, not so much because they suggest the narrowness of
Sterne's audience at this time, as because they indicate the popularity
which Sterne might have had if his style had not "rendered a work which
might have been the manual of all time, the possession and the study of
the few." [2]

However much Bulwer may have been indebted to Sterne, he made
at least partial reparation in some of the remarks in his *Caxtoniana,* a
series of essays first published in *Blackwood's* during 1862 and 1863.
He praises Sterne's style, asserting that none "of his contemporaries,
mighty prose-writers though they were, had, on the whole, so subtle
and fine a perception of the various capacities of our language" as Sterne.
"What delicate elegance he can extract from words the most colloquial
and vulgate," he says, "and again, with some word unfamiliar and
strange, how abruptly he strikes on the universal chords of laughter.
He can play with the massive weights of our language as a juggler
plays with his airy balls. In an age when other grand writers were
squaring their periods by rule and compass," he continues, "he flings
forth his jocund sentences loose and at random; now up towards the

early thirties (p. 380), and Bulwer seems to have maintained his reputation during the
forties and fifties, for he is frequently mentioned as being on a par with Thackeray and
Dickens. George Gilfillan was surprised "at the longitude of the ears of those critics"
who name Thackeray "in the same day" with Bulwer, since the latter is so superior;
"Thackeray," *Third Gallery of Portraits* (New York, 1855; 1st ed. London, 1854),
p. 218.

2. "*Tristram Shandy* or *The Caxtons?*," *Fraser's Magazine, 53* (March 1856),
253–67. See also the similar remarks of William Forsyth first published in the same
periodical in 1857, reprinted in *Essays Critical and Narrative* (London, 1874), pp.
186–7; and those of Vere Henry, Lord Hobart, also first published in *Fraser's* in 1859,
reprinted in *Essays and Miscellaneous Writings,* ed. Lady Mary Hobart (2 vols. London, 1885), *1,* 258.

stars, now down into puddles; yet how they shine where they soar, and how lightly rebound when they fall!" [3] Bulwer also speaks of the charges of plagiarism, dismissing them with the assertion that "little wits that plagiarise are but pickpockets; great wits that plagiarise are conquerors." [4]

When he comes to discuss the four great novelists of the eighteenth century, Bulwer finds that Fielding and Smollett are superior to the other two "in the conduct of the story," but Richardson and Sterne display "a finer order of art" in their "conception of character and in delicacy of treatment." The characters of both Richardson and Sterne manifest a "subtler and deeper" knowledge of the world than those of Smollett or even the "lusty heroes and buxom heroines" of Fielding. Though Sterne's "most exquisite characters are but sketches and outlines," they are universal types in "the boundless world of men . . . that world which has no special capital." "There is no reason," Bulwer concludes, "why Uncle Toby, Corporal Trim, Yorick, might not be Frenchmen or Germans, born at any epoch or in any land. Who cares for the mere date and name of the battles which Uncle Toby fights over again? Any battles would do as well—the siege of Troy as well as the siege of Namur." [5]

The critical controversies involving Sterne and his works during the years under consideration were fully as violent as those of the earlier periods. Bagehot's censure of the "fantastic disorder of the form" of *Tristram Shandy* is contradicted by Jeaffreson's assertion that Sterne has shown us "how to tell stories gracefully." While Thackeray "tossed and gored the unhappy Yorick" and Jeaffreson multiplied the charges many fold,[6] Fitzgerald cast down "the monstrous image . . . of the great Shandean" which Thackeray had set up. Though most critics accepted a large part of Thackeray's view of the facts of Sterne's life until Fitzgerald had corrected it in his biography, few of them agreed with his low estimate of Sterne's genius. Voices from further in the past commanded more respect with them, as they continued to refer to the judgments of Coleridge and Scott.[7]

3. "On Style and Diction," *Caxtoniana* (2 vols. Edinburgh and London, 1863), *1*, 126.

4. "On Some Authors in whose Writings Knowledge of the World is Eminently Displayed," *Caxtoniana, 2,* 289–90.

5. Ibid., *2,* 268–71.

6. See above, pp. 144–8 and 150–1. Thackeray suggests that Sterne was paying his addresses to three women in 1767; *Humourists,* pp. 166–7. Jeafferson speaks of his "making love to twenty ladies at the same time" during that year.

7. Johnson, Gray, Walpole, and Ferrier were likewise frequently quoted, though the judgments of the latter two were sometimes contradicted. One critic also revived the remarks of George Gregory and Anna Seward; see Katherine Thomson (pseud. Grace Wharton), *Literature of Society* (2 vols. London, 1862), *2,* 290–5. The author praises Sterne's characters and characterizes *Tristram Shandy* as "one of the most fascinating, witty, and dangerous works that has ever been penned in the English language." There is a copy of this book in the New York Public Library.

The attitude toward Sterne was inextricably bound up with the attitude toward the eighteenth century, which seems to have been one of mingled attraction and repugnance. However much they might censure the immorality and less polished manners of the previous century, the Victorians also appear to have felt something of a fascination in its darker side. This can be seen in their preoccupation with the gruesome legends of Sterne's friendless deathbed and the dissection of his corpse, as well as with some of the "questionable" incidents of his life. The concern with these stories represents more than merely a desire to point a moral, since the relish for details is apparent in many accounts. Even Fitzgerald plays up the "Shandean" element in his life of "the English Rabelais." Another critic went so far as to suggest that although Sterne was "not merely, like Fielding, a dissipated man, but, like Poe, a heartless scoundrel," nevertheless, "blackguard as he was, his vices, like those of Rousseau and Goethe, have contributed to the power and piquancy of his writings." [8] The Victorians had rejected for themselves, however, the kind of sensibility displayed in the *Sorrows of Werter* and *Letters from Yorick to Eliza,* works which they felt had been designed for "the especial cultivation of that adultery of the mind which the Reverend Laurence Sterne calls 'sentiment.' " [9] Their own "great sentimentalist," as Bagehot said, was a very different, though "an uncomfortable writer"; for Thackeray had a "peculiar and characteristic scepticism" which reflected the spirit of his age. Ruskin put it even more strongly a few years later when he said that "Thackeray settled like a meat-fly on whatever one had got for dinner, and made one sick of it." [1] The author of *Vanity Fair* never seemed to let up in his search for "humbuggery," and in the case of Sterne, he was convinced that he had found only too much of it.

The continued decline in Sterne's audience, already begun before the period under discussion, was due not so much to the accusations of insincerity, however, as to those of indelicacy. *Tristram Shandy* was relegated to the upper shelf of the library or the recesses of the club room, while others besides Thackeray doubtless thought with gratitude of the "sweet and unsullied page which the author of *David Copperfield*" had given to their children. Discerning critics realized, of course, that not all books were meant to be children's books, although they were forced to admit that the altered views of society were an inescapable fact. Bagehot regrets the necessity of having "a limited and truncated literature," fit for the perusal of young ladies; and Thomas Purnell thinks it strange that the English "are presumed to be so combustible a society that the tender passion must not be mentioned" in literature

8. Gilfillan, "Thackeray," p. 232.
9. Charles Knight, *Half-Hours with the Best Letter-Writers and Autobiographers* (London, 1867), p. 246.
1. "Letter 31," *Works: Fors Clavigera, 27,* 562.

(without an impending marriage), while detailed accounts of crime and stories in which "backbiting and reviling one's neighbour are exhibited as fine arts" may be placed "in the hands of women of character" without offense.[2] Swinburne, in a little pamphlet written in 1865 to defend his own poetry from the charges of immorality, complains that his time "has room only for such as are content to write for children and girls." There are "moral milkmen enough, in all conscience," to supply this function, he thinks, without forcing all literature to conform to the same standard.[3]

With the altered state of taste and the violent critical controversies over Sterne, probably for the first time a greater number of people may have read the criticisms of his works than the works themselves. It is important to realize, therefore, that the critics were almost unanimous in their agreement that he had genius, and his literary reputation remained almost as high with many of them as it had been in the preceding age. Though a few, like Thackeray, weighted the scales heavily on the side of his faults, the majority saw talents of the same order that the major literary figures of the Romantic Period had seen. David Masson felt that "one could have lived cheerfully and freely in the vicinity of Shandy Hall"; [4] and Elwin thought that "the entire library of fiction contains no more delightful pages" than many to be found in *Tristram Shandy*. Bulwer sensed that Sterne's characters were universal types who would be at home anywhere in "the boundless world of men." As Thomas Purnell said, the characters of *Tristram Shandy* "all are conceived and developed with a pathos that now for a hundred years has made them dear friends of the public, and will continue to make them favourites with our grandchildren in the next century." [5]

The first hundred years of criticism had certainly not always been kind to Sterne, but it had left him with his reputation established. Though relatively few of the grandchildren of the Victorians may have found "dear friends" in the characters of *Tristram Shandy* as Purnell thought they would, most of them would admit that Sterne belongs among those classics which, unfortunately, are sometimes more respected than read. When Vicesimus Knox criticized the discipline at English universities in an essay written a decade after Sterne's death, he gave a shocked picture of students who spent their time in "the

2. *Literature and its Professors*, p. 221.
3. *Notes on Poems and Reviews* (London, 1866), p. 14.
4. *British Novelists and Their Styles*, p. 152. He goes on to say that "it is only now and then, among the characters of Fielding and Smollett, that this attraction is felt by the reader" (pp. 152–3).
5. *Literature and its Professors*, p. 226.

amusement of cutting the desks, carving their names, or reading Sterne's Sentimental Journey," instead of attending to more serious pursuits.[6] He would not have believed that a hundred and fifty years later students would be studying Sterne in the same college classrooms.

Although the passage of time has enshrined Sterne safely in the realm of the classics, something has been lost in the process. Few readers today can feel the same exuberant delight that many of the contemporary readers of *Tristram Shandy* had, or the same emotional stimulation that was occasioned by the *Sentimental Journey*. With Sterne, more than with most writers, however, readers in any age are apt to disagree, as the violent controversies of the first hundred years of Sterne criticism so clearly show. To mention but a few examples, the enthusiasm of Boswell and Hume is in opposition to the severity of Johnson; the warmth of Anna Seward's defense stands in contrast to the "literary molism" of George Gregory; and the unfavorable remarks of Hannah More are at once contradicted in the eager defense of Mrs. Cavendish-Bradshaw. Byron's picture of "that dog Sterne" as a "villain—hypocrite—slave—sycophant" is balanced by the belief of Hazlitt and Scott that "the parent of Uncle Toby" could not be "a harsh or habitually a bad-humoured man." Thackeray's portrait of the mountebank and the "foul Satyr" is contradicted by Fitzgerald's presentation of the man who "had so many weaknesses but so many more redeeming features." From the very first appearance of *Tristram Shandy* and the *Sermons* in 1760, Sterne continued to be the subject of heated debate.

Literary controversies as to the character and writings of a man are not an unusual phenomenon, nor is the disagreement between different ages as to the way an author's life and works should be interpreted. Sterne's three great contemporaries in the novel have been differently regarded and received with varying degrees of enthusiasm by the various subsequent ages. In the case of Sterne, however, the controversies were especially violent and the differences in opinion more strongly marked. This may be explained by the presence of a rather unusual combination of factors, which sometimes raised critical problems quite different from those connected with the other writers of Sterne's time, and hence these factors often allow us to see quite sharply some of the differences between the various ages in their critical sensibilities.

First, there was the question of Sterne's private character. From the very beginning, many of the attacks and mock attacks on *Tristram Shandy* were motivated by the fact that its author was a clergyman, and through the years, down to and including the Victorians, there are always critics for whom this fact has a decisive influence in determining critical judgments. Furthermore, very little was known about Sterne's

6. *Essays Moral and Literary, 2,* 158–9.

life until Fitzgerald published his biography. Even the readers of
Sterne's own day had only a very scanty amount of knowledge in this
respect. Charles Johnstone's picture of Sterne in *The Reverie* in 1762
is nearly as harsh as Thackeray's picture in the *Humourists* ninety
years later, nor is it much fairer or more authentic, since Johnstone
retails at length one of the unreliable and scurrilous anecdotes which
were passing for biographical fact even in Sterne's own time. With
the passing of the years, unreliable anecdotes and legends of this sort,
many of them to Sterne's discredit, became more and more firmly
established. The calumny about Sterne's neglect of his mother pursued
him from the gossip of his own time until Fitzgerald's exposure of the
lack of basis for it, and the Eliza episode also tended to bring his
character into question with some critics in each age. There is no
time during the entire period from 1760 to 1868 when biographical
considerations do not have an important influence upon the criticism of
Sterne. The attacks on Sterne's character vary in severity and tone
with the different ages, however, for Thackeray's condemnation has
nothing of the playfulness which marked many of the mock attacks
during Sterne's lifetime. In general, strictures in Sterne's own time
were divided between those of serious moralists and those of literary
hacks, wits, and reviewers, who wrote in a spirit of banter. By the turn
of the century the attacks of moralists and serious critics were ever
increasing and hence the great Romantic critics felt it necessary to
defend Sterne's character, using the benevolence and good humor of
his work as proof that he could not have been really bad at heart. Many
of the Victorians, however, felt mingled attraction and repugnance
toward the supposed vices of their ancestors and were only too ready to
exaggerate Sterne's faults. Only with the publication of Fitzgerald's
Life did Sterne's character begin to come more clearly into focus.

Fully as warm debates raged over a related problem, the sincerity
and the tendency of Sterne's sentimental philosophy. These disputes,
too, had continued ever since Sterne's own day. After reading the
Sentimental Journey Mrs. Greville said that a man who chose "to
walk about the world with a cambrick handkerchief always in his hand,
that he may always be ready to weep," only turned her sick; and Mrs.
Carter, although she had not read the book, thought that Sterne's
sensibility was "no more benevolence than it is a fit of the gout," since
he had neglected his duties as a husband and a father. For Mrs. Greville,
Sterne's sentimentality was absurd, while for Mrs. Carter it was
dangerous. Other critics sometimes followed either or both of these
lines of attack, even during the period when the *Sentimental Journey*
was enjoying its greatest vogue and *Beauties of Sterne* was helping
to make his sentimental side so tremendously popular. During the
nineteenth century this side of Sterne was rated less highly by serious

critics as well as moralists. Coleridge found "little beyond a clever affectation" in the *Sentimental Journey* and Thackeray dismissed it as the work of a literary mountebank, to name but two of the later critics who objected to Sterne's sentimental side on aesthetic grounds. Coleridge also felt that "the sentimental philosophy of Sterne, and his numerous imitators" had done more mischief than "all the evil achieved by Hobbes and the whole school of materialists"; and many moral philosophers agreed with him.

The objections to Sterne's work on the ground of its alleged immorality also took another form. Thackeray and the Victorians were by no means the first to feel that a prurient element, running through *Tristram Shandy* especially, not only made Sterne's books unfit reading for the young, the "uncorrupted," and the modest majority of the fair sex, but also rendered his writing unpalatable and displeasing. In reviewing Volumes 7 and 8 of *Tristram Shandy* for the *Monthly* in 1765, Griffiths censured Sterne for including in his book elements which would "prohibit every modest woman in the three kingdoms" from reading it, and stated that Sterne had misjudged the public taste, since "obscenity is not in high vogue now, as it was in the time of Charles the Second." [7] Even though many of the contemporary attacks on *Tristram Shandy* were written in a spirit of banter, in Sterne's own time there were also numerous readers who felt disgust at this element in his work. Though most contemporary critics agreed that the immorality of *Tristram Shandy* was not such as to arouse the passions, this point of view did not go unchallenged. Even the agreement of Scott half a century later did not seem to settle the matter finally, for Thackeray implies that the "wicked allusions" which Sterne whispered "to honest boys," would have that effect, and Purnell feels it necessary to make the specific defense that nothing Sterne wrote "was capable of exciting unhallowed passion in the other sex."

More distinctly literary elements in Sterne's work also raised problems. Just as his supposed immorality was, in the view of the ablest critics like Scott and Coleridge, a question of taste rather than ethics, so, various elements in his style were also matters of individual judgment. Goldsmith disapproved of the initial installment of *Shandy* because he found both "bawdy" and "pertness" in it, and this latter quality was censured by many later critics, including Hazlitt, Coleridge, and Scott, under the name of "affectation." The elements of "oddity" in the "typographical wit" could be passed over if they did not amuse, but throughout Sterne's works the sense of the author's presence could be escaped on few, if any, of the pages. Perhaps it is largely for this reason that so many critics let biographical considerations play an even greater role in their criticism of Sterne than in that of other writers.

7. *Monthly Review, 32* (Feb. 1765), 123–4.

Furthermore, these elements of oddity and affectation in Sterne's style became especially obnoxious in the hands of unskillful imitators, and the sentimental side of his work likewise became ridiculous when attempted by those with inferior talents and unleavened by Yorick's wit and humor. For nearly sixty years after Sterne's death there were imitations of *Tristram Shandy,* and more especially of the *Sentimental Journey,* most of which were little better than caricatures; and these productions lowered the respect of some critics for the originals.

At the same time that the "odd" and "original" elements in Sterne presented problems, other questions were raised by the factor of his plagiarism, which was first hinted at when his books were originally published and which became an important issue after Ferriar's disclosures of the extent of his borrowings. The failure of Hazlitt and Coleridge to take the charges seriously might have been expected to end the matter, but Scott's too hasty acceptance of some of Ferriar's conclusions helped to prolong their influence and critics as late as the Victorian Period sometimes felt it necessary to defend Sterne from the accusation that he lacked originality.

Finally, the presence of so many diverse elements in Sterne often gave rise to misinterpretations of his work, for few readers, during his own time or later, saw the interrelationship of the different parts. Though the presence of satire, humor, and pathos in a single work helped to account for the initial success of *Tristram Shandy,* few critics could appreciate all three elements equally, and even fewer found them appropriately joined. Even Hazlitt spoke of Sterne's work as a collection of *"morceaux"* and "brilliant passages," and it is Coleridge alone who understood that "the digressive spirit" was "the *very form*" of Sterne's genius, with continuity supplied through the characters. No major critic during the entire period followed up Sterne's hint that the basis for his plan might be found in Locke's theory of the association of ideas. Since the *Sentimental Journey* seemed much more regular than *Tristram Shandy* in its plan and was better understood, the preference for Sterne's travels continued to grow until the great critics of the Romantic Period, with their superior insights, rediscovered the excellences of *Tristram Shandy,* which had been gradually coming into neglect since Sterne's death.

With the varied nature of Sterne's gifts and the many particular critical problems connected with his work, it is not surprising that there are such sharp disagreements in the overall estimates by each age as well as among the critics within the various periods. The initial popularity of *Tristram Shandy* was aided by the fact that its satire and its wit and humor appealed to the devotees of Fielding and Smollett, while its pathetic side won the admiration of many Richardson enthusiasts. Sterne's work was more quotable than that of any of his predecessors in the novel, for it had a certain aphoristic quality about it; and it likewise contained many set pieces and gems of wit and description which became favorite passages with anthologists and readers alike. The elements of benevolence and sentimentality won a high place for the *Sermons,* the *Sentimental Journey,* and the pathetic parts of *Tristram Shandy* in an age when the philosophy of Shaftesbury and Hutcheson was popular; and these parts of Sterne's work were anthologized in *Beauties of Sterne,* which reflected the taste of the eighties and nineties and helped to place the sentimental side of Sterne in the ascendancy. Ferriar's final conclusions in his *Illustrations* tended to have the same effect, but already another important factor was beginning to make its influence felt. The spread of the evangelical movement and the related change in taste at the turn of the century had two effects in judgments on Sterne. The indecent parts of his work were condemned even more strenuously than before, and the very basis of his sentimental philosophy was more widely questioned and more bitterly attacked. The "benevolence" of his work was found deficient because it did not lead to right conduct and some of the sentimentality of the travels was also beginning to be questioned on the grounds of its aesthetic validity as well as its sincerity. If the Romantic Period had not rediscovered the excellences of *Tristram Shandy* and raised it again to a place of eminence above the *Sentimental Journey,* it seems probable that the gloomy predictions of the moralists that Sterne's literary reputation would continue to sink might well have been fulfilled. The criticism of the major figures among the Romantics, and particularly that of Hazlitt, Coleridge, and Scott, helped to bring about the opposite effect, however, for during this period Sterne was rated more highly among nearly all the major critics than he had been before or has been since. While the dicta of these major figures were widely circulated during the thirties and forties, Sterne continued to maintain a high reputation with the critics, although continuing changes in the "refinement" of popular taste were gradually diminishing the number of his readers. By the time that Thackeray gave his lecture, there were probably many in his audiences who had never read the works of Sterne. When Hazlitt and Coleridge had lectured scarcely more than thirty years previously, this would not have been true. In spite of the hysterical tone of Thackeray's denunciation, his attack did not have as much effect as might have been expected, since his prejudiced estimate was contradicted by many critics who rose to defend Yorick's genius, though they lacked the materials to correct his interpretation of Sterne's personal character until the publication of Fitzgerald's *Life,* more than a decade later. After the famous dicta of the Romantics became known and accepted, Sterne's critical future was never really in doubt, as the quick contradictions of Thackeray's unfair appraisal so clearly show. Likewise, with Fitzgerald's biography, many of the old mistakes were corrected once and for all, though the picture was still incomplete.

More recent research, most notably that of Cross and of Curtis, has added many facts which have made possible a more accurate interpretation of Sterne's personal character. Modern criticism has likewise come to appreciate many elements of Sterne's artistry which had previously been neglected. The perceptive introduction and copious annotation of James A. Work's edition of *Tristram Shandy* have finally enabled the twentieth-century reader to read the book in somewhat the same way that contemporaries did. Even before the publication of Work's edition in 1940, Sterne had found appreciative readers in our time; and of the four famous eighteenth-century novelists, he has probably given the most in the way of creative inspiration to the twentieth century. "Sterne is singularly of our own age," in the words of Virginia Woolf, one of those who has derived no small amount of inspiration from Yorick. He is unique, she says, since "for all his interest in psychology Sterne was far more nimble than the masters of this somewhat sedentary school have since become." He is a great literary artist because he brings us "as close to life as we can be," combining "extreme art and extraordinary pains" with a seemingly careless familiarity with the reader. "No writing seems to flow more exactly into the very folds and creases of the individual mind, to express its changing moods, to answer its lightest whim and impulse," she says, "and yet the result is perfectly precise and composed. The utmost fluidity exists with the utmost permanence. It is as if the tide raced over the beach hither and thither and left every ripple and eddy cut on the sand in marble." [8] More than a century and a half earlier Sterne had chosen a more Shandean metaphor, but one which proved truly prophetic, when he thought that *Tristram Shandy* would "swim down the gutter of Time" to posterity.

8. Introduction to *A Sentimental Journey,* World's Classics Ed. (London, Oxford Univ. Press, 1928), pp. v–xvii.

Index

Addison, Joseph, 66, 71, 76, 77, 99. *See also Spectator*
"Admonitory Lyric EPISTLE to the Rev. Tristram Shandy," 29
Adventures of a Hackney Coach. See Kilner, Dorothy
Aikin, John, 87, 90
Alas! Poor Yorick! or, a Funeral Discourse, 3, 29
"Alciphron," 128
All the Year Round, 159
Almon, John, 89
Alves, Robert, 91
Amicable Quixote, 66
Analytical Review, 84
Anderson, Robert, 94
Anecdotes of Books and Authors, 134
Anecdotes of Polite Literature, 35
Annual Register, 23–4, 87, 92, 98
Anstey, Christopher, 71
Anti-Times, 30–2
Arabian Nights, 94
Arblay, Frances Burney, Madame D', 41, 104, 111
Arbuthnot, John, 57
Aristophanes, 72
Aristotle, 30, 72, 75, 115
Arthur, Archibald, 91
Athenaeum, 148, 159
Austen, Jane, 96, 110

Bachaumont, François Le Coigneux de, 85
Badcock, Samuel, 69, 76
Bagehot, Walter, 161–5, 170 f.
Barbauld, Anna Laetitia, 51, 88, 93, 100, 108–9
Baretti, Giuseppi, 66
Baring Family, 165
Barrett, Eaton Stannard, 101–2
Barrow, John, 99
Bates, Ely, 70
Bathurst, Allen Bathurst, 1st Baron, 5
Baxter, Mr. and Mrs. George, 146
Beattie, James, 72
Beauties of Sterne, 62–3, 65, 78, 95, 107, 136, 174, 177
Becket, Andrew, 88
Beckett, William à, Jr., 134
Beckford, William, 101
Beddoes, Thomas, 84
Bedford, Grosvenor, 96

Bedford, Horace Walpole, 97
Bellchambers, Edmund, 134
Bentham, Jeremy, 131
Berenger, Richard, 2
Berry, Mary, 108
Bevington, Merle M., 147
Bewley, William, 52
Blackwood's Edinburgh Magazine, 6, 132, 135, 160, 167, 169
Blake, William, 62
Blanchard, Frederic T., 3, 5, 141, 144, 150, 168–9
Boccaccio, Giovanni, 103
Boege, Fred, 1, 141
Bolingbroke, Henry, 1st Viscount, 92
Boswell, Alexander, 97
Boswell, James, 6, 8, 11, 16 f., 32, 34, 37, 69, 73, 120, 128, 173
Bouchet, Guillaume, 86
Bowdler, Thomas, 134
Bradshaigh, Lady Dorothy, 34, 42
Brewster, David, 134
British Magazine, 10, 13, 15
British Plutarch, 76
British Quarterly Review, 154, 160
Brontë, Charlotte, 143, 149
Brookfield, Mrs. Jane, 140
Brookfield, William Henry, 167
Brougham, Henry Peter, Baron Brougham and Vaux, 89
Browne, James, 133
Bulwer-Lytton, Edward George Earle Lytton, 1st Baron, 138–9, 151, 168–70, 172
Burke, Edmund, 23–4
Burney, Charles, 42
Burney, Elizabeth, 42
Burney, Frances. *See* Arblay, Frances Burney, Madame D'
Burns, Robert, 74, 107, 125, 126
Burton, John (Dr. Slop), 23
Burton, Robert, 81, 83 f., 86, 88, 133, 151, 158
Butler, Samuel (*1612–80*), 3, 71, 82
Butler, Samuel (*1835–1902*), 166
Butler, Weeden, 44
Byron, George Gordon, Lord, 54, 90, 96, 103, 110, 127, 132 f., 140, 165, 173

Campbell, Archibald, 29–30
Candid Review, 18, 26

YALE STUDIES IN ENGLISH

This volume is the one hundred and thirty-ninth of the Yale Studies in English, founded by Albert Stanburrough Cook in 1898 and edited by him until his death in 1927. Tucker Brooke succeeded him as editor, and served until 1941, when Benjamin C. Nangle succeeded him.

The following volumes are still in print. Orders should be addressed to YALE UNIVERSITY PRESS, New Haven, Connecticut.

137. BERGER, HARRY, JR., The Allegorical Temper: Vision and Reality in Book II of Spenser's *Faerie Queene*. $5.00.
138. YOUNG, R. B., W. T. FURNISS, and W. G. MADSEN, Three Studies in the Renaissance: Sidney, Jonson, Milton. $6.00.
139. HOWES, ALAN B., Yorick and the Critics. Sterne's Reputation in England, 1760–1868. $4.50.